Helping

Helping

Charlotte Towle
on Social Work
and Social
Casework

edited by Helen Harris Perlman

The University of Chicago Press
Chicago & London

SBN: 226-66026-5

Library of Congress Catalog Card Number: 69-19060

THE UNIVERSITY OF CHICAGO PRESS, CHICAGO 60637
The University of Chicago Press, Ltd., London

Printed in the United States of America

Contents

Part Two

Perspectives in Social Work

Preface

THIS BOOK HAS BEEN a labor of love. It was love of Charlotte Towle—for herself as person and for all she gave to me—that made me want to put between the covers of a book some of her writings that might otherwise be lost or too soon forgotten. I felt pushed to do that. What I did not know was the labor it involved. It was hard work, not in the sense of the usual drudgery it takes to bring words and footnotes and punctuation marks to rectitude, but, rather, because I found there were so many decisions to be made and then explained, first in imaginary conversations with Charlotte Towle herself and then to the prospective reader. It is the explanations to the reader that I set down here.

The decisions that had to be made were of several sorts. One was that of selection. Of the sixty-nine pieces of Charlotte Towle's published works (excluding her three books and her many book reviews), which should be chosen, which discarded or put off perhaps for another volume and another time? Any writings as rich in content as are Charlotte Towle's hold several lodes for the mining. And any "miner" will find one vein more promising or yielding than another. So a selection of some twenty pieces out of more than three times that sum must reflect the selector's special bent and interests. The final answer to questions of "Why this?—and why not that?" is simply that in the judgment of the decision maker and by his criteria one piece seemed more fitting or relevant than another. Yet the selector and compiler wonders all the while "Is my judgment sound?"

The single major criterion for my choices would, I think, be warmly approved by Charlotte Towle. It was simply and firmly this: that this volume's articles should be those that have contemporary applicability and usability. More, that their usefulness as guides and stimulators should be for the mainstream of social work practitioners and students, those who are as yet young and fresh in practice and for their teachers and supervisors and elder colleagues too. Charlotte Towle would want this. She loved nothing better than opening her stores of wisdom to the eyes of educable learners, whether they were beginning students or seasoned practitioners. And nothing delighted her more than to find —as the reader will also find—that she was so often ahead of her times that something she had written many years before was being rediscovered and found to be good and useful.

Two kinds of subject matter met the criterion of present-day relevance—that which dealt with factors and forces in social casework and that which dealt with the larger perspectives of social work, its nature, its values, its progress, and its problems. These I have organized in chronological sequence under two major sections, one "The Helper and the Helped in Social Casework," the other "Perspectives in Social Work." In the brief comments prefacing each article I have tried to highlight what seemed to me to be the points of closest connection or greatest interest for our present purposes.

The reader who knows the work of Charlotte Towle knows that within the last twenty years of her career she was the foremost theoretician and spokesman on education for the profession of social work. None of her many articles on education has been included here, partly because they are addressed more to educators than to practitioners and partly because in her monolithic book *The Learner in Education for the Professions* (1954) Charlotte Towle combined and integrated the contents of most of these published papers. Because, however, in some of them she had set down with clarity and authority the essence of social work itself and some of the problems to be anticipated by those who enter its portals, such sections have been lifted out of their education-oriented matrix and included here. The complete bibliography of Charlotte Towle's published works (excluding book reviews) is appended for those who would read beyond these excerpts.

One of the arduous aspects of editing the work of another is daring to change what has been thought, written, printed, and presumably given the stamp of approval by the author. It seems presumptuous to reshape it in any way—and one experiences some uneasiness in doing so. Again one must make explanations.

I took two major editorial liberties with these published pieces. One was technical. It was to break up overloaded pages into smaller paragraphs. Writing style reflects thinking style. Charlotte Towle's was concentrated, connected, tightly woven. Her paragraphs often ran page-long and concentrated, with no breaks of thought. But a reader, less intent, may lose his way in such thickly planted woods— or may lose sight of some of the individually interesting trees therein. So I presumed to cut some clearing spaces, to give the reader's mind and eye some momentary resting space. The paragraphing thus differs from what it is in the original printings. Further, in a few places—very few—I have corrected punctuation and blue penciled an occasional redundancy. Footnotes have been renumbered when some references have been dropped. On some articles titles have been changed to better express the content after deletions were made; but always the original title will be found in the footnote.

As for content change, there has been none, except for

deletions of sections of articles—sometimes several sentences, sometimes several paragraphs. The reason for such editorial cuts were twofold.

For all that Charlotte Towle was often ahead of her time, she was human enough to be *of* her time, too, and in some of her earlier writings there appear concepts and notions which she herself, as a continuously learning and progressing person, later discarded. For example, in one piece she classified people into the "adequate and inadequate," the latter being social work's clients. This was an idea she herself quickly got rid of. In several early pieces she wrote of the relationship between client and caseworker as a child-parent relationship—an idea she was not long thereafter to modify considerably. I was afraid that if these and like outdated notions were let stand in the context of otherwise up-to-date thinking the reader might cast off the whole piece as "old hat." So I excised such sections, but, I hasten to add, I never did so unless they were only incidental to the major content, and I did so with the added assurance that any scholar, seeking to know the whole of Charlotte Towle's thinking, or perhaps to trace the evolution of her ideas, would have access to full texts in the original publications.

One further condition led to editorial deletions—the problem of repetition. A thinker, one who develops a thought fragment into a notion, thence into an idea, and thence into a formulation with explanatory and applicatory power, is bound to be repetitive. He nurses and pats and coddles his ideas in order to make them grow, and he shows them off to friends and acquaintances whose reactions affect him. If the reactions are praise and pleasure, the thinker, understandably, shows the idea again, hoping now that some wider group will also find it good. If the reactions are pallid or thin, and the thinker remains convinced that his thought-child deserves better or further consideration, he, understandably, trots it forward once again, perhaps in a new place or context. Add to this the fact that Charlotte Towle long knew that repetition, in differing contexts, entrenches learning. So she repeated many of her salient ideas in her writings. Sometimes she paraphrased them, but sometimes she transferred them verbatim from one context to another. Over time this has—and had—entrenchment value. Within the confines of one book, however, repetition becomes an irritant. I have deleted those I found unnecessary, but only when their omission left no gap in the article's essential content. Beyond this, a few time-bound names and references have been cut since they would have small meaning for this day's reader.

Shortly before Charlotte Towle's retirement her colleague and mine, Rachel Marks, suggested that Charlotte put together a volume of her selected writings. I talked with her about this prospect several times, urging that she do so and suggesting a format similar to the one that has been used here. With her usual and honest modesty Charlotte Towle was reluctant to do this, partly because she was not sure her perspectives on her own work were objective enough and partly because she was unsure about the cogency of what she had produced for the present generation of social workers. My undertaking to do what I would have wished Charlotte Towle herself had done is based on my belief that I am able to view her work with objectivity and on my conviction that much of what is presented here is not only cogent but holds deep and long wisdom about the helper, the helped, and the helping processes of social work.

There remain my acknowledgments of gratitude. First and foremost I must speak of Mary Rall who over many years was Charlotte Towle's dearest friend and boon companion. It was Mary Rall, inheritor of Charlotte Towle's published and unpublished papers, who persuaded me to take on this task. It was she who presented me with an ordered file of the publications. I am particularly grateful and appreciative to her, however, for giving me the right

and the freedom to select and present the materials as I saw
fit. I know how hard it is to relinquish the works and interpretations of a beloved person to another, even when that
other is a friend.

To the following holders of copyrights on published
articles of Charlotte Towle's go my thanks for permission to
reprint articles or excerpts: *American Journal of Ortho-
psychiatry*, published by the American Orthopsychiatric
Association, Inc., New York City; *Child Welfare*, published
by the Child Welfare League of America, Inc., New York
City; Council on Social Work Education publications, New
York City; *Mental Hygiene*, published by the National Association for Mental Health, Inc., New York City; *Social
Casework*, published by the Family Service Association,
New York City; *Social Service Review*, published by the
University of Chicago Press; and *Social Work*, published by
the National Association of Social Workers, New York City.

As for the prospective reader, I can only hope that he will
experience in his reading the pleasure and stimulation of
meeting or becoming further acquainted or renewing his
fellowship with Charlotte Towle.

H. H. P.

Charlotte Towle:
An Appreciation

CHARLOTTE TOWLE WAS BORN in the rugged mountain country of Montana in November, 1896. She died in the age-gentled mountains of New Hampshire just before her seventieth birthday, in October, 1966. In the course of her seventy years, she was daughter, sister, friend, colleague, student, social worker, teacher, scholar, writer, and leader, and in these varied and always richly invested roles she touched thousands of other lives and left a vital impress upon many of them. Within her profession she came to be recognized as one of its outstanding standard-setters and spokesmen. Yet she never lost touch with common human needs and aspirations, and she retained that rare capacity for wholeness that binds head and heart and hand together: she thought, felt, reached out to act at once, in harmony and simultaneity. In this lay her uniqueness and her stature.

How does one write a brief biography of a many-faceted person? There are the bare-bone facts of where and when the person moved from one to another life stage or life role. There are the open, public meanings of those facts. There are the underlying, personal reactions and interpretations of them made by the person who lived them out. There is the biographer's interest bias that constitutes a selective sieve through which certain parts are captured and held and certain others allowed to drain away. And, always, there is the haunting wish to bring this person to live again before

1

the reader's eyes and, along with it, the fear that the confines of space and the implacability of print make flat what should be many-dimensioned. Charlotte Towle would have understood this because she understood how subtly complex each human life is and how no single account, factual or diagnostically astute as it may be, can capture it. With this assurance one goes forward.

Charlotte Towle was the second of four children, three daughters—Mildred, Charlotte, Elise—and the youngest, a son, John. Her father, a jeweler, had come from the midwest; his forebears had lived since pre-Revolutionary days on the eastern seaboard. (When she was an adult and a social worker, Charlotte Towle rejected an invitation from the D.A.R. to join their membership with a firm and careful explanation of how her social philosophy differed from theirs.) She was, one sister reports, "the apple of her mother's eye," and the warmth and loving nurturing and responsibility that permeated her adult relationships attest to her having been much loved. And small wonder. Pictures of her as a baby and youngster show a beautiful feature-perfect child, her round, brown eyes open and trustful to the world. She was a lively child, physically and intellectually. Those who knew Charlotte Towle only in her later years, when family responsibilities had taken their toll of her energy and spirit, would scarcely believe the carefree, mischievous, roof-climbing, fence-walking tomboy she was in her childhood and early adolescence. Snapshots confirm her own stories of herself as a laughing, hoydenish "cut-up." She rode, hiked, played tennis, climbed mountains. She was a deadly mimic. Those who knew her intimately knew she never lost her capacity to take off, privately, on the idiosyncrasies of speech and manner of others she encountered. (Perhaps, indeed, it is the ability to get "under the skin" or "into the shoes" of another that bespeaks a person's spontaneous capacity for empathy.) Her imitations of Charlie

Chaplin were held, by her family and friends, to be hilarious, and she briefly went through the period common to all vivid adolescents of wanting to go on the stage.

In a western mining town, now rich and heady with the demand for copper, now pinched and tight-belted when economic vicissitudes closed the mines, where rugged capitalism and rugged immigrant labor strove for power or rights, it was inevitable that even a middle-class child should come to know the ups and downs of fortune. "From my earliest years," Charlotte Towle once wrote, "I overheard heated discussions of labor-employer rights and obligations. In these my mother was always aligned with the working man against the capitalist. She was an ardent 'trust buster.' . . . I also recall my mother's interest in social reform . . . [and] later when I was well embarked in social casework my mother expressed disappointment that I had chosen this area [casework] of social work. . . . She thought casework rather hopeless, like spooning the ocean."

Writing further of the social milieu of her childhood that made its imprint upon her: "Butte was a wide open town—the gambling joints, road houses, etc. of the pioneer west persisted throughout my life there. . . . I knew the roaring twenties from birth. There was a superficial sophistication about the town brought in by leading citizens who worked for 'the Company' and by the copper magnates who wintered in New York City and San Francisco. Butte was not a town divided in two by the tracks . . . people shifted back and forth, economically, morally, culturally . . . it was impossible for me as a child in Butte not to come to know very early the kinship of the Colonel's lady and Judy O'Grady."

These few glimpses of Charlotte Towle's childhood environment cast light upon her later capacities as a social worker—the sense of obligation that security so often breeds, the sense of freedom that an open social system inculcated, the tolerance for and interest in diversity, and the buoyant belief that people who have, or are given, the wherewithal can and do better themselves and their life conditions.

Her intellectual curiosity and competence were keenly appreciated by her parents and her teachers, so when she finished high school Charlotte Towle was packed off to college in the East where education and cultivation were long and soundly established. Her freshman year was spent in a women's college in Virginia and her next three years at Goucher College in Baltimore. Indicative of her independence of spirit (was it seen then as rebellion against the establishment?) she was the first "bobbed-hair" girl in her Goucher class. Her short-cut hair with little forehead bangs that turned over the years from chestnut brown to grey became her characteristic style. Again bespeaking her lively curiosity, she spent hours off campus prowling about the docks and markets and slum areas of Baltimore, soaking up the atmosphere of an old history-haunted American city, taking its traditional grace and its uglier backwater pockets into her ken. The slums of Baltimore troubled her, and on the Goucher campus she struggled unhappily with a wish to resign from her sorority when, unbelieving, she learned of its exclusion policies.

It was a time when women's vocational choices were constricted. Charlotte Towle majored in education with substantive courses in English and psychology to prepare herself for teaching in grade school. Two things made her turn from teaching to social work on her graduation in 1919. One was that she had done volunteer work for the Red Cross while in college. Her awareness of human troubles and of social forces could only have been heightened by this experience. The other intelligence that came in upon her with her practice-teaching experience is one of which she herself has written. It was that in order to teach Latin to Johnny, one needed not only to know Latin but to understand Johnny. And it was to understanding Johnny and his peers and his parents and his internal pushes and external pulls that she chose to devote herself.

The aftermath of World War I swept Charlotte Towle into work with the Red Cross for two years following her graduation from Goucher in 1919, first in Baltimore, then in Denver. In 1921–24 she was a caseworker at the United States Veteran's Bureau in San Francisco. (Her later stories were of her love of that city and of the great scarlet and pink efflorescence of geraniums in her window boxes). She went from this to be a "psychiatric caseworker" in Tacoma, Washington, in the United States Neuropsychiatric Hospital there, where she worked between 1924 and 1926. (Forty years later, in 1966, she received a letter from the chief psychiatric social worker of that hospital reporting on one of their patients: the one person he remembered who had helped him and had brought hope into his dismal life had been a young social worker named Charlotte Towle.)

The sensitive, responsive, growingly responsible young Charlotte Towle must have become increasingly aware of how much there was to know about human sickness and strength that she did not know, how little equipped she was, except by her natural caring and talents for relationship, to cope with the social and emotional problems she had already experienced in breadth. So she applied for and won a Commonwealth Fellowship to attend the New York School of Social Work. In 1925–26 generous fellowships were competitive, literally won for excellence and potential promise. In those days, too, it was possible to complete professional training in a year, since past practice experience, when it was rated "good," was credited as fieldwork and courses were fewer than they are today. In 1926, then, Charlotte Towle got her certificate of completion of the New York School's psychiatric social work curriculum. Perhaps her most influential teacher there—and one who remained a lifelong friend—was Dr. Marion Kenworthy who taught both the human development course and the seminars in psychiatric social casework. (Charlotte Towle's own account of this teacher's impact on her is to be found in her article on Marion Kenworthy, excerpts from which appear herein as "Reflections on a Teacher.")

With her basic professional preparation completed, Charlotte Towle went as director of its home-finding department to the Children's Aid Society of Philadelphia. This agency offered her an opportunity she had not yet had—to work with and in behalf of young children, to study their needs and growth patterns, to try to prevent in the still malleable young the hurts that hardened into the emotional and mental warpings she had long known as a caseworker in adult psychiatric hospitals. In her two years in foster-home work Charlotte Towle did indeed learn, and, further, she consolidated much that she had partly known before. Her writings show this. Except for one earlier printed piece on the treatment of neuropsychiatric patients, her first published writings were toward the articulation of what foster homes were and could be—and later and more sophisticated articles drew from her experiential knowledge of foster-parents' motivations and of family interactions and role relationships.

In her "Philadelphia days," as Charlotte Towle called them, she came to know and have professional interchange with a number of people whose ideas she found stimulating to her own thought. Jessie Taft was one of them, Virginia Robinson another. Jessie Taft had already been profoundly influenced by her analysis with Otto Rank. Virginia Robinson must already have been at work on her *Changing Psychology in Social Casework*—that first articulation in casework of the potency of relationship. Perhaps it was her having early tasted, liked, and digested some aspects of what was later to be called the "functional school" of thought in social work that made it possible for Charlotte Towle to maintain her balance and interested openness all through the period of the late thirties and the forties when many social work leaders were locked in paroxysms of conflict over the differences between the Freudian and Rankian or—translated into social work—functional and diagnostic schools of thought. At any rate, Charlotte Towle spoke of Jessie Taft and Virginia Robinson with understanding and respect for their thinking even when she differed with their theory or practice. Almena Dawley and Dr. Frederick Allen of the Philadelphia Child Guidance Clinic, both also "Rankians," were two other Philadelphia personages whose thinking Charlotte Towle encountered and held in respect.

In New York City under the aegis of the Commonwealth Fund there had been established one of its model clinics, the Institute for Child Guidance. Charlotte Towle went to work there in 1928 as caseworker and field supervisor of students for the New York and Smith College schools of social work. The Institute was a model in more than intent. It had attracted a group of outstanding practitioners in psychiatry, psychology, and social work, people who, along with Charlotte Towle, came to have considerable influence subsequently upon the practitioners and students whom they taught because they were among the most productive professional theoreticians. Fern Lowry, who was later to teach at the New York School and to write for many other learners, and Madeline Moore, whose articles on "attitude therapy" and whose supervision of students influenced casework practice far beyond the confines of this clinic, were among Charlotte Towle's colleagues. Dr. David Levy was one of the clinic's several outstanding psychiatrists. His classic work on maternal rejection, his therapeutic cogency and skill, his rigorous research stance all deeply impressed the always open and thoughtful Charlotte Towle. As far as casework attitudes and practice were concerned, Dr. Levy's emphasis upon the mother (or father) of the child as emotionally involved, as an affected as well as affecting person, gave new direction to caseworkers whose tendency had been to view the parent as "cause" or "cure" for the child. It pushed them to relate to the parent as one who herself (or himself) was hurt, disturbed, emotionally needful. Sometimes this was called "attitude therapy," sometimes "relationship therapy"—the former being in effect the result of the latter.

Charlotte Towle found this approach, this compassionate effort to nurture the needful parent, in complete consonance with all that her practice and her growing practical wisdom told her was real and valid. Her earlier work with neuropsychiatric patients and with children whose foster parents were being expected to provide what their own parents could not give them had told her in myriad ways that, as she later wrote, "the parent who fails frequently has been failed . . . none of us can give from a vacuum." So her four years of practice and teaching at this teaching and experimenting clinic (it was closed early in 1933 with the end of its funding) were years of rich new learning and integration for her.

In 1931, the University of Chicago's School of Social Service Administration began to eye Charlotte Towle and then to try to persuade her to join its faculty. At that time dynamic psychiatry and psychiatric social work were largely confined within, roughly, a three-hundred-mile radius around New York City. But Chicago began to be drawn into this orbit of influence by several forces. One, probably, was the importation into Chicago of the dynamic and articulate Franz Alexander who established Chicago's Institute for Psychoanalysis. In the course of his brief appointment to the faculty of the University of Chicago, he drew many knowledge-hungry social workers to his lectures. More immediate motivation and its implementation were provided by the Commonwealth Fund, which offered the School of Social Service Administration student stipends if psychiatric field placements could be developed and if psychiatric concepts would be brought to illuminate casework. Dean Edith Abbott was herself dedicated to social provision and policy reform and was militant and tireless in her active involvement and leadership in social issues. Yet she was prescient enough to recognize the wave of change that was rolling onto social casework's shores, and to give its potential values an attentive consideration.

So, on recommendation of several New York social workers—Gordon Hamilton among them—she asked Charlotte Towle to come to Chicago to teach psychiatric concepts to selected students, to develop psychiatric field placements and, perhaps, to do some direct supervision on the side. She might also, Dean Abbott wrote encouragingly, find time to do some of the writing she was interested in doing.

Charlotte Towle came in 1932. She took on all these tasks. She carried them—a staggering load, because her classes grew larger and larger, and demands for the special knowledges she brought burgeoned from all sides, including her faculty colleagues and agencies' personnel—over many years with great competence, at considerable personal sacrifice, but with reward and pride, too.

The references that came to Dean Abbott on Charlotte Towle are noteworthy for their identification of the qualities that remained constant in the thirty-some years that followed. Those qualities must already have been firmly entrenched. References note her ability to work harmoniously with members of other professions—chiefly psychiatry—whose theoretical positions might be different from hers, without need either to deny her difference or to impose it. They characterize her as frank, responsive, thoughtful, interested in students. They speak of her capacity to integrate thinking, to formulate clearly, and of her enjoyment of teaching and writing. Asked whether she was interested only in psychiatric casework, Charlotte Towle responded, in a vein that was to affect the casework content and total curriculum of the University of Chicago and later all schools of social work, that she was interested in seeing all social work infused with psychiatric—that is, psychological—understandings. Dean Abbott, not given to hyperbole, noted that she found Charlotte Towle "an extremely attractive, rather brilliant person."

Some persons have a profound influence upon others by their impact, by their powerful projection of ideas or personality. Others influence people deeply by a kind of infusion or suffusion, by a steady, omnipresent, tender input of ideas, actions, and relationships that feed and develop the receiver's own growth potentials. Charlotte Towle was one of the latter. Under her thoughtful, knowledge-and-wisdom-directed activities, the content of casework courses became three-dimensional for her students, field centers of high quality were established and maintained, but, more, her colleagues and teammates as well as her students found themselves learning and changing in response to Charlotte Towle's patient nurture and firm convictions.

She, in turn, was strongly influenced by her coming to the University of Chicago. She came at a time when all thoughtful social workers were deeply shaken by the catastrophes of the depression and the threatening tides of European fascism. The fact that the economic collapse had shaken the foundations of her own family's security must have made this a period of personal anguish for Charlotte Towle. She joined a faculty at the School of Social Service Administration whose voices were strong and clear in the causes of social legislation, whose eyes were open to the social problems that undercut decent human life, who were activists as well as scholars. Charlotte Towle found herself inspired and caught up in the social concerns of the Abbotts, Grace and Edith, and Sophonisba Breckenridge. What she did, characteristically, however, was to carry forward, consciously and surely unconsciously, too, her continuously ongoing mental work of integration and synthesis. She never saw the individual as separate from his society nor social problems in the mass only. She strove to understand social stress and disorder in the light of her understanding of people's drives and behavior. More successfully she lent herself to the careful study of the interrelationship between the human being's physical, social, and emotional needs and their satisfaction, of the psychological import and impacts upon the individual of having his "common human needs" met or denied. Her article "The Individual in Relation to Social Change" (1939) expresses her struggle to find connecting links between the psychology of the individual and the spirit and drive of social forces. Her book *Common Human Needs* (1945) presents, with the simplicity that can only be achieved by one who has carefully distilled her deep and varied knowledge, an interpretation of the psychodynamic forces at work within the everyday social experience of the everyday man.

It was this distillation and achieved integration which sent Charlotte Towle forward on the path she had marked when she left the Institute for Child Guidance: to make the insights and understandings of dynamic psychiatry a basic part of the education of all social caseworkers, whatever their specialization, and eventually of all social workers. In collaboration with her casework colleagues—a faculty which by the late forties had grown both in number and quality—she began the painstaking work of identifying the generic elements that could be found in all the persons, problems, places, and processes embraced by social casework. We looked to find and to formulate the generalizations of psychosocial, organizational and action theories that could be taught across the board for caseworkers, regardless of the particular settings in which they worked at any given time. Charlotte Towle's active participation on curriculum committees of the (then) American Association of Schools of Social Work gave impetus to this effort. The result was a long forward step in the building of social work theory because of the extraction, formulation, and then rapid dissemination of the "Chicago pattern" of preparation for casework practice, a pattern that bound caseworkers together in recognition of their joint concerns and knowledge base in place of the former fragmenting and fence-building of specialties.

It was in recognition of Charlotte Towle's leadership in the development of generic casework theory that the London School of Economics sought her out to be an educational consultant in its Applied Social Studies sequence. As a senior Fulbright scholar she spent 1955 at that school working in collaboration with her admirer and friend, British social work leader, Dame Eileen Younghusband. Within that year, with her habitual dedication and industry, she taught classroom and field teachers of casework, she developed case materials with them (heretofore the case method had been used only sporadically in England), identified common and basic teaching points, helped groups to find their footing in that often hidden but solid ground between abstract theory and rule-of-thumb guidance. There has been repeated and continuous testimony that the work of Charlotte Towle in that short year shaped the concepts and content of social casework education in England in fundamental ways.

Two incidents occurred in the fifties, one in 1951 and a sequel in 1954, that, in their course, rallied the whole profession of social work around Charlotte Towle. Briefly, in 1951 the president of the American Medical Association, paging through *Common Human Needs,* found the word "socialized" used as a desirable goal for individuals and for our society. "Socialized" he translated to mean "socialistic," and in a published article he leveled this charge against the Federal Security Administration under the aegis of which *Common Human Needs* had been published. The book was ordered destroyed by that agency's executive. There was, of course, high indignation throughout the field of social work, but letters of indignant protest both from social workers and from defenders of civil liberties brought no revocation of the order. Instead, the National Association of Social Workers picked up *Common Human Needs,* republished it, and gave it wide circulation.

Three years later, as Charlotte Towle was about to leave for England as a senior Fulbright scholar she found that her passport was being withheld because of suspicions of her "communist" leanings. Her suspect activities had consisted of membership in two organizations "cited by the California Committee on Un-American Activities as a Communist front," and she had signed a petition for clemency for the Rosenbergs who, as spies, had been given the death sentence. Again, letters from prominent persons and strong support from the university cleared her, and she was on her way. Her inevitable scars from this experience were perhaps soothed by the loyal rallying to her defense of scores of social workers and friends.

These two incidents might have been written off as small but vicious stupidities except that, like many small stupidities, they had their wider repercussions. One was that Charlotte Towle became a cause, a rallying point for social work and for many of its friends. Another was that the wanton "book burning," the silence or backing down of government and press in the face of the irresponsible accusations, the illustration of the vulnerability of any individual in a reactionary era—it was the time of Joe McCarthy—drove deep into the hearts and minds of all who treasured democratic freedoms and reminded social workers yet again of their inevitable involvement in social issues.

Charlotte Towle herself was most articulate. In a letter to the Federal Security Administrator on the destruction of her book she wrote, "As a social worker I care what happens to recipients under the Federal Security programs and notably the public assistance programs. The morale of an agency affects its services. To strengthen public confidence rather than to strengthen public fears is decisively important for the fulfilment of the intent of the Social Security Act. Hence what you do in your important position concerns me both as a social worker and as a citizen." And in defense of her action on the Rosenberg case she wrote, in part, to the Department of State, "I did sign the petition for clemency for the Rosenbergs. . . . I thought that the death penalty was excessive in view of all the circumstances. . . . I was not at all in sympathy with the Rosenbergs as Communists, but I would not hold belief in Communism against an individual in a court of law when he is being tried for another offense. I would punish him for his *offense*, but not for being a Communist. Were I to do otherwise I would regard myself as acting not in the Anglo-American legal tradition but like a Communist."

In the five years or so that followed her return to Chicago, Charlotte Towle was heaped with honors. Her stature as social caseworker had now long been recognized, known through her continuous productivity as a speaker and writer on subjects of concern and interest to all social workers, through her membership and always cogent and useful participation on vital national professional committees, and, of course, known and carried in the memories and actions of the hundreds upon hundreds of people who had had her as their teacher. Added to her funds of casework and social work knowledge, she had begun in the fifties to focus upon education for social work, upon its subject matters, its methods of transmission, and upon its "object matters," the student-learners themselves. In this pursuit Charlotte Towle was both an innovator and, again, an integrator.

To the complex task of preparing young men and women to use themselves—"head, heart, and hand," in her own phrase—with compassion and competence to help people in trouble, she brought now not only her own years of practical experience as a teacher, not only her carefully perused study of current educational theories, but, at base, her permeating bone-and-marrow knowledge of human motivation, aspiration, capacities, and behavior, and all the intrapersonal and external factors which could affect them for good or ill. She had attained that fusion she knew was needed when she left college: the knowledge of Johnny as learner, as well as the knowledge of what it was he needed to learn. Its attainment is stated in the title of her 1954 book, *The Learner in Education for the Professions*. The profession of social work, its practitioners, teachers, and theorists gratefully received and rewarded her achievements.

In 1956 Charlotte Towle was given the Florina Lasker Award for distinguished service to social welfare. In 1957 Tulane University, citing her contributions as teacher, author, and leader in education, awarded her an honorary LL.D. degree. In 1961 and 1962 she was again honored with LL.D. degrees, one from her own college, Goucher, and one from Western Reserve University. In 1962, further, she received the National Conference of Social Work Award, and she was given a citation honor by Loyola University in Chicago in 1965.

Charlotte Towle's service and solid contributions to various national committees have been mentioned. For the record, a few of those she held to be most important are set down here:

Chairman, Social Casework Section, National Conference of Social Work, 1943; chairman and member, Committee on Casework, American Association of Schools of Social Work, 1941–45; chairman and member, Curriculum Committee, American Association of Schools of Social Work (dates not clear); vice-chairman and member, Committee on Advanced Education, Council on Social Work Education, 1950–57; board member, Council on Social Work Education, 1951–54; social work consultant, Group for the Advancement of Psychiatry, 1946–48; chairman and mental health consultant, subcommittee on Training in Psychiatric Social Work, U.S. Public Health Service, 1947–49, 1953; editorial board, *Social Service Review*, 1944–62; executive committee, American Association of Psychiatric Social Workers, 1946. Social work advisory committees: National Red Cross, 1945–48; Veteran's Administration, 1946–48.

There are other services she gave, too numerous to set

down, including many consultations to local agencies that kept alive her awareness and sense of the practical problems in social work.

Charlotte Towle's retirement year was 1962, although she worked part time for four years thereafter. In her thirty years on the full-time faculty of the University of Chicago's School of Social Service Administration she had taught in both the master's and doctoral programs, had taught casework courses at all levels, had developed and taught courses in the dynamics of learning (for doctoral students preparing to teach), and also courses in supervision of students and staff.

The last course she developed and taught for several years was probably her favorite, the one in which she put together all she knew and understood about human development and behavior—a year-long course given to first-year students in human growth and development. It is a course which by long tradition (and perhaps by necessity, too) has been taught in schools of social work by psychiatrists, or, more recently, by a variety of "behavioral scientists," stitched together by a social worker instructor in some effort to achieve unity and continuity. In her break from this old pattern, Charlotte Towle was, again, an innovator and a persuasive one. She had long argued—quietly, firmly —that normal human behavior and normal personality development was no one profession's "property." Child development knowledge had entered the public domain. Psychiatric insights could no longer stand alone out of relationship to the insights that the social sciences were newly providing. The social work teacher, she said, needed to be the selector from among these burgeoning bodies of knowledge of what would be "knowledge for use" by social workers. Therefore she set upon this formidable task—to gather and study and winnow out and organize material for teaching the course in normal development of the human personality. To the knowledge of others she added her own, sifted through her wisdom and vision. But, more than this, she could bring to this course some of her own creative interpretations of ego functions which, for those fortunate ones whose notes recorded them, were true contributions to ego psychology.*

When she came to her last lecture in this course Charlotte Towle wept a little, and so did her students. Because, as she spoke then of old age and of the end of living, we knew that she was in part speaking of herself. In the latter years of life, she used to say, one looks back and says "I have lived on a treadmill—or on a pilgrimage." Charlotte Towle's life was the latter.

And on this pilgrimage what had happened to the person who had involved herself in it? What was Charlotte Towle like as a person, shaped by and shaper of the lifelong tasks she carried? What a person is "like" departs from objective fact. It is an interpretation by the viewer; it reflects the way he reads the other. Aware of this, I set down here what is in part my subjective experience of Charlotte Towle but what in large part I know to have been the experience of many others, too.

Once she had entered social work Charlotte Towle was *in* it and *of* it. She was never a halfway person; her decisions were carefully considered—to write or not to write this paper, to accept or not to accept this or that appointment, to go or to stay—but once she had decided she put herself whole, unstintingly, into what she had undertaken. It was a mark of her freedom from unresolved conflict that this sunny, bobbed-haired college graduate could give herself over to nurturing and caring for others. Because she trusted, because she had had and had used freedom well, because she knew herself to be loved and secure, because her lively curiosities and active initiative had been given latitude, she came to young adulthood free to invest herself in work and people. When she invested herself, when, in

---

* Some of these formulations are to be found in *The Learner in Education for the Professions*, pp. 52–85.

Erikson's terms, she was able to be "intimate" in object
relations rather than isolated within her own skin, she
found that the people she dealt with and the tasks she undertook responded to what she put into them. So she was
rewarded and herself fed into enough that she could give
out again in the fullness of nurture of which she was re-
markably capable. Free of self-doubt, secure in her personal
identity—a clarity and security that repeatedly shows itself
in her writings about the identity of social work—she was
able to fuse herself with her meaningful professional role,
to enter and carry it fully, wholeheartedly, concentratedly,
and with dedication. There were times later in life when it
came to demand too much of her, when it drained her
waning energies and left too little margin for herself. But
that self had many facets that remained, always, in play.

Maturing is sobering for all of us. Charlotte Towle's maturing years took place in the threatening shadows of the
depression, the Fascist holocaust, the war. But more than
that. Financial losses and years of sickness in her family put
their heavy weight of anxiety and continuous responsibility
on this devoted and sturdy young woman. A disciplined
patience and compassionate forbearance began to take the
place of her earlier gaiety and spontaneity. Students who
knew her only slightly or who only skimmed her courses
often saw only this surface combination of wisdom and
world-weariness. But those who were lucky enough to come
close to her or who took the trouble to look and listen
closely found the pleasures of her personality.

She had many small and delightful talents beyond those
large ones that she poured into her professional life. In her
later years she had stopped painting, promising herself that
she might pick it up in her retirement years, but the paint-
ings she had done some years before of seascapes and rocky
coastlines show not only talent but her great and buoyant
love of nature in motion. Alex Elson, a neighbor and friend,
in his memorial address quoted her as having written once,

"I love the seashore and the mountains. I also love as intensely the prairies and the desert—in short, when it comes to the out of doors, I am not difficult to please. To me the mountains and the sea are akin. The mountains are the sea in arrested motion. The prairies and the desert are sea bottoms embraced by the sky that is a sea and many a storm at sea is approximated by the movement of angry clouds. . . . Its moods and movements do not cause restlessness and melancholy of a disturbing degree—but only a finding of self through empathy."

She was, as these few lines suggested, a sensuously sensitive and responsive person, always. Beauty in nature lifted her heart. She found it in small commonplace things every day—in the subtle colors or shape of a stone, in the fine veining of a leaf, in the grey furry flash of squirrels that scuttle about the campus. Her fine feeling for colors and textures and forms showed itself in the grace and decorative charm of the apartment she and her long-time friend and companion, Mary Rall, maintained. Again she wrote, "As for apartments, I thoroughly dislike efficiency ones, nor do I like modern glass houses. I am one who likes to be inside or outside rather than inside out or outside in. Viewed from the outside I do not like the vacant stare of their façades. They look feeble-minded. I like particularly apartments built in old houses, high ceilings, fireplaces, irregular shaped rooms, like those here in my neighborhood in Chicago."

In the country—particularly in the gentle quiet of New England where she and Mary Rall most often vacationed—she loved hiking, climbing, finding rapture in a suddenly disclosed vista or wild flower or odd-shaped rock. Dame Eileen Younghusband, who came to know Charlotte Towle intimately in England, wrote, "Her enormous capacity for pleasures in simple things was one of the most characteristic things about her. . . . She kept all her life this vivid visual sense."

But she was a wicked one, too, was Charlotte Towle. Her

"wickedness" lay in her irrepressible sense of humor. Humor bubbled up in her like the leap of a fountain. Trying to control it when she held it to be inappropriate, her eyes would be aswim with tears of inner merriment. Sometimes, in serious faculty meetings or sober working conferences she would express something deadpan and understated—and it would take a few seconds before her listeners were aware that they had heard something very witty, sharp, discombobulating, something made all the funnier by its coming from that modest, grey-brown, small giant called Charlotte Towle. After hours or on vacation, when she could briefly let responsibility slip off, there would pop out that lively mischief humor of her earlier days. Her takeoffs or her wry and sometimes salty accounts of people and events could be hilariously funny to her hearers and to herself, too. But they were never malicious. Even when she "made fun," it was warmed and softened by her permeating empathy for her subjects.

Sometimes, akin to her wit, there was sharp edge to her comments, but, in Eileen Younghusband's discerning words, "The fight was always against ideas and never against people as such. Someone, to whom she had sent the draft of a red-hot memorandum, toned it down and returned it. Charlotte replied: 'I sent you pepper-pot soup, and you have turned it into cold consomme.' There was nothing cold or jellylike about that warmhearted, steadfast little figure. 'We cussed and discussed,' she said in a letter. And again: 'If there is anything more dumb than a dumb intellectual, I have yet to encounter it.' "

Mothering—in its best sense of nurturing combined with respect for the separate self of the other—permeated Charlotte Towle's personality. It found its fullest expression, of course, in her teaching and in relationships with students. But one saw it consistently, too, in her love of children, of animals, of growing plants. She looked at children and related to them unobtrusively but with keen attentiveness and receptivity. Her face came alive with responsiveness. She listened to them sensitively, feeling always for the meaning of what they said and did. And, as her lectures on child development showed, she understood them deeply.

So with animals, too, especially with dogs. She always had a Scottie—first Friday, then Paddy, then Tammas—loving this breed, she had said, for their feisty independence of spirit. Indeed they had that, and the little figure of Charlotte Towle ostensibly walking her dog but actually being pulled raggle-taggle here and there by him was one of the regular morning and late-afternoon sights on the University of Chicago campus. She would look at dogs and listen to them as if she were trying to find the human being in them—and often she did.

Gardening was a spring and summer pleasure for Charlotte Towle. Her long, green, Chicago-type back yard bloomed joyously in response to her patient and loving labors. Helping things grow, it could be said, was her lifelong push. Gardening was in this quest. So was learning and teaching.

Charlotte Towle was the teacher of thousands of social workers, some of whom had never seen her. Her expositions and interpretations of human beings under stress, of ways of helping them, of the matrix and mission of social work has been disseminated by her prolific writings and from her students to theirs in turn. In her work as consultant with numerous agencies and practitioners and in her colleague relationships she did not presume to be "the teacher" but she always became that for those who were open to her, because she was deeply knowledgeable, and sage, and because she was a generous sharer of her abundance.

In a paper that was partly a tribute to Charlotte Towle, "—and Gladly Teach"* I tried to analyze what a great

* Presented at the 1967 meeting of the Council on Social Work Education, Salt Lake City; published in *Journal of Education for Social Work*, Spring, 1967.

teacher is made up of and to see Charlotte Towle in the light of that analysis. Because I cannot now say it any better, I presume to quote from it.

The probability is that great teachers are born, or shaped in childhood. There is a charisma about them, a giftedness that is grounded in some secure sense of self. There is some generosity of mind that is the result of an inner life so abundant and rich that it spills over to give its content to others. There is some free and open receptivity to encounters with new knowledge or ideas or people that makes them able to take them in with interest and delight. And there is their obvious pleasure in the exercise of mind and action that continuously shapes their subject matter to the need of the students they teach.

These qualities were Charlotte Towle's.

One could not be with Charlotte Towle for an hour without recognizing what a store of knowledge she possessed about the individual personality and the human condition, about all the living transactions between man and his social environment. She did not just "know" these things in a static way. What she knew was constantly at play in her, lighted up, now in one area now in another by a continuously lively intelligence and probing curiosity. It was continuously being added to, not in some monolithic accretion, but in sifted, reshuffled, reorganized, newly connected ways, by her continuous study combined with a wide and varied non-professional reading, and her insightful taking in of every new person and situation she encountered. Continuously she wove, unravelled and rewove her ideas and observations and learnings so that the fabric of her knowledge was elastic and continuously in growth and change. You knew, when you opened some subject with her, that you were in the presence of a person who *possessed* what she had learned. Because she had made it her own she felt comfortable with it, with neither the need to display it nor to feel uneasy when she was faced with a gap. When she said "I don't know" it carried neither embarrassment nor annoyance but rather some pleased sense that here was something new that deserved exploration.

Charlotte Towle also had know-how. . . . One knew it with immediacy and validity in the encounters with her as teacher, consultant, colleague. She knew how to draw out and to feed into a person's own potentials and strengths, how to free initiative in others, how to empathize and support, how to differ without rancor or threat, how to criticize without hedging but also without attacking. She had the know-how, in short, to deal with another person in ways that undergirded him at the same time as he was being influenced to change.

The influence of Charlotte Towle made a deep impress upon those who learned from her because

... she loved learners as she loved learning. I have never known anyone who continuously gave so much of her time, energy and thinking to helping others work on their learning tasks. Her comments on student papers were running dialogues with them, praising or taking issue as the case might be, never simply marking right or wrong, good or poor, yes or no, but spelling out the issue that was overlooked, supplementing the under-developed idea, pointing the alternatives. She did not for a moment forget the dynamic matrix of the supporting relation-ship that provides the learner's safety island. But she was also clear about the difference between an educational and a thera-peutic focus and in the former she understood the many aspects of ego strength, cognitive among them, that empowered the learner. Her belief in the "impulse toward progression" com-bined with her love for the learner. Never was the learner her creature; rather he was seen as a self-motivated source of poten-tial professional power. The dialogue between Charlotte Towle and a learner—whether that learner was a first-year student or a colleague—was a matter of respectfully shared knowledge, opinion, judgments. If in the end you disagreed there was no threat to her or to you. Rather she took pleasure in seeing difference asserted and therefore she left one free to be himself.

This is probably the truest mark of the great teacher: that he gives generously of his knowledge and notions and attention to the student and then, having offered such nurture, he does no violence to the independence of the learner; he leaves him free to be himself. Partly it is belief in the learner's own drive for competence. Charlotte Towle combined this care and belief.

June of 1966 was the time she had set for ending. At long last—having waited on the settling of obligations and re-sponsibilities to relatives and friends—she was to be able to reap her leisure rewards, to travel, to read, perhaps to paint again, to play imaginatively with ideas she had had to tuck into her mental filing system until she had time enough and space. Late in September she and her good companion, Mary Rall, along with waggle-tailed Tammas set off for their beloved New Hampshire country. They had one week of sun and walking and breathing deep and free in the sparkling mountain air. Then, suddenly, there was a hemorrhage in that finely articulated brain and two weeks followed when she was locked in speechlessness and part-coma, and then she died.

There is nothing more to say. Except that, as her writings will show, Charlotte Towle on her life pilgrimage carried a large and goodly company with her and nourished and cared for and lighted up the sky for them all.

HELEN HARRIS PERLMAN

Part One:
The Helper and the Helped
in Social Casework

The Mental Hygiene
of the Social
Worker

MORE THAN A GENERATION of social workers has been born and come to full maturity since "The Mental Hygiene of the Social Worker" was written. It is thirty-four years old. Yet its insights and its usefulness are as pertinent today as they were then. Indeed, they may be even more readily grasped and understood, because in 1935 they ran ahead of most caseworkers in their psychological understanding or in their capacity to translate such understanding into action.

"Self-awareness" has become a shibboleth in social work and at times with the neophyte it has become a fixation upon the delicious revelations of one's self that transactions with clients call forth. Charlotte Towle's concept of self-awareness as it is revealed here was always focused upon the worker's self-in-service to his client.

What one finds here are ideas that have fresh relevance in today's focus upon client-worker transactions: the recognition not only that self knowledge is the basis for knowing another (the ancient Greeks said that) but, beyond this, the recognition that the client as he is seen and assessed is reacting not simply in expression of his characteristic self, not simply to his problems, but to the person and behavior of the caseworker. The caseworker as *actor* is pointed up here—

Reprinted from *Proceedings: Illinois State Conference of Social Welfare*, 1935.

as a vital determinant of the client's response. Today's concerns with "transaction" and "communication" are based on this recognition.

A number of other vital concepts are put forth here that had only been touched on before in writing about casework. The idea of the necessity for the worker's firm, clear sense of his own identity; the phenomenon of the two-way identification between client and worker; the reasons for and import of projection; the transference elements in relationship; the difference—still not fully absorbed by most of us —between emancipation from old parental relationships and rejection of them.

In brief one finds in this early and little-known piece (it was all but lost in a regional publication) a number of basic trenchant ideas which still govern and deserve integration with present-day thinking and practice in social work.

H. H. P.

To be effective the social worker must acquire a body of knowledge which constitutes the profession of social casework. This knowledge of methods, procedures and techniques is a recognized essential, which few would dispute as attested by the enrollment in graduate schools of social work and as affirmed by the ever widening curriculum which these schools are requiring of the individual who meets professional standards.

There is a growing recognition, too, that this content of skills and procedures alone will not enable the social caseworker to help human beings unless he understands them. A basic understanding of the cause and effect relationships in human behavior has become a significant requisite. Why the individual reacts the way he does, and how to meet his needs so that he may be enabled to react differently is a vital concern of the social caseworker—a concern which graduate schools of social work have been endeavoring to meet through courses in psychiatry, psychology, personality development, psychiatric social work, and the like. Once launched in this field the social worker has found that there is much to be learned in a field in which there still is much to be known.

A little knowledge can be a dangerous thing—with the result that there has been an increasing clamor for more and more courses, with a resultant piling on of more advanced and more technical material by the schools, together with a deeper delving by students. The caseworker, baffled by the realization that in spite of certain knowledge he was not necessarily enabled to help people, sought more and more knowledge *about* people. Unable to apply certain first principles given him in the basic courses, he has sought and still is seeking wide elaboration of first principles and an overwhelming superstructure of technical knowledge. One might ask,"To what end?," and answer sometimes, "To his greater confusion." Crichton Miller, English psychiatrist and educator, has described three phases of development in the teaching profession. The first, when the teacher of Latin needed to know Latin; the second, when it was recognized that in order to teach Johnny the teacher must know Latin and Johnny; and the third, when it was realized that she must know *herself* in order to be an effective teacher. We have come through the same phases in social casework, and today some of us are accepting these three aspects as equally essential integral parts of the whole social worker if he is to function completely and with full effectiveness.

Self ignorance has defeated many highly trained, well-informed, and widely experienced social caseworkers. Frustration day after day in dealing with people because one does not truly know or understand them in spite of extensive information *about* them, can react in such a way as to deepen personal need and further complicate and confuse the worker in his professional relationships. It is essential for us to realize that we can have much knowledge about people without really knowing people. Self-knowledge is basic in knowing people. Penetrating insight enables us to be penetrating and deepens our understanding of those to whom we relate ourselves. We see the world through our own eyes and what we see is subject to the limitations of our range of vision and to any disfunction in our visual capacity. Likewise, as we relate ourselves to people, the reaction we induce is not *solely* the reaction of the other individual, but is the product also of what we inject. His reaction is the composite interplay of two personalities, each of whom is the product of his total life experience. An individual's reaction to a given social caseworker is not his reaction in general, but his reaction to that social worker as an individual. That is why the same client may be free with one worker and constrained with another, secure with one, and defensive with another, or amenable and hostile by turn in response to the individual worker. Therefore, since the worker determines the client's response, he cannot understand the client unless he understands himself. He must see himself in others, and be aware of his own part in the client's response in order to see the client more nearly as he is. It is essential that he see himself as he is not only for a more adequate understanding of the client, but in order that he may handle his own needs, and inclinations, in short, deal with his tendency to project, in such a way as to interfere as little as possible with the client's full and free expression of himself.

What of this tendency to project? We may think that this is a rare and unusual tendency, pathological in nature by reason of the technical term, and a human ill to which the average caseworker would not be heir. Projection, however, is a common human tendency. We are all prone to more or less habitually vent both pleasurable and unpleasurable emotions onto people and circumstances which are in reality unconnected with their true cause. In projecting we may demand of others what we demand of ourselves in the way of moral standards, achievement, mode of living, and the like. Because we have certain values, we may superimpose those values onto others for whom they are illogical and without reality.

This projection of self colors much of our work and innumerable examples could be cited. It is particularly prone to occur in those individuals who lack insight, who have much unsatisfied emotion accruing from past frustrating experiences, and who, therefore, must fulfill themselves or realize satisfaction in present individuals, or circumstances. It may occur, also, to a marked degree, in individuals who are in considerable conflict and whose personality difficulties have not been worked out to the extent that they are relatively free from conflict and have gained self-acceptance, which implies an acceptance of frustration and of their own limitations, as well as awareness of their own capacities. Recognition of this tendency to project ourselves into situations, and to react to people and situations in terms of our own personal experience and personal need has influenced many aspects of our work. . . .

There is no need to elaborate the changes which have come in our philosophy of social casework through recognition of this tendency on the part of the social worker to project his own needs into the lives of others, thereby defeating his well-intentioned efforts to help individuals realize basic growth. Present-day trends which emphasize the identity of the client and which stress the opportunity for self-determinism as his inalienable right in any casework situation are based on our growing awareness of how the worker's personal needs have interfered and may continue to obstruct the client's development. In this connection it is well to note that because of the reciprocal nature of the relationship between worker and client that in frustrating the client, the worker inevitably has interfered with his own development. Insofar as the worker enables the client to develop, he himself realizes growth. In so far as he projects his own needs, he entangles himself in the other individual, and experiences the frustration, the defeat which is almost inevitable when the client is exposed to the ensnaring experience of being lived in and through by another, rather than left free to live his own life.

Closely related to the tendency to project is the process of identification. In case work we all identify in some measure with our clients. In fact, the human tendency to identify may be regarded as the very core of altruism—and the motive force in all social work. Because we have all experienced defeat, frustration, deprivation, despair in some degree, because we have all known pain, unhappiness, and hunger at least in slight measure, we are enabled to put ourselves in the place of those who are disadvantaged and to feel with them and for them. This capacity to identify is a vital factor in social casework. A caseworker with meagre capacity to identify would be definitely handicapped in relating herself to people. It is an essential element in all human relationships. Identification occurs sometimes, however, in excessive degree in response to deep personal need and in such emotional pressure, when we are frustrated in our own desires and urges in life, when we are feeling deprived and defeated, in short, when we have much unsatisfied emotion to unload, and when we do not *understand* our needs and urges, then unconsciously we may give vent to them through close identification with others. The human being identifies in accordance with his emotional need. The urge to be completely at one with others is a fundamental human urge through which we seek security, the primary pattern for which is rooted in the child's identification with the mother, so that this urge symbolizes an attempt to re-identify with the mother throughout life. Consequently, it may be utilized to excess in times of extreme need, particularly if we are not consciously aware of this tendency and of our need.

What happens when a social caseworker identifies rather closely and completely with a client in the fulfillment of his need? The result is that he ceases merely to feel *with* the client but feels *like* him. This implies that he may react like him—that he may throw all the emotional pressure of his own unsatisfied feelings into fortifying and intensifying the client's feeling response. In short, the worker virtually becomes the client—or the patient. When this occurs he cannot help him, but instead probably will intensify his insecurity and his need—whatever that need may be. A caseworker who has led and is leading a meagre unsatisfied life, who is suffering deprivation through straitened financial circumstances, who has little security in any present relationships, and who is feeling embittered and defeated, may feel so identical with the client that he may augment the client's feeling of hostility and defeat and intensify his antagonism toward the organization and the social order. Or in such an instance, he may find his identity with the client so painful and unacceptable, because the client's predicament and feeling reaction recreate and intensify his own life situation, that he may need to reject the client. In such a case we might find the worker blocking the client's expression of hostility, arguing with him in defense of the social order, defending the organization and negating the client through dominating measures, or through deprivation. Such a reaction might mean an inability to experience identification with the client whose lot in life and whose feelings are as unacceptable to the worker as his own. . . . In either instance, this worker would be unable to help this client handle his own feelings in such a way as to attain a more comfortable acceptance of his life situation.

One could cite innumerable examples. In a clinic situation, a worker whose own childhood experience had been unsatisfying, who had experienced marked hostility toward her overauthoritative parents, and who still was feeling antagonistic toward them and thereby toward parent persons in general, identified closely with an adolescent girl whose foreign parents seemed overauthoritative in contrast to the parents of her associates. She wanted the freedom of the American girl. The worker, through feeling completely at one with the girl versus her parents, bent all her efforts toward getting the parents to give the child more freedom. The youngster apparently fortified by the worker reacted with intensified hostility toward her parents, becoming more and more self-willed and disobedient. To quote the father—"she went wild." Sexual delinquency and pregnancy resulted. It is needless to state that the parents condemned the social worker, saying—"She was always against us." This worker was not sufficiently free from her own emotional need to identify in any measure with the parents, or to see the total situation. Reared in an overprotective environment and having experienced throughout life the domination of her parents, this patient was not prepared to use the new freedom wisely, nor was she able to handle the released feelings of hostility toward her parents. The worker not only was unable to help her cope with her feelings but she was also too involved to see that probably it would have been more wise to have helped the patient accept the limitations of the parents, as a first step in a gradual emancipation. Obviously, she could not have done this, limited as she was through her own non-acceptance of the parents. It was only through emotional acceptance of all the members of this family that this worker could have helped the various individuals in their relationships with one another.

Acceptance of others implies self-acceptance. The individual who has self-knowledge in the true meaning of the term, not only understands but accepts himself and thereby is enabled to accept others because he does not have to fulfill his own limitations in others. Some people react against the term self-acceptance. To them it connotes self-satisfaction, or abject resignation and a defeatist attitude. It does not imply any of these attitudes, however, nor does acceptance of others imply indifference or apathy as arising out of a feeling that people cannot be changed.... The self-accepting individual sees and feels his likeness to others and his difference from others. He is no longer anxious about his likeness or his difference for, having realized emancipation from dependence on parent persons, he neither fears absorption by others or separation from others. His security lies within himself. He is therefore free to identify, or to remain apart—in short, he is free to relate himself to others, and he is enabled also to accept their likeness and their difference. Because he is secure within himself, he does not need to fulfill himself in them. Instead, therefore, of implying self-satisfaction, resignation, or defeat, self-acceptance implies freedom to develop and to permit and to help others develop in accordance with their need. . . .

The client has need for the worker to maintain his own identity—for therein may lie his source of security. In this connection it is well to comment on identification on the part of the client. The person seeking help identifies in accordance with his need. The person who is disadvantaged, who for the time being is feeling inadequate in meeting his life situation in one respect or another seeks difference in the caseworker. He does not need to feel completely at one with someone whose feelings are identical with his own. To do so would not promote security. He needs to feel that the worker is different in the sense of *feeling* different—that he has a certain adequacy which he, the client, at the present moment lacks. He strives to gain adequacy through identification with the worker. Accordingly the client may need to go through a phase of identification with the worker. One sees him taking over some of the worker's attitudes, the worker's ways, and one sees him also striving to meet situations as the worker would meet them. This is a period of emotional dependence on the part of the client—an inevitable growth phase—which unfortunately may frighten the worker if he does not understand the client's need or his own reaction thereto. With dependency as the bugaboo which haunts the case worker's mind as being that something which must never be induced, he may flee meeting this need—through discouraging or frustrating the client, or through withdrawing his interest and his effect from the client. Because of this tendency on the part of the client, it is doubly essential that the worker understand himself, for it is his therapeutic responsibility to direct the relationship so that the client's need may be met without indulging his own identification needs. . . .

An illustration of the individual's frequent need for difference in the social worker follows:

A thirteen-year-old boy had been referred to a clinic because of delinquent behavior which seemed to have been of sudden onset and which represented a radical change in personality. This lad was undersized, underweight, and during his early years had been closely guarded by an anxious mother because of prolonged illness which had resulted in cardiac involvement. . . . He was the youngest child and the only son whose father, on whom the mother had been quite dependent, had died when the boy was an infant. Four older sisters had contributed to the infantalization of the boy through coddling him and dominating him. The boy had suffered throughout his early school years through social isolation. . . . He could not play games and frequently was annoyed by the teasing of his schoolmates who derided him for being teacher's pet. This boy's attachment to a lad of fifteen who was a bully and the leader of a gang of a notoriously rough crowd is quite understandable. He became the hero-worshipping, abject follower of this youth whose ways he was emulating. He found this identification very satisfying, not only because of his need for masculine adequacy but perhaps also because in the aggrandizing, antisocial behavior which he was enacting through the identification, he found an outlet for the repressed hostility which is so often an accompaniment of dependency.

When the boy was brought to the clinic, he was troubled by the consequences of his behavior and showed some remorse over having hurt his mother. He seemed accessible and was responsive to the psychiatrist to whom he revealed fantasies about his father and longing for a father relationship. The psychiatrist recommended a male social worker with whom the boy might identify as a substitute satisfaction for the present delinquent companion. The man assigned to the case was a physically frail individual, a shy passive person who gave the impression of being somewhat dependent. There were indications that he had not resolved his own mother dependency. He evidenced considerable zeal in his work with delinquent boys—and was imbued with the urge to reform them. In his work with this boy he was moralistic. He could not understand or accept the delinquent behavior. He stressed good, conforming behavior and tended to project his own ideals, standards, and patterns of behavior upon this boy—to whom obviously they were unacceptable, since they typified the kind of adjustment against which this boy had been reacting. The boy could not identify with this worker. Instead he came into instant combat with him, and in his flight from this relationship he was driven to further lengths in the enactment of his delinquency. In this connection it is of interest that he always regaled the worker with detailed accounts of his misdemeanors. This may have been an expression of hostility toward the worker, or it may have been a plea for acceptance of his masculine, aggressive behavior. If the worker could have been understanding and accepting of this, perhaps he would have taken on some masculine values for the boy—and an identification, thereby, might have been facilitated. As it was, he could only frustrate the patient and intensify his present need for antisocial behavior.

The worker needs self-understanding in order to understand the transference which may occur in the casework situation somewhat as in the psychoanalytic situation, even though there may be less distortion and less intense feeling in the displaced affect occurring in the former instance than in the latter. In psychoanalytic terms the transference is the process of transferring to the analyst . . . emotion left over from some earlier relationship or experience. Sometimes this emotion is expressed in positive affect—as love, admiration, affection—but it is quite as often expressed negatively in terms of hatred, anger, resentment, or scorn. During analytical treatment much old and forgotten emotional experience comes to the surface which relates to people who have been significant to the individual in the past. . . . As these associations are revived, the individual unconsciously transfers to the analyst the emotions he has felt in the past for this or that person. The analyst becomes in turn the father, the mother, the sibling, the lover, and onto him is projected the patient's feeling of irritation, dissatisfaction, jealousy, devotion, childlike dependence, etc. This process has the effect of freeing the patient from old, frustrated, largely unrealized and confused relationships through giving him the experience of living through these various relationships with an individual who accepts him in each and every role; who meets the varying situations between himself and the patient without emotional involvement and who, by means of free association and by analysis of the transference, helps him bring to consciousness the real origin of the emotions, disentangling reality from fantasy. Having experienced acceptance and understanding in these varying relationships through the one therapeutic relationship, the individual gains self-acceptance which implies a capacity to work out his own identity in an untrammeled fashion. . . .

In casework there is growing awareness that the worker encounters the transference as just defined. To be sure in many instances the feelings of the client may be more diluted and the projections less distorted—but they are there in shadow form and consequently may be less clear and less comprehensive. They must be understood and accepted just as in the analytic situation if the client is to work out his own identity through being freed from entangling and unfulfilled personal relationships which continually interfere with his social adaptation. When a social caseworker meets unexpected hostility in a client which seemingly is unrelated to the superficial circumstances in the service situation, it is well for him to ask himself, "Who am I to this individual?" "Who is he making of me?" If he is aware that the hostility is not necessarily directed toward him as a person but toward him insofar as he symbolized someone else, then the worker will not be so prone to react defensively—but instead, conceivably would become interested in understanding the client's projection, and in helping him to understand and cope with his feelings. How often we see well-intentioned caseworkers arguing defensively with hostile clients, thereby perhaps repeating old frustrating parental relationships. Or we may see them meeting demanding dependency needs in a flustered, protesting, but nevertheless, anxious and solicitous parental fashion, thereby frustrating the client in the working through of his authority-dependency problem. In such an instance a client might readily need to experience a relationship which in no way resembled his own early parental situation. There is no growth opportunity for him in recreating his own early life situation. In fact, there is the possibility of intensifying his social difficulty through so doing.

It is obvious that in order to understand the client's use of him, the worker would have to be well oriented as to his own part in the interplay of client and worker. A worker needs to see and understand what he himself has done or is doing to determine the client's reaction. He needs this understanding also to enable him to be nonjudgmental and uninvolved emotionally. He needs it, furthermore, in order to help the client understand his own feeling response. There is a growing awareness that in addition to affording the client a unique relationship—in the sense of making no emotional demands through which he can re-experience former frustrated relationships—the caseworker should enable the client to bring his feelings for the worker to a conscious level through verbalization. The purpose of this is to clarify and objectify the relationship for both worker and client. Dr. Temple Burling, in an article entitled, "The Value of Explicit Acknowledgement of the Transference,"[1] discusses the value of this procedure in social casework. Understanding of self is essential in this process, otherwise fears and emotional needs may block the worker. . . .

Throughout this discussion of the worker's need for self-awareness in order to avoid projection of self, in order also to avoid strong identification as determined by deep personal need, and in order to understand and handle the transference, there is repeated mention not only of the need for self-knowledge but also for self-acceptance if he is to understand and accept others so that they, in turn, may be helped in self-understanding and self-acceptance. What are the implications of self-acceptance and how does one become accepting of others? One sees here a certain continuity—the worker's self-acceptance predetermines acceptance of others—the client must experience this acceptance in order to gain self-acceptance, and thereby acceptance of others which implies improved relationships and a better adjustment to the limiting realities of his life. At what point does the worker's acceptance of self begin? The worker likewise must have experienced acceptance in some relationship in order to have gained this capacity. The worker's effectiveness is therefore predetermined by the nature of the relationships which he has experienced.

When one considers that from infancy onwards the conflicts and inhibitions of life are concerned largely with tan-

1. *American Journal of Orthopsychiatry*, vol. 4, no. 4 (October 1934).

gled or unfulfilled personal relationships, it seems natural, in fact, almost inevitable, that many of us may bring to the social casework situation much unfulfilled need as predetermined by frustrating relationships. In considering the relationships which the social caseworker has experienced, we get back to the early parental relationships just as we do in the life of any other individual. In discussing identifications, August Aichorn states that "they are the product of the early attachment of the child to his parents. . . ." "The child's attachment to the family, the continuance and the subsequent dissolution of these love relationships within the family, not only leave a deep effect on the child through the resulting relationships; they determine at the same time the actual form of his love relationships in the future." He further states that "Freud compares these forms, without implying too great a rigidity, to copper plates for engraving. He has shown that in the emotional relationships we can do nothing but make an imprint from one or another of these patterns which we have established in early childhood."[2] The nature, therefore, of the early parent-child relationship may predetermine the caseworker's effectiveness.

When one considers that the parental patterns were likewise predetermined, we can face our early parental relationships and what they mean to us—wherein they were dissatisfying and frustrating or wherein they were fulfilling—without any sense of condemning our parents but instead with a sense of understanding them and with a feeling of greater acceptance of them. That many of us experienced parental relationships which frustrated our growth, interfered with the working out of our identities, induced dependency, instilled hostility is a natural and inevitable reality in the evolution of parenthood. It does not imply that many of us were unloved, grossly neglected, or experienced rejection at the hands of our parents. It means merely that the adult throughout generations has been prone to superimpose his own standards, desires, and needs upon the child just as these standards, desires, and needs were imposed

2. August Aichorn, *Wayward Youth* (New York: The Viking Press, 1935) p. 118.

upon him. The child long has been regarded as a plastic model in the hands of the parent. The most conscientious and devoted parents have sometimes intruded upon the child's development with well-intentioned efforts. How many parents are sufficiently free from emotional involvement to permit the child to develop his own individuality? Instead they are prone to make him do this or that, or be the kind of person which may fulfill their own need. One parent may want his child to be a replica of himself, another may want him to be and realize all that he failed to be or realize—all of this occurring unconsciously out of the parent's self-love or unacceptance of self and in either instance the parent may have been molding the child against his inclination. If he were to be himself he would be some one entirely different from that image for which the parent had been striving through him.

How many of us, if we were to know ourselves, would find that we have ever really been ourselves? Many of us go through life enacting a part projected onto us and accepted by us out of our need for security in the parent, which implied being accepted by the parent. We felt accepted perhaps insofar as we were *not ourselves*. Therefore, we may not have experienced a relationship which offered acceptance of our *real* selves. Thereby, we may not have realized much basic satisfaction or security—but it perhaps afforded the most satisfaction and the most security we could derive under existing circumstances. It represented the best possible adjustment we could make, but even so it may have left us with certain basic needs which must be met through projection of our frustrated desires onto others and through close identifications with other persons in accordance with our needs.

Parental relationships in which the individual has not experienced acceptance of his real self complicate the emancipation process. In such instances the individual sometimes has gone through life enacting a role which has been projected upon him by the parents. The parents thereby contince to be the source of his identity. If he were to separate from them he would have no security in himself, for

his real self is undeveloped. . . . Many individuals may feel
that they have emancipated from the parents because they
live separate from them, support themselves, or because
at some point they have perhaps reacted against the parent. Sometimes we confuse separation, self-maintenance,
and rejection of the parents with a gradual growth away
from parental dependence. Cutting off and growing away
may have entirely different implications. The former may
leave one dependent and in need of re-enacting parental
identifications. The latter should leave one free to enact
one's own identity. How many of us are living our own lives
instead of being lived in and through by subtle likes and
dislikes, biases, prejudices, aspirations, and traditional
urges which we little understand because they are not our
own—but which we did not lose in the process of being
severed from the parent, since separation did not necessarily imply growth.

Some social caseworkers may have experienced parental
relationships which have afforded them growth opportunity—in the sense of actual emancipation from parental ties
and the realization of self-identity. Others may have experienced subsequent relationships which have implied an acceptance of the real self thereby achieving emancipation
and self-identity at some later point in their lives. In these
instances one would expect a minimum of difficulty in accepting and utilizing psychiatric and casework concepts and
in meeting the needs of people. Others may find themselves
continually meeting personal defeat, reacting with tension
or strain to the impact of the many lives with which they
are inevitably in contact; others may find themselves unable to face reality—as implied in the acceptance of the
treatment limitations in a case situation; the reality limitations in what they can accomplish, the reality limitations of
time and of energy. They may find themselves persisting indefinitely in handling situations which are beyond their
professional scope and capacity; they may be unable to
terminate case situations, or they may need to close them
prematurely because the client does not need what they
need to give. . . .

And throughout they may find themselves completely at loss in utilizing the wide information *about* people which they have derived through prolonged study. Feeling inadequate they may react to this with a quest for more and more knowledge, thereby building up the aforementioned superstructure of technical knowledge, which may prove to be overwhelming because it grows progressively more and more useless. Frustrated in spite of their intensive study, they may at some point experience disillusionment, at which time we might expect a projection to ensue—in the form of a reaction against psychiatry or casework. Psychiatry becomes the logical target for this projection because presumably it is the main source of knowledge about human behavior. One may see in such instances a strong reaction against psychiatry and hear such comments as "There is nothing in it!" or there may be warm protests against the limitations of psychiatry. "It accomplishes too little," "It is not a cure all"—*valid protests*, for psychiatry has limited scope at its present stage of development in the present social order. One meets here, however, the rage at limitations which comes when the individual does not understand or accept his own limitations, or is not free to function effectively.

Some workers at this point of disillusionment do not project in this fashion but instead face themselves and seek help. Hopefully the day has passed when there is any professional stigma attached to the social caseworker's . . . getting help because of the growing realization that the experiencing of a therapeutic situation in which they may work through previous tangled or unfulfilled relationships enables them to be more effective in their professional relationships.

In stressing the tendency of some social workers to escape the source of their inadequacy through fortifying themselves with more and more technical information, I am not minimizing the importance of a wide knowledge. The caseworker cannot know too much about human behavior and the social order in which we live. When the caseworker, however, meets with difficulties in applying first principles, it is to be hoped that he will be helped to see his difficulties in relation to himself, so that he will be directed toward a pursuit of self-understanding, rather than encouraged to escape himself through the acquisition of more technical knowledge at a time when he is unable to assimilate and utilize it.

In graduate schools of social work the responsibility of so guiding the student social worker may fall upon the field-work supervisor. In organizations this responsibility may be that of the casework supervisor. All of the thinking brought out in this paper on the mental hygiene of the social worker applies also to the supervisor of casework. Insofar as he has been an effective caseworker he will probably be an effective supervisor. As he relates himself to the workers under his supervision he will be confronted with the same need for self-awareness—lest he project, identify, or handle the relationship with the work in such a way as to obstruct the worker's development. At all times the responsibility of the supervisor could be said to be that of affording the worker a relationship through which he is afforded a growth opportunity, which implies understanding and acceptance of his individual needs in order that he in turn may be enabled to express himself as freely as possible in the casework situation. It is only through such an opportunity that the worker may gain self-understanding in his casework, for if the supervisor intrudes his needs the situation may be complicated in such a way as to obscure the worker as an individual. He will not appear as he is either to himself or to the supervisor, and the latter will be limited in helping the worker see himself in his relationships with the client. A realization of his bearing upon the development of the worker, and thence upon the worker's effectiveness with the client, has induced a new awareness amongst casework supervisors, amongst whom there is a growing concern about their supervision. . . .

The field of social casework is swept almost annually with a hue and cry of new methods, new approaches, new emphases. Every national conference has its keynote of this or that emphasis or overemphasis. Avid and needful for a solution, social workers respond with a hectic pursuit of the last word, in a reaction so widespread and so compulsive that one is reminded of the sweep of flames through dry grass, only to experience again the acrid smoke of frustration and disillusionment. When will we get a realization of self which will enable us to experience our work in the full sense of the word and to work freely in such a way as to evolve methods that are effective for ourselves as individuals, or to apply effectively those which have been evolved and to realize in practice the knowledge which right now presumably is a part of our equipment? When one looks at the contributions to the field made by those who have been free to experience self-identity, one is impressed by the wide difference in techniques and emphases, a difference which frequently leads to controversy and confusion but which should not confuse us. The approach or method used by one individual does not necessarily become a natural part of another individual's way of relating himself to people in a therapeutic situation. Individual difference in the utilization of concepts is inevitable if each worker is functioning completely and effectively as an individual. Our need to take over in stereotyped fashion another person's way of working may indicate dependence, a need to identify completely because we have no security within ourselves. Perhaps we are still enacting roles projected onto us by others and we may need to continue to do so. As supervisors and instructors of casework, we may need to project our ways of working onto others because in so far as we see ourselves enacted through others we may get a sense of personal adequacy and reassurance about our methods. Unfortunately, however, when we do this we meet with much personal defeat, for the supervisor seldom recognizes his methods, so distorted do they become in the practice of another when they have been superimposed out of his own need for self-fulfillment.

Increasingly as caseworkers realize growth one may expect a growing freedom in the utilization of concepts and a more effective use of their professional orientation. Present-day supervisors have a definite responsibility for the professional development of the caseworkers of today. On our shoulders rests the responsibility of imparting content in such a way as to facilitate growth through affording the worker a relationship which gives security without engendering dependence—one which offers him an opportunity for self-acceptance through our acceptance of him as an individual, different from ourselves, with capacities which hopefully may far outreach our capacities and with limitations which he may not need to fulfill in his casework.

Factors
in Treatment

A NUMBER OF IDEAS shine forth in this down-to-earth, practice-based paper, ideas which were to become nuclear to Charlotte Towle's theory of casework practice. One is the idea of *motivation:* "consideration for what the client seeks is a first principle." A second is that of *capacity.* The client's capacity for relating and using relationship is seen as a central criterion for treatability. Third, one sees here that firm beginning of Charlotte Towle's continuing efforts to formulate, in systematic ways, the accruing practice knowledge of casework. Thus she identified and organized the signs by which relationship capacity might be gauged as good or poor, criteria which stand as relevant and useful today as they did when she identified them thirty-three years ago.

Only touched on here are a number of other comments Charlotte Towle made in passing (those who knew her learned to examine the wake of her thought for the bright particles of "throw-away" ideas), comments worth further

Reprinted from *Proceedings: National Conference of Social Work* (Chicago: University of Chicago Press, 1936).

notice today. Among them: the agency function as a treatment determinant; the criterion of the problem's pervasiveness or chronicity in prognosticating treatment means and outcomes; the need for assessment of and intervention in the client's living environment; the uses of treatment in yielding diagnosis; and the reader will find more.

H. H. P.

In general three sets of factors interplay in casework treatment. The function of the agency, the professional qualifications of the worker, and those factors inherent in the client's total situation together determine the treatment possibilities in any given case. So close is the interaction of these elements that it is difficult to isolate one set of factors for separate consideration.

Many cases have been closed with the notation, "Client untreatable," when he may have been treatable within the limitations of his purpose, within the scope of the agency's function, and within the professional grasp of a well-oriented social worker. The social worker's orientation then can be regarded as the core of the treatment situation. Her ability to understand the client and to accept his limitations, her understanding of self together with the degree of her self-acceptance, as well as her acceptance of the agency's responsibility to the community as implied in its functional limitations will determine the treatment possibilities in any given case. Valid statements regarding treatment potentialities emerge only in those instances wherein the social worker has brought into play an integration of these factors.

Every simple casework procedure may have fundamental or superficial treatment value depending upon its meaning to the individual. Every casework contact from the initial interview to the termination of treatment likewise has the treatment implications which may have deep or casual values, depending again upon its meaning for the individual. He may gain increased self-understanding and self-acceptance with a resultant increased capacity for solving his difficulties through the treatment interview in which he is helped to secure release of feeling and in which he experiences acceptance of that feeling. In the average casework situation this may not occur in clearly defined treatment sessions divorced from usual casework activity. In all casework contacts there is opportunity for this process to occur. Caseworkers may render specific services or give suggestions about handling of critical problems at any point in the treatment contact, but in so doing it is their primary concern to release the feeling necessary to enable the client to utilize these services and suggestions in a growth direction. It is essential, also, that they direct the emotional interplay between worker and client so that the relationship results in development of the client—which implies that they direct it so that he experiences acceptance and understanding. Specific services may create tensions or they may facilitate the release of feeling, but inevitably they produce a response which has to be met by the caseworker in a progressive treatment process.

One sees, then, that we do not function categorically. There is no such division of labor as implied in simple routines on the one hand, and complicated treatment sessions on the other. Treatment in any case implies a flexible meeting of the needs of the individual. This involves diagnostic skill unhampered by unprofessional bias, and a capacity for relationship which is not obstructed by personal need for self-gratification in the treatment process. The nature of treatment is not predetermined by the social worker, but is determined by the response of the client.

We are confronted in every case with the need for one or more exploratory interviews. In these interviews the client presents the nature of his problem as he sees it and feels it. He is given freedom to elaborate what he thinks and feels about his situation. He is led to express his purpose in bringing his problem to us, as well as to tell us what he himself wants to do about it. During these interviews the worker not only is observing and evaluating but also is participating in his exploration of his problem. The primary purpose of these interviews is that the individual may be given an opportunity to reveal himself. First, that we may understand him and thus be enabled to assist him. Second, that in revealing himself he may experience increased self-understanding with a resultant reorientation in his life situation, providing, of course, that he is able to use this opportunity in that direction. Sometimes reorientation at this point may imply a clarified decision as to whether or not he wishes help and wants to continue with treatment. In these interviews as throughout continuing treatment contacts there should be on the part of the worker a capacity for sensing what the client wants. This implies an understanding of the unconscious meaning of his words, and a realization that his feelings about his experiences are as important as the facts of his experience. She should be able to allow a free development of the relationship with the client and be sensitive to the use that he is making of it.

While few criteria have been established for determining the treatment possibilities in a case, certain indicators have emerged which guide the worker as to general direction, emphasis, duration of treatment, and the need for termination. Some of those which have been rather definitely formulated are as follows.

Recognition of the importance of the client's purpose, in determining the nature of treatment and whether or not he can be served by a particular agency or individual, is so general that it will not be elaborated at any length even though it has many implications. Consideration for what the client seeks is a first principle among caseworkers today. This does not mean that every treatment situation is rigidly limited to a specific objective which he brings and which may be relatively trifling as compared with other problems evidenced in his total situation. It does mean, though, that the caseworker meets the need which he brings with understanding. She grants him the reality of his feeling about his problem so that in process of revealing his needs he may experience help, which may lead him to seek further assistance in other areas.

A client applies for relief. In handling the relief situation, either in granting relief or in withholding it, the worker's acceptance and understanding of the client's feelings about this problem may induce him to seek help about other troublesome matters. If the worker has perceived his wants, if she has followed his feelings and allowed free development of the relationship, one would expect a developing changing purpose in the client in accordance with his further needs. If this development does not occur under these circumstances, we can well question whether or not he wants further help. One can question, also, his capacity for relationship. If he does not want help, it would be futile to impose it. If he has diminished capacity for relationship, then he will be unable to respond except within the limits of this capacity. This does not mean that he would not be served in regard to external needs if these came within the function of the agency, but it does mean that the casework service would proceed in accordance with his wants, at any given time. Change in external circumstances might gradually effect some modification in his feelings and attitudes so that at some later time he might become accessible for further treatment, at which time his needs could be met.

In any situation the use which the individual makes of his problem—that is, the emotional value which this behavior has for him—will determine what he can do about modifying his behavior, or what the social worker can do in helping him. If his problem is irritating, if he suffers discomfort, then he may respond to the available help unless the irritation and discomfort are meeting a deep need for self-punishment to the extent that he could be said to be enjoying his misery. If his behavior is meeting some basic need to his satisfaction, and there are no alternative satisfactions available toward which the social worker can direct him, then she may be unable to help him. In this connection it is essential that the social worker understand the unconscious motivation in order to know the treatment possibilities. It will not be her task to treat the unconscious problem, but she will need to use the meaning of his behavior in terms of the unconscious factors in order to deal with the conscious manifestations which are of concern to the client.

The duration of the symptomatic behavior may also signify treatment possibilities. Since persistent behavior is for the most part satisfying, or it would not persist, long-standing symptoms imply prolonged satisfaction in a certain mode of behavior. Again, one confronts the factor of satisfaction or dissatisfaction as a determinant in what the individual may or may not be able to do about his problem, with this additional complication. Changing circumstances in the life of an individual gradually may have rendered certain long-standing behavior less satisfying, or even irritating. But because of the crystallization of the patterns, the rigidity of related attitudes, and the immobility of the response of others who continue to contribute to his reaction, he may be unable to change without very fundamental help. In this instance the techniques of the psychiatrist might be more effective, because the client would need a deep regenerative experience which would involve direct treatment of unconscious problems.

Closely related to this factor of duration of the symptomatic behavior is the extent of the area of life-experience involved in the individual's behavior. A person may be having difficulty in a given life-relationship, with some recognition of his part in the problem and some desire for help in working out the relationship. Such a person might readily utilize social case treatment which would enable him to release his feeling and gain further insight about his difficulty through his having been afforded a relationship in which his feelings are accepted and understood. In this experience he might gain self-understanding and an increased capacity for relationship which would help him in working through his present problem. Another individual, also presenting difficulties in a given life-relationship, might be found to be having difficulties in all of his relationships. Furthermore, one might find that the present extensive problem was not of recent origin—that disturbed vital life-relationships in the early life and throughout the intervening years preceded the present more extensive involvement. The treatment implications here would be quite different—in fact, one questions whether social case treatment would be indicated—and again the need for psychiatric treatment arises.

Another example in relation to the extent of involvement is given because this is a significant point and often an ascertainable one which can guide the social worker in determining the direction of treatment. A client presents an evasive attitude toward certain realities in his present life-situation. It would be important for the social worker to ascertain the following: whether this attitude was confined to a certain area of his life, or whether it was justified by the nature of the reality situation—that is, has the client withdrawn under the pressure of overwhelming circumstances or has he consistently reacted to vital life-experiences with evasion. In the former instance the individual might be helped to face reality issues through an easing of environmental irritants, if this were possible, as well as through the casework interviews if he has not grown too protective to participate in this situation. In the latter case, however, one might have a person who would be unable to use any help directed toward enabling him to meet reality.

Frequently in such an instance one meets an interplay of factors: first, there is the long duration of the difficulty; second, one suspects deep satisfaction in the dependency which is implied in escaping responsibility; third, one may encounter meager capacity for relationships as predetermined by long-standing withdrawal; fourth, one questions the individual's desire for help since escape measures may have brought a comfortable nirvana from which he is loath to emerge, when in contrast the realities of life would seem harsh. Here we would have a dubious case for either psychiatric or social case treatment directed toward a reintegration of the personality or toward changed attitudes. In this instance, the person probably would utilize any treatment in furthering his dependency. In rendering essential case services, then, one would recognize and accept the fundamental dependency factor and not expect a growth response. Social caseworkers are sometimes criticized for withholding services from such individuals, out of their well-intentioned desire for active participation in the growth interests of these persons. It is essential that we recognize basic limitations and do not impose our standards of how a client ought to react if he is to grow when he is incapacitated for growth.

This leads to another point in our diagnostic thinking—the question of related attitudes. A client may present problems in a certain area which have induced attitudes which contribute to reinforce, or further, the crystallization of the original problem. For example, an individual may have enjoyed dependency to such an extent that he has clung to infantile satisfactions. In meeting the reality issues of life, however, he felt inadequate, thereby developing anxieties and fears. In spite of enjoyment of dependency, some hostility may have been induced toward those who had infantalized him, with perhaps resultant feelings of guilt for his hatred of those to whom he felt deeply obligated. The guilt, in turn, may have engendered further anxiety. Thus one sees a ramification of feelings and attitudes arising out of the original dependency problem.

One may find that the related attitudes are quite fixed. The client cannot relinquish them, for as long as he is fearful he is justified in withdrawing, while his hostility persists also because it motivates a continuance of dependency—perhaps with the purpose of punishing others. One must consider then the purpose which these related attitudes serve the individual. If they enable him to protect himself, through justifying basic need, then they may not be readily modified. When one finds a rigidity induced by the purposeful interplay of feelings and attitudes, one has a situation which is not adapted to social case treatment measures. The release of emotional tension or the redirection of the behavior arising out of unconscious drives probably will not be effective. Again, one has a case in which direct treatment of unconscious problems is indicated, which in turn implies referral to a psychiatrist for basic treatment, if available and if the individual is receptive to this procedure. The social caseworker's role in such an instance might be that of easing the environmental situation, in so far as it is possible to do so.

Another factor significant to social caseworkers is the environment. The client's subjective feelings imply careful consideration of the objective reality of his environment. How mobile is his environment? Frequently we are unable to help him realize growth and thus manifest changed attitudes because we cannot effect environmental change for him, or assist him in effecting that change. Any attempt to evaluate the treatment possibilities in a case, therefore, must take into account the potentials for change within this area. We have met many overwhelming obstacles herein during recent years. Frustrated in this regard, social caseworkers perhaps have in some instances attempted more exhaustive direct therapy of the individual than was indicated in view of the total situation. The futility of such efforts has been demonstrated and should lead social caseworkers to an acceptance of their limitations. Facing reality on this score might direct energy otherwise wastefully consumed toward a more purposeful interest in social action.

The nature of the relationship which it is possible to establish with a client may determine the treatment possibilities in a case. Understanding the manifestations of relationship is, therefore, essential in our diagnostic thinking. So much emphasis has been placed upon this factor that we are prone to be anxious about it. We become self-conscious, tense, less free in being ourselves as we strive for relationship, and in so doing we obstruct its development. A person who is seeking help may withdraw or become antagonistic in response to the emotional pressure of the striving social worker. He needs to have his emotional need met and is not able to meet the demand of the worker. In such an instance there may occur a reversal of roles in which the client is forced into the position of meeting the worker's demands, rather than the worker being free to meet his need. Confusion in relationship inevitably results under these circumstances. Perhaps we should be more at ease if we understand that this element develops naturally out of the following conditions:

The individual's need will determine whether or not he will want a relationship with us. Unless he wants something he probably will not participate. Or if his needs are excessive, he may be frustrated in any attempted relationship because we cannot meet the depth of his need. In such instances one may find him resorting to many material or service demands, by utilizing the interviews for an endless, repetitive dramatization of himself on an attention-getting basis, or by being hostile and negativistic. His reaction in many cases might represent an attempt to get something from the worker to compensate himself for what he is unable to realize in terms of his basic need, or it might be an attempt to retaliate for the frustration which he has experienced.

The caseworker's ability to follow the individual's feeling, and her capacity for acknowledging the reality of his feelings and directing treatment with consideration for them without imposing her values, her judgments, or her need to win a response, are other vital factors in the development of relationship. In short, the worker's capacity for relationship in contrast to an inclination to identify subjectively may determine the nature of the client's response.

The client's capacity for relationship is another essential element. Some individuals have been so deprived throughout life in the vital relationships which make for growth, that they seem not to have developed an inclination to relate themselves to others or any ability to do so. Other individuals have experienced so much frustration, through having been deeply hurt in their vital life-relationships, that they have become fearful about relationships to the extent that they withdraw from any closeness to people. They will not be hurt again. In either instance one may note a marked protective reaction, a deep-lying kind of narcissism as frequently evidenced in self-love and also in self-aggrandizing trends. In using the casework situation to his own ends a person in this condition is prone to be demanding, hostile, suspicious, and casual, and though sometimes superficially responsive, he is not basically so. He may be prone to demand from the worker what he wants when he wants it in terms of material things or specific services, and any denial will spell rejection and re-create his lifelong frustration in such a way as to intensify his need. Sometimes these persons are quite obviously withdrawn and show their incapacity for relationship through their apathy, and through inability to participate conversationally in the interview. Often, however, they may talk glibly and offer a pretensive response which is misleading. Whenever there is this diminished capacity for relationship induced by deprivation and frustration, the individual is prone to be very sensitive to emotional pressure from the worker.

The worker who strives for relationship may become anxious, and therefore, more striving with these individuals as she experiences frustration in their response to her overtures. They, in turn, experience increased anxiety because of their inability in meeting the worker's emotional demands, and one may note increased withdrawal, more marked hostilities and suspicions, and a greater need to protect themselves against invasion. One may see this meager capacity for relationship evolving also through the individual's having experienced extreme indulgence and infantilization in previous life-relationships, so that he is unable to relate himself now in any situation which will not sustain his infantile omnipotence. Whatever the causes of this condition, and they may be manifold, it is essential that the caseworker develop understanding of this factor, for it will determine in large measure what she can help the individual to do about his problem, and certainly her understanding of this basic element would influence the treatment emphasis.

In attempting to gauge the individual's capacity for relationship through his response in the present treatment situation, we must always take into account those other conditions in which relationship develops—that is, whether or not there is urgent need for help and whether or not the worker has been able to follow his feeling without obstructing him through the injection of her own need. A safeguard here lies in understanding the life-experience of the individual. One should check his response in the present situation with his previous relationship experiences in order to determine to what extent these protective response patterns have evolved gradually out of his total life-experience. . . .

There is a tendency to confuse a so-called "good" contact with a vital sort of treatment relationship. A person may use the sessions with the worker for certain immediate satisfactions which have no basic treatment implications. We therefore note certain dominant tendencies, any one of which suggests that the individual might be unable to respond to treatment directed toward fundamental change in attitudes:

First, an exaggerated striving for the worker's attention with a tendency to take up her time in aimless conversation, in which he may show marked need for approval and sympathy. If the worker has been free to relate herself and has not withheld herself in such a way as to frustrate him, one questions his absorption merely in getting a response from the worker, rather than in working out his difficulties.

Second, revealing a lack of focus to any particular area, as he recounts his difficulties, as evidenced in continual transition from problem to problem or repeated introduction of new problems, without facing those previously enumerated. If so, we may expect that he is blocked in bringing through the problems that matter; that there is a tendency to evade facing any problem; that he needs the worker's anxiety and concern; that he revels in problem situations because of certain satisfactions in them.

Third, a persistent tendency to be engrossed in his own aches and pains, in his own dramatic life-experiences, in his own interesting personality reactions, and the like, to such an extent that he could be said to be dramatizing his life-situation. When this occurs, one suspects that he cannot reveal himself through being himself with the worker, because of a basic inability to face reality.

Fourth, a glibness in which he recounts intimate details with an apparent lack of feeling, suggesting that he has no conflict about what he tells or no feelings of obligation to others. In such an instance one would question his capacity for relationship. This casual response suggests an emotional shallowness, and one would expect the treatment relationship to have negligible values for him.

There are certain positive reactions, also, which orient the worker as to the meaning of the relationship for an individual which it is not possible to discuss inclusively, some of which briefly are as follows:

First: The person should become increasingly free in bringing through problems about which he has had conflict and formerly withheld because of his deep feeling about them. In this process he shows the need of removing any barriers between himself and the worker, because of his desire for the worker's acceptance of his whole self, which in the last analysis indicates his own urge to face himself and his reality.

Second: There should be a growing tendency to focalize —to talk to the point. There should be lessened tensions as evidenced in change in mode of speech, mannerisms, and all the outward physical signs of anxiety. In this connection, as time goes on there should be lessened need to talk, and diminished need for contacts with the worker; one might see him gradually terminating treatment through seeking the worker less often.

Third: One should see the individual gradually assuming more and more initiative in working out his external difficulties. If this does not occur—if he does not become more free in handling his own life-situation—one can question the values of treatment for him. Prolonged contacts through which he gains no increased capacity to function on his own may well cause concern, for frequently such contacts further dependency or intensify his feelings about the difficulties which he discusses.

In considering significant treatment factors one might reach the following tentative conclusions:

1. The social caseworker is the core of the treatment situation. Her orientation as to agency function, the degree of her self-understanding, and her grasp of the client's total situation as well as her knowledge of casework method will

determine in large measure the nature and direction of treatment.

2. The efficacy of treatment will be determined by its values for the client—values which frequently are unpredictable and will have deep or casual implications for him in terms of his needs, inclinations, and capacities. The client's response is not inherent in the mode or type of treatment utilized.

3. We have been obstructed in developing more exact criteria as to the treatment possibilities in any given case because the factors inherent in the client's situation have been obscured by the qualifications of the worker and the agency's function. While it will always be difficult to isolate the client and his situation for separate consideration as to treatment potentialities, still this may become more possible as social caseworkers gain a more adequate professional orientation.

4. In spite of the limiting factors certain criteria have emerged to guide us in our work, a few of which have been tentatively formulated in this paper. Social casework as a profession affords us the challenging task of widening this area of knowledge in so far as we also are able to accept the challenge of knowing ourselves, of perceiving agency function, and of realizing responsibility to the community.

Comments
on Social Casework
and Psychiatry

CHARLOTTE TOWLE ONCE SAID, with a kind of weary humor, that when older people disengage themselves from the current scene it is not so much because of their reluctance to

A discussion of papers presented on "Therapeutic Criteria in Social Agencies," reprinted from *American Journal of Orthopsychiatry*, vol. 9, no. 2 (April 1939). Copyright 1939 by the American Orthopsychiatric Association.

grapple with what's new but rather their ennui at seeing what's old repeated yet again.

In this symposium of thirty years ago five papers were presented, two by leading social workers, three by leading psychiatrists. Charlotte Towle was introduced as a discussant who, as "an academic person," could view the issues with "a certain amount of detachment."

In her discussion Charlotte Towle tackles some of the problems that over the years repetitively raise themselves. Where do social caseworkers leave off and psychiatrists begin? What are the areas of their joint and separate authority and knowledge? and what, therefore, can be the valid expectations of each and each of the other? What one sees in her argument is, first, a social caseworker secure in her own identity. She is familiar and experienced enough in her work with psychiatrists and in psychiatric settings to have no naïve illusions about their magic. Nor must she defensively underestimate their legitimate areas of expertness. The same balance of knowledge about social work's limitations along with its special areas of potential power shows through in her assessment of casework help.

Especially noteworthy is her point-up of how the presence of a concrete social problem, known and felt by the client, makes him accessible to therapeutic influence and how this entré occurs more frequently in social work than in psychiatry. Her criteria for the client's treatability—whether by psychiatry or by social work—are essentially the same as those put forward in "Factors in Treatment" but they are affirmed with the greater confidence that the several in-between years built up. Her own capacity to work collaboratively with others, unafraid of their usurpation of her "rights" because she was a fully self-accepting person, able thus fully to accept others—that capacity shows through in her clear identification of boundary lines and crossover lines between psychiatry and social work.

Finally she affirms her belief in the values of social supports for "untreatable" people. ". . . man must live even though he may be psychotherapeutically inaccessible." Thus she stated social work's cause.

H. H. P.

. . . It seems that the wide range of cases which flow through a social agency in any considerable period of time would fall into the following groups: first, those in which there is a simple and obvious connection between the individual's emotional upset and the social situation; second, those cases which present gross pathology; third, frequently a larger group of persons in whom there is apparent personality disorder, perhaps less fundamental and certainly not so obviously pathological as in the second group, and in which the relation of the disorder to the environmental factors is not always clear as in the first group.

The first group of cases unquestionably is the responsibility of the social worker. Treatment here does not imply routine service, for fundamental understanding of human behavior is essential if the integrity of the individual is to be safeguarded. Thus the same orientation about the function of the agency and the same ability to relate self to the client and to understand his purpose is inherent in effective work with these people. Social workers have learned a great deal in this area of their work, in fact, I believe that certain strengths which they bring to those individuals who are more seriously involved have been derived in their work with the relatively more normal group, in which the focus has been upon emotional attitudes centering about certain social dilemmas. This entré into the case, afforded by the social dilemma, has enabled them to help people without involving them totally as a result of which they have become experienced in helping people, sometimes basically, without encountering the resistance which the psychiatrist may meet. Dr. Emery has mentioned how the psychiatrist may be blocked through not having an entré that is acceptable to the client. In this respect social workers have had an advantage over psychiatrists and to this one might attribute their greater facility in limited treatment situations.

The second group of cases obviously are the primary responsibility of the psychiatrist. The social worker may serve these cases in effecting environmental changes or in assisting with a social plan, but no well-oriented social worker attempts to effect fundamental personality change in these individuals. They have to deal with many of these people, however, and frequently have been confronted with the task of easing their life situations or with the complex responsibility of securing their cooperation in social plans. This requires a fundamental understanding of the personality structure of the individual, for only as social workers perceive the significance of his attitudes can they influence him, even superficially. One hears frequent negative comment to the effect that social workers are *treating* cases in which there is gross pathology, but I wonder if this is not inferred erroneously in many instances wherein they are functioning in a discriminative fashion in meeting certain social issues and wherein their *treatment* is quite different from that of the psychiatrist.

Those persons who present personality disorders which are not always clearly related to the environment, the extent and depth of which is frequently obscure, comprise the group which is causing the greatest confusion and contention in the field today. They belong to both psychiatrist and social worker. There is quite general thinking and feeling that we ought to be able to define explicitly the difference between a social work case and a psychiatric one. But at present we can make no precise differentiation, a source of anxiety to many of us. Feelings of fear of social workers and confidence in them have been expressed by psychiatrists. In those instances wherein psychiatrists and social workers have functioned together to sufficient extent to have gained some understanding of one another, one would probably find feelings of mutual confidence, as expressed by Dr. Levy. Where neither group has had the opportunity to become oriented about the other we can expect suspicious and competitive attitudes.

At the present time we might comment tentatively as follows on the division of professional responsibility within this group:

1. Certainly social workers will frequently need the diagnostic aid of psychiatrists in determining the nature, extent and depth of the personality disorders encountered.

2. Obviously psychiatrists will in many instances need the diagnostic aid of social workers in clarifying the social situation so that the individual's emotional disturbance will not be unduly weighted on the psychogenic side.

3. Having diagnosed any given case we probably would find: that some clients may require psychiatric treatment, whereupon helping the individual to see and accept this need might be the area of casework service. In other instances, joint treatment by psychiatrist and social worker might be indicated. In many cases either psychiatrist or social worker might meet the treatment needs. In this event, the greater availability of the social caseworker together with the fact that she may have already entered the situation, might determine social casework treatment rather than referral to a psychiatrist. In such an instance the social worker would not function as a psychiatrist. It is with this group of clients that social caseworkers are being most effective and most ineffective. Insofar as they have a well-formulated conception of the possibilities of social casework methods, as distinct from psychiatric techniques, they are being effective and in many instances have an advantage over the psychiatrist.

We look to the psychiatrist then for diagnostic help with cases in all the groupings mentioned in this discussion; we depend upon him for the treatment or disposition of the definitely pathological cases; we refer to him those individuals who need more intensive kind of psychotherapy than we can give, but we do not need to depend upon him nor can he help us much in the treatment of many individuals whose emotional difficulties are rooted in social dilemmas and who seek help about these difficulties as well as about their feeling response to them.

The social worker has gone far in developing interviewing skills suitable to such situations; in fact, I would go so far as to say that many social workers have gone further than have many psychiatrists in formulating skills in these limited therapeutic situations. The strength of the psychiatrist does not seem to lie in this area. When he leaves intensive therapy behind him, frequently he departs from any application of psychiatric and psychoanalytic concepts, in interviewing the client about his practical life situation, social plans, and the like. The social worker has learned to make these concepts part and parcel of her work with people as she deals with them in all aspects of their external lives. In making this differentiation, I wish to emphasize that I am not generalizing about all psychiatrists and all social workers. There are exceptions in both professional groups.

It has been said that many social workers are lost in a maze of words and there have been expressions of anxiety about our general state of disorientation. It is doubtless true that considerable confusion exists within some of our members, but that the profession as a whole is blindly groping in the dark would be a false implication to be drawn from this discussion. I refer you to much of the case work literature of recent years . . . in particular to the various papers on differential treatment which have emerged during the last few years for evidence that there has been some formulation of our professional field.

Inevitably our thinking is tentative but at least we have some signs to guide us in determining the treatment possibilities in any given case. For example we look closely at the client's purpose, and give full consideration to what he seeks in determining whether or not we can help him. We consider also the duration of his symptomatic behavior and the extent of his emotional involvement as well as the degree of satisfaction accruing from his behavior in determining whether or not he can use our help in the modification of his attitudes. There is focus also upon the client's subjective feelings in relation to the objective reality of his environment for we recognize that change in feeling response may be stymied by an immodifiable environmental situation.

Also, we are very aware of the significance of the client's response as an indicator of his capacity for relationship, realizing that in some instances the client may be unable to use anything more than superficial help because of a diminished capacity for relationship. We realize that the nature of the relationship which it is possible to establish with a client may determine the treatment possibilities. When we encounter an individual who evidences meager capacity for relationship and in whom the symptomatic response is of long duration, the related attitudes rigid, and the behavior deeply satisfying, we recognize that such a person is beyond our therapeutic scope. Or when we find a client whose environmental situation is overwhelming and immobile, we know that our deeper therapeutic efforts probably will be futile.

What do we do in such instances? I think where we have been confronted with our own ineptitude, the tendency has been to postulate that because he needs more than we can give, he should have a deep regenerative experience such as might be afforded through psychiatric treatment. Our tendency then has been to refer our untreatable clients to the psychiatrist. Certainly in many instances this is valid practice for we do need the psychiatrist's diagnostic skill in affirming or negating our opinion. But whether these are the cases which we should be referring to psychiatrists for treatment is a very real question. Surely the frequent refusals of psychiatrists to treat these individuals should tell us something. Disappointed in the fulfillment of our hopes, perhaps we have been prone to assume indifference rather than discrimination on the part of psychiatrists. . . .

In referring cases for treatment, I wonder if we should not be making psychiatric treatment available for our responsive clients rather than the unresponsive ones. The individual who uses the casework relationship dynamically, and who becomes more effective in dealing with his life situation through casework help afforded him, might well make vital use of a deeper therapeutic opportunity. In short the casework situation might well serve as a proving ground for the psychotherapeutic referral. I wonder if we were to exchange thinking with psychiatrists on the subject of criteria established for determining the treatment possibilities in a case, if we would not be in close agreement as to the factors which constitute a treatable and an untreatable condition.

We come then to this tentative opinion about the third group—those cases presenting personality disorder which are not always clearly related to the environment, the extent and depth of which is frequently obscure. We can make no precise differentiation as to which cases are the psychiatrist's responsibility and which are the social worker's. Instead of moving toward a separation of this group into two professional entities, we move toward both professions working on the same group of cases. This tendency would seem to make increasingly essential some clarification of our thinking about each other. As for those individuals from this group who prove to be unresponsive, responsibility for them seems fairly clear and here the psychiatrists have the advantage, for they undoubtedly will come to the social worker. The social worker in many instances will serve them in a supportive way, but if she is well oriented she will not go beyond this point. And in her efforts, may she have the psychiatrist's understanding and his blessing rather than his condemnation, for man must live even though he may be psychotherapeutically inaccessible.

Some Uses
of Relationship

BY 1940 A LARGE number of caseworkers, practitioners, and teachers had been heavily influenced by the then-current psychoanalytic model of treatment in which the helper was "neutral," a screen on which the client—or patient—pro-

Excerpted from "The Social Worker and the Treatment of Marital Discord Problems," *Social Service Review*, vol. 14, no. 2 (June 1940).

jected and then discovered himself. Not only did the literature of psychiatry and casework abound with the alleged therapeutic values in this relationship stance but many caseworkers, themselves the patients of psychoanalysts, had experienced it as "good."

Charlotte Towle, always with her two feet planted solidly on the ground and her eyes searching out not what was fashionable but what she observed clinically, was among the first to see the possible pitfalls in the helper's neutrality. She saw what has only recently been established by several researches: that the helper's silence or noncommittal response is continuously being read and interpreted by the client, often incorrectly. She knew the frequency with which the client of the social worker—particularly he who is not verbal, nor introspective, nor sophisticated in protocols of psychological treatment—wants responsiveness in his helper, wants indications that he is felt with and that his helper can and will take action in his behalf.

Thus, in these comments, Charlotte Towle points to the need for social casework to differentiate the casework relationship from that of analysis and to use it differentially in relation to client needs and capacities. She points to— though she does not answer—a question that often permeates the relationship in social work: how to inject authority, to "impose demands and not be destructive."

H. H. P.

[The author examines some of the assumed values of talking through emotional difficulties in a "neutral but understanding" relationship.]

Caseworkers today are familiar with this therapeutic concept and seduced by it. It sounds so very simple when recounted. . . . It is not simple to apply and carry through, however, for the formula must be subject to continual modification in endless variation, depending upon the needs of the individual as evidenced with each changing response.

Effective help of this nature depends on several factors: (*a*) the professional orientation of the worker, (*b*) the capacity of the client to use this sort of relationship in a growth direction, (*c*) the nature and urgency of his need.

In considering these factors one is confronted first of all with the possibility that the experience of unburdening may not be wholly and immediately gratifying. For some individuals the urgency of their need with reference to the neutral but understanding attitude of the worker may stimulate such a precipitous production of confidences and such a free expression of negative feeling that strong guilt feelings with resultant anxiety may follow. We are all familiar with the individual who, after confiding freely, responds in some one of the following ways: withdraws and seems blocked in going further; enacts his retreat overtly in broken appointments or cessation of contact; in other instance resistance to compromising himself further may be expressed in anxious apologies for having told so much; in submissive compliance to the worker's will (collapse into dependent state) or in the opposite reaction of antagonistic and hostile attitudes toward the worker. The worker must be aware of the significance of such responses in order to help the client deal with his anxiety and guilt. This may be done in many ways, notably: (*a*) setting limits to check his precipitous response; (*b*) clarifying the relationship as he makes anxious apologies in comments such as "he has never told anyone not even his own mother so much before"; (*c*) reassurance as to the confidential nature of the relationship and his safety here; (*d*) interpreting the significance of his response as when he breaks appointments or is hostile toward the worker.

It is only as the worker is able to deal also with the additional problems which this therapeutic process creates that the client is assured of help with the difficulties originally brought to the treatment situation. That the patient may get worse as a result of medication before he gets better is a well-known phenomenon in medical practice. It has its corollary in psychotherapy. Knowing when and how to utilize these various measures requires professional skill, derived from training and experience. It requires also on the part of the worker a great capacity for objective handling of his own emotional response to the impact of the client's demands, needs, and pressures.

As for the client's capacity to utilize this kind of relationship constructively we note wide variation. Note, for example, Mrs. X.

Mrs. X came to a clinic for advice as to what she might do about her husband, who had evidenced great irritability since the birth of their child and who had been drinking to excess for the first time in his life. At first she could bring through only criticism and condemnation of him. He was wholly to blame, and she felt unjustly treated. She wanted advice as to what psychiatry could do for him and how she could contrive to get him to a psychiatrist. Within two interviews her condemnation gave way in large measure and was replaced by assumption of some responsibility for his difficulty. She was able to face her husband's need of her and to accept his limitations as implied in recognition of the fact that he needed to rival his child and would have to have his dependency met if her were to function adequately as huband and father. In this case we could see clearly the woman's ready utilization of the emotional immunity granted her in the worker's response. As the worker refrained from seeming to defend the accused husband through immediately interpreting him and his needs to his complaining wife, the latter, apparently through experiencing release of resentment and through testing out the worker's response to human limitations, gradually ceased projecting all blame onto her husband and edged into her part in the problem. As she gained security through the worker's acceptance of her own human limitations, she brought through freely her failure to understand her husband and wondered if it were possible that he had been jealous of his own child. Worker granted this possibility since husbands sometimes are jealous and explored this question with her. As she talked about his early deprivation and hard life, in contrast to her own more satisfying one, she became sympathetic with his need and warmly responsive to her own responsibility for meeting it. She left the second interview deciding to postpone the question of psychiatric care for him, saying she would like to try to deal with the situation herself. How might we explain her response?

The worker's skill was an undeniable factor here, but the client's capacity for relationship was also clear. Satisfying and constructive early parental relationships, a minimum of frustration in her own life-experiences obviously were basic in giving this woman the capacity to face her own failure and the capacity for giving to her husband in terms of his need. Having been given to constructively in her life-relationships, she now had inner resources for giving.

In contrast to this case, we have Mrs. L. Mrs. L. was given an opportunity to work through her marital difficulty with a relatively skilled worker, who offered her the same sort of treatment approach. It was soon clear that she could not use the opportunity. While she experienced certain emotional release, that is, always felt better after talking to the worker, she became no more active in relating herself to her husband differently, nor did she move in the direction of assuming responsibility for having any part in the problem. Her production within the interviews remained a stereotyped recital of complaints against the husband. Furthermore, repeated recounting of them seemed to be strengthening her conviction that she was wronged. She used the worker's neutrality in this direction, commenting to others that the worker agreed with her. Apparently since the worker did not take issue with her ideas, that is, actively disagree with her, her wishful assumption was that the worker was on her side. It was also clear before long that the relationship to the worker had become a gratifying end in itself, and because she was so satisfied in the worker as an interested and responsive person, her need to improve her situation lessened, since if the marital relationship were to improve, she would have to forfeit the worker.

An endlessly understanding worker who indefinitely grants the client the reality of his feeling can be a seductive person for some very deprived individuals and can offer keen competition to the ordinary husband with his realistic demands. How might we explain this woman's regressive response? Certainly lifelong deprivation and frustration in parental, sibling, and other relationships, together with frustrated achievement and economic deprivation seem to have combined to create an exaggerated dependency need. This woman had meager capacity to give in relationship, and today she finds herself married to a man with no capacity to give more than his share in the marital relationship or who even may be as needful as his wife. Because she can endure no denial, since denial spells deprivation, she has not been brought through this therapeutic approach to accept the limitations that her husband presents.

Actually, when we come to evaluate the efficacy of therapeutic relationship as many social workers conceive of it today—in the terms above described—we find that certain clients seem to be unable to use it in a growth direction. In fact, it is probably used in an uncomplicated and smooth way by the relatively more mature clients and those whose problem only partially involves the person so that his guilt is not so great but that he can be readily brought to face himself, and his anxiety is not so extensive or so deep but that it can be eased through this approach.

The evidence in other cases suggests that many individuals become confused, anxious, and frustrated through this approach, so they may enact their disturbed feelings in ways which vary from a demanding kind of dependency to withdrawal in one form or another from a situation which they find either too threatening or quite empty of value. It is precarious to generalize as to the reasons for this. . . . At the risk of oversimplification, however, the tentative impression is ventured that many individuals find this neutral relationship too unsupportive. Many individuals are quite dependent upon the approval and disapproval of others. They have gone through life with their "feelers" out for the "yes-no" attitudes of others to guide them in their thinking, acting, and, to some extent, even in their feeling. When drawn into this relationship which withholds approval and disapproval and which presumably then grants them the freedom to "find themselves," that is, their own set of values through which they may become more self-determining, they are lost. The very strangeness of this unique relationship may create anxiety for any client, and the unresourceful, dependent person is prone to respond with intensified inadequacy rather than to be stimulated to focalized activity in and around his problem. We could give many examples in which the client has used the worker's response in destructive ways. Sometimes they interpret the worker's neutrality as indifference and are driven to clamor for a response which signifies to them that the worker cares; in this connection they may enact a demanding kind of dependency. If there is deep guilt around the original problem, they may seek authority in the relationship as a kind of self-punishment and may be driven to further and further lengths in the expression or enactment of unacceptable attitudes with a view to implicating the worker in a punitive role. Or they may use the lack of emotional demand in this relationship as an opportunity for evading issues and settle down to a comfortable enjoyment of the worker's time and attention.

. . . Even with a relative degree of skill, however, in the control of this type of therapeutic relationship, it is our conviction that many clients cannot use it. Our present concern is one of affording the client a relationship which he can use to some advantage. This implies laying aside any rigid ideal as to the kind of therapeutic role a social worker should play. It implies a flexible meeting of the client's need at his particular level of personality organization, which in turn makes imperative a supportive relationship in many instances.

Today we are concerned with the "how" of being supportive in a relatively constructive way. How may we inject authority, meet dependency, impose demands, and not be destructive to people? Can this be done in a sustaining way so that gradually the individual may become more self-determining or at least less self-destructive? How may we be more helpful to people in dealing with their emotional difficulties whether they lie in the area of the marital relationship or elsewhere? We have drawn heavily on psychiatry for help in this area, and we need to continue to work hand in glove with the members of this profession for the further formulation of knowledge and skills in understanding and in controlling therapeutic relationships. Exploration of this area with a view to clarifying certain differences between casework relationship and the psychoanalytic transference situation, perhaps, is indicated.

Underlying Skills
of Casework Today

TO THE "SCIENTIFIC METHOD" in social casework—which is to say the systematization and organization of its knowledge and action principles and the objective, controlled application of them—Charlotte Towle was a continuous contributor. Like any scientific worker worth his salt, she would stop now and again to assess what misuses might be occurring or what misinterpretations of generalizations warranted attention. This she does in the following article.

Her concern here is that adherents of any formulated methods should "guard against the subjective enthronement of those observations which are personally gratifying." Supporting the development of generalizations drawn from the case-by-case experiences of practitioners, she stresses the fact that skill is based on individualization within a theory framework. She takes several assumptions governing casework in 1941 (perhaps still dogma in some places)—that self-determination is a major desideratum, that discomfort is inherent in help-taking, that the release of hostility is therapeutic—and she examines them in the light of individual human differences. Chiefly she alerts the

Reprinted from *Proceedings: National Conference of Social Work* (New York: Columbia University Press, 1941). Copyright 1941 by The National Conference of Social Work. Also in *Social Service Review*, vol. 15, no. 3 (September 1941). Originally presented at the National Conference of Social Work, Atlantic City, June 2, 1941.

caseworker to the seductiveness of theory which supports his personal bent and which, then, may blind him to the singular and unique factors in any individual case.

H. H. P.

The term "skill" has come to mean the art of dealing properly with specific situations. Because in some technical fields it has been possible for workers to gain facility in performing certain tasks without comprehension of the basic laws and principles of the field as a whole, skills have come to be regarded as techniques and procedures which can be imparted in and of themselves in relation to a particular problem. In social casework we have had phases of trying to formulate skills in this narrow sense of the term. Confronted with the untrained worker, the pressure of time, the complex demands of a profession, and armed with our own not too adequate professional education, we have longed for a magician's bag of tricks or the technician's well-defined techniques to pass on to those entering the field in order that they might become quickly effective. As we consider skill within a professional field, we are drawn back to the early meanings of the word which originally signified understanding, discernment, differentiation, comprehension, and judiciousness. Apparently those who understood, who were discerning, who were able to differentiate, and who were judicious came to think and act with an ease synonymous with our concept of skill. And the very ease implied in skill was deceptive. We came to believe that its simple secret might be lifted out, abstracted from the whole, and attained without experiencing the whole. The error of this assumption, I hope, will emerge in the course of this discussion.

I shall discuss social casework skills from the standpoint that they cannot be thought of apart from the content of knowledge and a body of principles or general conceptions underlying this branch of learning. They cannot be thought of apart from that particular integration of knowledge, philosophy, and experience which a worker brings to a specific situation. They cannot be divorced from the purpose or function of the particular agency in a given case. And most important of all, they cannot operate without reference to the client's needs and person.

With reference to skill in investigation or social study, the comments of Robert F. Hoxie on social research method seem relevant to this aspect of social casework.[1] In our early gropings with scientific method we became historical, and frequently we were narrative historians of a sterile sort rather than scientific historians. Facts were neither well selected nor always relevant to the specific person or problem. We knew somehow that history was important and that it had within it the power "to evoke and to solve problems still unstated or unrecognized." Because our investigations were undertaken in furtherance of some definite human good, our scientific interest has been practical rather than academic. Our inquiries quickly came into accord with dynamic scientific method in becoming highly selective. Absorption in history as an end in itself readily gave way to a use of history for light on the present problem. As stated by Hoxie, we have gone to the past in our scientific social studies because we have recognized that "living individuals are not altogether what we see them to be in immediate thought and action." In this field we have come to use the process of scientific inquiry also as a therapeutic tool, and this function has modified the process in a way peculiar to the fields of psychiatry and social casework.

The experienced social worker is aware of the skill implied in a differential history which meets the specifications of scientific inquiry and which serves also as a treatment process. He may find it difficult to analyze what went into this skill and may only be able to single out this and that factor which contributed to its development. Among these he may recall that period when he explored a specific social situation in that random, unfocused way which resulted in the indiscriminate historical narrative which Hoxie de-

1. *Trade Unionism in the United States* (New York: Appleton, 1920), Appendix 1, "Notes on Method," pp. 376–79.

plores as a travesty of the scientific historical method. He may remember that in this period gradually he learned to find the relevant in the mass of irrelevancies, that he learned to build up hypotheses and to infer cautiously. He may recall that in his undirected browsings he got a grasp of the complexities of the individual social situation and felt the need not only of knowing what to find but also of testing that knowledge in relation to what he found.

Probably every social worker new to the field relives in some measure this developmental phase experienced at one point by the field as a whole. Fortunately we cannot take this experience away from him though we may shortcut it dangerously. Many of us inched along through a long period of inductive thinking in which we participated in formulating many of the hypotheses, theories, and systems which we now hand over to the novice. In contrast, the novice enters the social situation heavily armed in terms of what to find and of what to think, and perhaps it is not to be wondered at if hypotheses prematurely become theories and theory, dogma. How to shorten the time through instruction and supervision without depriving the worker of the opportunity to experience the scientific method in a gradual evolutionary way so that it becomes an integral part of his professional approach is one of today's baffling educational problems.

If the experienced worker can analyze further the gradual emergence of his skill, he may recall that at an early point in the study process he began to diagnose and to use his grasp of basic treatment principles and that his skill as an investigator increased in direct proportion to gains in diagnostic ability and with deepened understanding of treatment principles. He began to secure valid diagnostic material in so far as he was therapeutic in his approach to people. These skills developed hand in hand in an inseparable fashion. Diagnostic and treatment skills imply a capacity for precise analysis of a case situation into its parts, for comparative thinking of the parts in relation to the whole, and for synthesizing the parts into a comprehensive interpretative statement in which the essential elements of the case situation are still discernible and, therefore, may serve as a treatment focus. It implies also some generalization, for each case takes on meaning in the light of other cases and in turn contributes to the gradual formulation of a casework philosophy to serve the worker in other instances. Professional skills are directly related to, in fact they emerge from, the development of valid generalizations.

The caseworker who remains absorbed in each case and regards it as absolutely unique is one who has not grasped its general import and who, therefore, must grope his way through each new fact situation as though it were an initial venture. Generalization with resultant formulation of ways of working lies at the core of skill. Since the purpose of social casework, however, is to help the individual rather than to work in certain ways, diagnostic and treatment skills rest, in the last analysis, upon the worker's ability to see the particular relatedness of the factors within *this* situation which make it *this* situation and not another one. Skill breaks down when formulated methods and philosophies are enthroned and when generalizations are rigidly applied without reference to the person presenting certain needs. The past few years might be characterized as a period of generalization, in contrast to the initial phase in the development of a science of social casework in which we were absorbed in individualization. We have made headway in formulating thinking derived through years of individual-by-individual experience and in applying thinking formulated elsewhere, notably in the field of psychiatry. It has been a productive period in that much theory that is sound has emerged to guide us in our present and future work provided we do not abandon the scientific method through which it was achieved. This implies a continued weighing of evidence, a testing of hypotheses, and a questioning of theory in relation to the individual situation in which it is being utilized. Theories are seductive, however, and unless we consciously guard ourselves against their wiles we may seize on them or be possessed by them so that unwittingly we come to serve them rather than the individuals whom they were designed to serve. A few examples may clarify this point.

The idea has been advanced that it is quite general if not universal for the individual to experience discomfort in asking for help. The assumption is that the activation of basic dependency inherent in this experience engenders anxiety over helplessness and anxiety over loss of one's identity. Another assumption is that in the relationship established between the helping person and the one helped, anxiety is aroused because of the guilt activated, for insofar as this relationship re-creates the parent-child situation, unresolved conflicts sometimes of a psycho-sexual nature emerge in various forms and in varying combinations of symptoms which express dependency, hostility, anxiety, and the like. In either instance, regardless of differences in the interpretation of the basis of the conflict, there has been agreement on the point that it is essential that the worker deal with this conflict so that that discomfort which is so productive of demoralizing effects be relieved in order that the individual may make constructive use of help. This concept has validity when used with close reference to the individual situation. Skill is obstructed, however, when the worker hangs tenaciously to this assumption as in one case.

A woman revealed marked anxiety as she sought help in the form of relief and placement of two children. The worker became absorbed in trying to deal with the discomfort over getting help. The interviews were highly repetitive in worker's overtures to come to grips with these feelings which she thought it essential to clarify before working out the placement plan. Finally the worker gave up; the feelings of discomfort were not forthcoming, and when relief was given and the children placed, the mother moved into the experience with obvious serenity. If the worker had focused on this woman rather than on the theoretical assumption as to how she must be feeling, she would have seen at a much earlier point that in being helped this person found comfort. Help in any form was comforting to her as a sustaining symbol of being loved. The childlike dependence which she brought to the experience had none of the relatively more adult conflict elements in it. If conflict over being helped was present here, it was so deeply repressed, so long latent, that for all practical purposes it was nonexistent in the casework relationship.

A commonly accepted idea in casework practice is to the effect that the casework relationship should offer the individual the opportunity to be self-determining. Dedicated to this idea—an idea which is greatly reinforced by the trends of the times in which we are defensive of this right—many of us lose sight of the responses which clearly indicate that some individuals are unable to use the relationship in this way. We have learned that when this opportunity has been imposed it may constitute an authoritative demand which the individual may be unable to meet; and if so, he may react with resultant hostility, anxiety, and a response that may vary from aggressive demands to a collapse into abject dependency. Thus we may do the individual more damage in the long run than if we had met his dependency at the start. Our own fears may operate here as in many other areas against discriminative help, which is synonymous with skill. Accordingly the skilled worker is endeavoring to meet the individual where he is in terms of capacity to carry responsibility in any area whether it be in responding within the interview, expressing feelings, or initiating and effecting plans.[2] The caseworker who staunchly maintains that he can help only the person who can use a certain kind of relationship, frequently is saying that he can relate himself only to that individual who least needs help. At this point, perhaps, we need to remind ourselves of the purpose of our profession; and while this stand may be reconciled with the function of some agencies, it cannot be reconciled with our profession's purpose as a whole.

In recent years we have gained a deepened understanding of the import of hostility both as it affects the personality

2. This point has been more fully discussed elsewhere. See Charlotte Towle, "The Social Worker and the Treatment of Marital Discord Problems," *The Social Service Review*, 14 (June 1940): 211–23.

adjustment of the individual and as it affects the treatment relationship. We have learned that the repression of hostile feelings is not only the core of many an individual's difficulty but also that in helping him it is frequently beneficial from a twofold standpoint for him to give expression to these feelings. (1) He may be relieved of hostile impulses in his life-relationships and thus be freed for more satisfactory relationship to others and for greater assumption of responsibility for himself. With the easing of guilt over hostile feelings he may no longer need to project responsibility or to punish himself through failure and suffering in one form or another. (2) As he brings through the hostile impulses in the casework relationship directed either toward the worker or toward others, the worker's objective response may not only ease guilt but may also enable him to enter into that positive relationship with the worker, essential for, or at least conductive to, a constructive use of help.

As we learned this, our initial assumption was that we had found a simple answer to the woes of mankind and to the establishment of more effective treatment relationships. As we have worked with this concept, however, we have experienced its complexity. We have become acquainted with the marked anxieties, even the panic responses, that may be engendered as hostilities are released. We have felt the impact of the troubles that ensue in some instances when hostile aggressions find an outlet. We have seen that a more intensely negative casework relationship may result insofar as the individual blames us for this discomfort or resents our acceptance of his negative self. In short, we frequently unleashed forces with which we were unable to cope. The skilled worker has learned to move slowly in this area and to observe intently the individual's response in relation to all that he has learned about him as a person so that hostility and anxiety may not be released beyond the capacity of the individual to deal with it, or beyond the circumstances of his situation to afford opportunities for the redirection of hostile impulses and the constructive utilization of anxiety.

The skilled worker also has learned ways of limiting the

person if a precipitous response is generated within the casework relationship. He may set time limits or help the person handle his guilt through bringing out positive feelings to offset the negative ones; he may interpret, reassure, permit, or even help the person maintain some of his rationalizations and defenses; he may direct the individual to activity in the social setting or to activity comprised in steps in agency procedure through which the hostile impulses may be atoned and the anxiety eased. These "techniques" for dealing with or controlling the individual's response imply great skill in knowing when and how and what to say and do—a skill which emerges from intensive observation, close listening, and the diagnostic ability which stems from knowledge and experience. They are not "techniques" that can be handed over to the novice as a body of well-established procedures or routines to be utilized in general or in this or that situation. When they are so used they inevitably are misused.

In the child-placing field a theory has been advanced that the parent himself must initiate and be responsible for accepting and actually taking the steps in the placement process in order to give the agency a sound basis for placing the child.[3] This is done not only in the interests of helping the client to be self-determining but also with the conviction that this process will be therapeutic, that is, help the individual work through his conflicts over placing the child and separating from him. While we see this as a desirable method, perhaps even the most desirable basis on which to effect placement, still we have noted that the individual's capacity to do this has varied widely so that the statement that the parent must initiate and be responsible for actually taking the steps in a placement process raises questions. I refer here to those parents who are not free and cannot become free to do that which they might even like to do. Therefore, the burden of the decision only activates guilt, and anxiety while acting out the steps may so intensify these same feelings as to precipitate a retreat.

3. Jessie Taft, "Foster Home Care for Children," *Annals of the American Academy of Political and Social Science*, 212 (November 1940): 179–85.

I recall a case where the placement could be effected only on an authoritative basis, even though the referral of the mother by a clinic to a children's agency came in response to her own voluntarily expressed wish to place the child.[4] In considering the placement she showed a strong impulse toward it, but in acting out the steps in the process, anxiety mounted and retreat ensued. The relatively skilled worker tried to ease the guilt through nonjudgmental attitudes toward placement, through interpretation of its appropriateness in this instance, and through trying to help her ease her guilt in seeing and feeling the placement as something she was doing in the child's behalf. Finally she could only take this action "on the doctor's orders" and with the worker taking the major steps in effecting the placement. Since the mother's condition endangered the child, it would seem that her need made this a sound basis for placement. It would be sound, however, only if the subsequent relationship with this parent were defined on this same basis. Perhaps placements in such instances have proved to be unsound because later the agency has reversed its position and permitted the parent freedom to decide the kind of relationship he will have with the child in the foster-home. We are familiar with the parent who has projected full responsibility onto the agency and who then becomes demanding on both the foster-home and the agency, interfering with the child's adjustment. Skill here would imply a consistent use of authority in response to careful diagnosis and a capacity on the worker's part to deal with his own feelings about playing this role. In the process of careful diagnostic thinking the worker's anxiety about authority may be eased in some measure.

Since the major *modus operandi* of the social caseworker is the personal interview. I shall consider briefly how skill in the use of scientific method may be affected by what the worker brings to the interview. We see the world through our own eyes, and what we see is subject to the limitations of our range of vision and to any disfunction in our visual

4. See Charlotte Towle, *Social Case Records from Psychiatric Clinics* (Chicago: University of Chicago Press, 1941), pp. 369–92, "Doris Carey."

capacity. Likewise, as we relate ourselves to people the re-action we induce is not solely the reaction of the other in-dividual but is the product also of what we inject. An indi-vidual's reaction to a given social worker will typify his way of responding to that kind of approach, but it does not give us a conclusive picture of the kind of person he is. Too often we conclude summarily and prematurely, this is a depen-dent person or this is a deeply anxious person when any one of us could well ask: Is this person being dependent to meet my demands, or is this anxiety a response to my un-certainty or aggression? In diagnosis and treatment, there-fore, we are led to consider what the worker brings to the client. What he sees, feels, and thinks as well as the re-sponse he begets will be determined by (1) experience (per-sonal and professional), (2) knowledge and skill, (3) per-sonality needs with particular reference to capacity or incapacity to objectify those needs.

Today we are aware of the importance of the emotional needs of the social worker. In fact, it has become such a dominant concern of supervisors, instructors, and case-workers themselves that we tend to overlook the other de-terminants when they may have a direct bearing on this factor.

Consider first the relation of experience to what the social worker observes. A young worker records her visit to the home of a family applying for relief. She gives a vivid de-scription of the bleakness of the home, of its disorder, of its deplorable lacks. She notes that the mother is unfriendly and untidy and records the impression that she seems shift-less and unco-operative. She expresses the opinion to her supervisor that Mrs. X cannot be a planful person and feels hopeless about working with her. Things looked badly man-aged, the children were grimy, and money had been spent for nonessentials. Shortly thereafter the supervisor, a woman of some years' experience, visited this home. The differences in observation may be due in part to chance factors, but one is aware also of a different perspective. She finds a home that is in relatively good condition as com-pared with the homes of other factory workers in this same

district. Fundamentally it is clean, but disorder prevails,
though perhaps no more disorder than is inevitable with
overcrowding and four active young children. She notes
touches here and there that bespeak the mother's effort to
make it homelike. The artificial flowers, the children's toys,
the varied diet in relation to the income, and the improvised
sunbathing contraption in the one south window so that infant Jimmy may get the sunshine recommended by the "In
fant Welfare" all bespeak resourcefulness rather than shift-
lessness and a normal yearning for something more than
bread alone. She sees an intelligent sense of values within
the superficial disorder and meagerness of this woman's
world. She does not find an unfriendly woman so much as a
weary and discouraged one; an untidy woman, so much as
a shabby one; an unco-operative woman so much as a person with ideas of her own. Case developments confirmed
the soundness of the experienced worker's observations.

One might suppose that the young worker was unsympa-
thetic or that she was a punitive person; that she had some
basic need to reject the disadvantaged or that she tended to
dramatize and distort in response to her own personal
needs. Her response might be symptomatic or any one or
all of these difficulties. Further acquaintance with this
worker, however, indicated that her previous experience—
that is, her social and economic background together with
a lack of professional experience—combined to give her no
comprehension whatever of such factors as what constitutes a normal way of life among poor people; how much
order is possible with overcrowded housing; what constitutes planfulness when one has meager resources with
which to be planful; that a weary woman who has always
been socially and economically disadvantaged may not relate herself to a stranger with the gracious manner of her
more advantaged sister; or that one may feel defensive at
having to ask for help. Actually this worker's subsequent
development showed a capacity to be understanding, and
no marked hostilities or punitive attitudes were revealed.
One would say that the second worker was more accepting
of the limitations of others. We accept what we understand.

Probably there is very little acceptance of the unknown or the strange. Therefore, the capacity to accept may grow with widened experience.

Likewise the worker's lack of experience may affect not only what he does or fails to do in a situation but also his response or emotional attitude in the very doing. Recently a psychiatrist expressed concern about a worker in whom he had noted anxiety and tension as he had had several brief contacts with her in a case situation. This worker had not impressed her supervisor as being anxious or tense in general. Inquiry into the case situation revealed that she had been drawn into the assumption of more direct treatment responsibility in the case of a deeply neurotic young woman than she was professionally prepared to carry. A strong relationship had developed between the worker and patient with the latter giving full confidences, then reacting with hostility and becoming inordinately aggressive not only in relation to the worker but in her social situation.

In a discussion of the worker's difficulty emphasis was placed on the fact that this case probably was activating the worker's basic conflicts. That may be so; we should not be ready to say it was not so, or that this factor may not have entered into her response. But before deciding that this was the whole difficulty we should want to know how much she knew about handling this kind of response. It was found that she had a vague impression that in some mysterious way it was therapeutic for a client to unburden. She had no comprehension of the possibility of resultant anxieties or of the import of released hostilities. Nor did she know, nor had anyone helped her to learn the ABC's of how to deal with anxiety, how to set limits—in short, how to direct or control the therapeutic relationship. In view of this, I wonder if she may not have been intelligently "anxious and tense."

Knowledge and skill attained through experience and through professional education continually operate to determine the worker's emotional response within the interview. One could cite many examples. The overauthoritative tendency of young or inexperienced workers to routine and exhaustive inquiry emerges frequently from their need to know in order to feel adequate and capable of helping. The overauthoritative tendency to instruct, to guide, to tell, even to dictate may be produced by a need to reassure themselves as well as others that they have something to give and probably will subside when they are more secure in professional knowledge and skill. An eagerness to reassure, to minimize the problem, and to encourage invalidly may arise from a need to be liked personally—a need which will diminish when security in their professional contribution brings them the client's acceptance on a realistic basis. Absorption in and glib use of terminology may characterize the worker who has not yet grasped the full meaning of the terms. When this comprehension comes, language will grow more simple and understandable. The vague uncertainty and lack of direction frequently noted in interviewing lessens when knowledge enlightens and gives meaning to what the client is saying and doing.

As human beings entering this field of service, inevitably we bring personal needs and a wealth of lay attitudes, biases, and prejudices, their content and depth varying with backgrounds and previous relationship experiences. Furthermore, as human beings we continue to live in spite of the fact that we are social workers, so that throughout our training and professional experience we are subject to the full range of frustrations, stresses, and strains to which those whom we serve are heir. We bring from life's gratifications and from the self-realization which has been our lot the strength and capacity to help. Probably also through our frustrations and other negative experience, providing it has not been too great, we are attuned to feel with the disadvantaged, and almost inevitably there will be times or instances when we will feel like them and, therefore, at times more against them than with them. In these instances our effectiveness as helping persons will be undermined. Inevitably the person entering this field will tend to project his own feelings and needs onto those whom he is trying to help, and certainly he will identify with those whom he serves. In casework we all identify in some measure with our clients. In fact, the human tendency to identify may be regarded as the very core of altruism and one of the motive forces in all social work. It occurs, however, sometimes in excessive degree in response to deep personal need, and in such instances it can obstruct the development of a helpful relationship. When we are responding to unresolved emotional pressure ourselves, when we are frustrated in our own desires and urges in life, when we are feeling deprived and defeated—in short, when we have deep conflicts and needs to appease or resolve and when we do not understand our needs and urges—then unconsciously we may use the client to meet our need rather than be free to meet the need which he brings to us. . . .

I shall touch briefly upon some of the effects of projection and overidentification in the interviewing process. In those instances where this occurs we become more demanding than usual. Not only may we take over responsibility for certain services but in the interview process itself we may reveal certain overprotective practices, such as giving undue reassurance, minimizing the problem, anticipating the client's story, or changing the subject when the client's discomfort becomes unbearable, not so much to him as to ourselves. Such overprotection may prevent him from giving full expression to his feelings, thus depriving him of the therapeutic benefit of release; insofar as we minimize his problem he may feel that we just do not understand, but if he needs our service, he may talk to please us rather than for his own benefit. On the other hand, we may oversympathize, get unusually absorbed in the detail and flow of his story, become markedly seductive to him as a sympathetic listener, and be powerless to set limits or to ease the resultant anxiety, because we are caught in that anxiety. Or if we experience negative identification—that is, find in him our unacceptable self—we may be unusually judgmatic, condemning, withholding, and show meager capacity to accept his feelings together with a marked urge to change his response, outreaching the client's readiness in interpretation, giving insight, and directing him.

Other indications of emotional involvement in a given

case may be evidenced in a need to stretch the agency function, and we find ourselves making a marked exception of
this person, giving him more time, a more personalized relationship, more material help, or waiving certain procedures.
For example, we may feel somehow that this person's confidences should not be recorded; he should not be treated
like other clients in this regard. . . . This case cannot be
terminated when indicated but must be clung to for the fulfillment of our additional goals, or if we are leaving the district, an exception must be made and this case must go with
us. Or conversely, our own need may lead us to an authoritative use of agency function so that we subordinate the
good of the individual to our own will expressed through
the functional limits of the agency—a tendency which may
well be reinforced by current social trends.

In these cases our wishful thinking will crop out; our
need to defend the client, protect, or deny him will make it
difficult for us to think logically; we may be less autocritical
than usual and in staff conferences we will find ourselves
less receptive to the perspective which our colleagues bring
to the discussion of the case. And finally, perhaps, defeated
and frustrated, we will terminate the case abruptly and
sometimes vindictively. The feeling we experience in termination is sometimes very revealing indeed.

In these instances also the client may reveal our involvement. There will be a lack of movement which will be revealed not only in general lack of progress in his social situation but also within the interview. Frustrated in finding
help or irritated by the pressure of our emotional need, he
may become resistive, hostile, or markedly anxious. He may
defend himself against us in various ways through evasive
talking, stereotyped production, through resistance or projections, or through taking himself out of the situation. In
clinics this frequently happens, for few patients feel sufficient need of psychiatric help to endure an uncomfortable
worker for long. In some other settings the client's imperative need for the service does not leave him free to escape,
so he makes an adaptation of one sort or another, and one
frequently encountered is endless, unproductive talking; or
sometimes very ingenious productions to meet the worker's

need. He soon knows what provokes our anxiety or interest so he earns his way, and in the long run may feel unobligated and entitled to the service.

We have a host of good stories in this connection—the comments of clients who have been more aware than we have been of the nature of the relationship. Or if our involvement has gratified the client, as when our punitive attitudes meet neurotic need for punishment, or when our protectiveness has fostered his need to be dependent, he may give himself over to enjoyment of the relationship which becomes an end in itself. This will be reflected in his response in the interview, and here again we would expect to see repetitious productions, or endless bringing-in of new problem situations to engage our aggression or protection.

Time prohibits an inclusive discussion of the innumerable ways in which our personality needs may affect the interview or the many ways in which the client may respond to our need. The involvements discussed as well as many others are very usual ones to which any of us may be subject at any moment. When we find them occurring in general so that our interviewing skill is seriously impaired, then we may suspect fundamental difficulties which may not be met in the educational process. It would seem that since we all bring personal need to the casework situation, our professional effectiveness cannot be based on an absence of such need but instead on our capacity to deal with it, a subject which I have discussed elsewhere.[5]

Finally, it is important to recognize that in attaining a scientific approach we must accept the limitations of science, namely, that there are no short cuts, that there are no substitutes for its slow and painstaking ways, that there are no escapes from its complexities, that its theoretical formulations must ever be tested and, therefore, are ever subject to change, and that its generalizations cannot be abstracted and adapted to unquestioned usage as well-established techniques or arts.

This creates a common problem for all of us in passing our present formulations on to the younger generation. It is

5. See "Some Basic Principles of Social Research in Social Case Work," by Charlotte Towle, *Social Service Review*, 15 (March 1941): 66–80.

a problem peculiar to no one school of thought. It appears to be a prevalent one, in keeping with the trends of the times and characteristic of our developmental stage in the use of scientific method. It is one which must be solved in some measure if the caseworker of tomorrow is to surpass in skill the case worker of today. Indeed there is danger that the caseworker of tomorrow may fall short of his predecessor if he merely annexes the results of our thinking without the basic thought processes through which our skills have been attained. When the social worker looked at the human individual from a scientific standpoint, man as man became important, for differentiations based on social and economic status, racial, national, or sex factors, conditions of body or mind became incidental to his identity as a person. Science then has served as a humanizing force in giving a deeper understanding of human nature. It is important to remember though that science in any field may reinforce our tendency to generalize, and its adherents must guard against the subjective enthronement of those observations which are personally gratifying or which in some way serve their user's purpose. One has only to look out to the broad social scene today to see the inhumanities that man is committing against man in the name of this or that so-called scientific generalization. May social casework avoid this misuse of scientific method.

The Place of Social Casework
in the Treatment
of Delinquency

THE PAPER BY KENNETH PRAY and its discussion by Charlotte Towle, which follows (and which restates some of

Reprinted from *Social Service Review*, vol. 19 no. 2 (June 1945).

Mr. Pray's major points), are among the first forthright grapplings with the caseworker's problem of dealing with unwilling clients and of combining coercive authority with a therapeutic relationship. (The reader may remember that earlier Charlotte Towle had asked "How may we inject authority . . . impose demands, and not be destructive to people?" in "Some Notes on Relationship.")

Here it can only be said of Kenneth Pray's paper that it deserves reading as a small classic of a position on the creative uses of agencies and of reality limits. Charlotte Towle gives this full recognition. But her position offers a necessary balance: that we must not identify so completely with "the authoritative system that we are not able to see its defects and limitations," and, further, that correctional systems themselves are often blatantly in need of correction.

Charlotte Towle goes further to point up the strong emotional responses that are, naturally, roused in caseworkers who encounter lawbreakers and social deviants. True to her habitual examination of the caseworker's feelings as unconscious determinants of defenses against or with the client, she points to the necessity for self-awareness. True to her continuous press for individuation, she notes that acts of delinquency may have multiple and different meanings that will call for differential treatment.

Beneath the surface of this discussion between Pray and Towle may be heard the echoes of the functional-diagnostic battles that, in 1945, were in full cry. The struggle in this instance was pitched in terms of the acceptance and uses of the function and realities of the agency versus the assessment of the agency's validity and the focus on individualization of the client. Charlotte Towle did not fear or blindly fight the "functional" position, as a careful perusal of her writings reveals. Here as elsewhere her clear-sighted realism combined with her secure self-identity to make her open to examine objectively ideas that were different from her own, to reject them, or to incorporate them when they seemed

congruent and useful. Thus, she is with Mr. Pray on a number of points and she differs with him on others.

                                                        H. H. P.

Mr. Pray has presented the problem which confronts the
caseworker who must work with the individual in a situation in which his services are imposed rather than sought.
He has emphasized the fact that we cannot fulfill our dual
function—that of safeguarding the community and of helping the individual—by identifying with him against the
authoritative system responsible for his supervision. Instead we must help the individual in such a way that the
demands of society, as conveyed through a correctional
agency, may become sufficiently desirable that he himself
regulates his behavior.

We have learned that, just as this end is not attained by
identifying with the offender versus the law, it likewise is
not attained by such a complete identification with the
authoritative system that we are not able to see its defects
and limitations and to understand what the individual is
feeling as he must submit to the drastic restrictions involved in imprisonment, and to society's mistrust as expressed in supervised parole. It is probably true that much
of our ineffectual work in authoritative systems has been
due to an extreme alignment on the side either of the individual or of the correctional agency. It is clear that we must
accept and maintain our identity as representatives of the
law and at the same time extend to the individual help
which may become desirable to him because he feels our
kindly purpose, our understanding, and our respect for him
as a person who has an identity other than that of the offender. This seems so obvious that we might well wonder
why caseworkers in general have not functioned this way
to a greater extent than they have. Time does not permit
discussion of the many factors which may have operated
against our relating ourselves both to the correctional system and to the individual. I shall mention only those that
seem to me to be particularly significant.

Workers as human beings have had strong feelings which have led to marked alignments and which have determined their thinking and their action. Many of us have come to adulthood with intense feelings about offenders. These feelings have ranged, varying with the offense, from mild distaste to extreme repugnance and from mild anxiety to extreme fear. The very feelings which in part enabled us to inhibit our own unsocial impulses operate, *warningly*, to make us condemn their enactment by others. Any acceptance or understanding of antisocial behavior may be reacted to with the fear that we are condoning and thereby perhaps lowering our own standards. These feelings gradually give way in many workers as they experience professional education. In some instances, however, vestiges may remain. Feelings of condemnation may give way to sympathy and understanding, as workers study human behavior. This may occur as they come to know the effects of frustrating and hurtful relationships, as they become acquainted with the effects of adverse social and economic conditions on family life and of the effects of disturbed family life on the individual. They see the individual not as having sinned so much as having been sinned against. At this point there may come a marked swing away from their former attitudes. There may emerge as strong an identification with the individual against the law as formerly there was with the law against the individual.

At this point there may come also through study of human behavior and through knowledge of the mechanisms operating in some instances of antisocial behavior an appreciation of the need of these individuals for supportive moral judgments and for help given by consistent discipline and understanding authority. When workers see this, they are less fearful of identifying with the correctional agency. They may then come to use the authority of the agency and the supportive judgments of society objectively and effectively because they use them now in response to the individual's need rather than from their own need to punish and condemn.

But right here, at a time of psychological readiness to represent the law-enforcing agency and to help the individual incorporate its dictates, they are driven back by the very nature of some institutional programs either into alignment with the individual or into a defensive alliance with the agency. Insofar as caseworkers care mightily what happens to people and insofar as they truly understand the factors and forces which shape men to unsocial ends and which undermine possibilities for their rehabilitation, they find it difficult indeed to accept the programs and the administrative procedure of some correctional agencies. When these regimes are destructively restrictive, caseworkers are driven either to reject or to defend *blindly* the agencies which theoretically they should be able to use in the confident, resourceful, and creative way described by Mr. Pray. This occurs, almost inevitably, in systems which are administered by people who are harshly punitive and who lack respect for the individuals they serve, that is, when everything is done to defeat rather than to attain the aims of a rehabilitation program. Until many correctional institutions are corrected, it is probable that caseworkers will find it difficult if not impossible to work constructively within their authoritative framework.

The creative use of this framework which Mr. Pray's stimulating discussion envisages presupposes an acceptable regime, administered by reasonably well-qualified personnel, oriented to human needs and to the import of their work. When these conditions are not present, it is important that we not become blindly worshipful of restrictive and depriving systems on the assumption that in and of themselves and even by reason of these qualities the caseworker can help the individual make constructive use of them. It is important to remember that in some instances institutional reform is prerequisite to effective casework service. If social workers put first things first, they will make known the need for program change rather than assume that in their skilled hands a poor instrument may be wielded effectively.

Within a well-planned and constructively administered correctional system we would do well to note the therapeutic possibilities inherent in helping the individual learn to live within social limits. In some instances this may come about in so far as the individual finds in the caseworker a person who understands his anger and his frustration, who at the same time helps him to understand the purpose of the social demands, who values his efforts at fitting in, and who through trusting him shows confidence in his ability to modify his behavior. As he is thus understood and encouraged, he may come to feel different about authority and he may move into identification with the worker's attitudes toward social restrictions, gradually making them his own apart from the worker. This will occur when the individual has considerable capacity for relationship, considerable capacity to endure denial, and a relatively active conscience —in short, a character structure which enables him to come to grips with reality.

Little other than sometimes a temporary "institution cure" may take place in such instances as that of the adult offender with a markedly infantile character. This is particularly true when his inability to inhibit his unsocial impulses stems from life-long deprivation and from the lack of sufficiently meaningful relationships to have developed a normal conscience. The juvenile offender when behavior is on this same basis may experience through imposed authority more lasting ability to inhibit his unsocial impulses, providing conformity and consideration for others gives him new patterns for relating to others which are more gratifying than the old ones.

Socially acceptable behavior will be more firmly intrenched, however, if within the institution the young person is afforded meaningful relationships through which he develops genuine feelings of love and hence of obligation to others. Benefits to the individual through the use of imposed authority may not occur in those instances of adult or juvenile offenders where the delinquency is a solution for some deep neurotic conflict, as, for example, when it serves the purpose of obtaining punishment, or of punishing others, etc. Many adult offenders and some juvenile delinquents are persons who may not be able to make use of imposed limits without help other than has been described. Their irrational strivings, that is, their inability to think, has derived from an excess of deprivation, of frustration, and of measuring and bruising themselves against limiting circumstances. For some of these individuals direct psychotherapeutic help will be indicated. Institutional regimes which are permissive rather than restrictive in character also will be needed in some instances.

It is true that caseworkers sometimes have undertaken direct psychotherapeutic work inadvisedly. In my opinion more often than not these abortive attempts have not derived from a lack of respect for usual casework measures. Instead these attempts have been motivated by the caseworker's comprehension of the individual's need and his lack of realization of the full extent of knowledge and skill demanded for competent service of this nature. We would all agree with Mr. Pray that the sick delinquent is a large order for the average caseworker, and we would not recommend ambitious efforts at direct treatment for which he lacks adequate preparation.

It is important, however, that caseworkers focus on understanding what purpose delinquent behavior serves the individual in a given instance; also on what the correctional experience is meaning to the person in relation to the needs expressed in his delinquency. Finding the answers to these questions will imply history-taking, that is, exploration of the past for light on the present problem and the present experience which we are trying to help him use constructively. As the trained worker attains skill through experience, his inquiries will become differential. They will not be a random collection of facts unless in the present problem of determining what help the individual needs and can use. Nor will these inquiries be used blindly as an escape to the past or unjustifiably as an excuse for not coming to terms with the present reality, if there is evidence of capacity for facing that reality. They may be used, however, as a safeguard against misguided hopes and mistaken assumption as to the benefits of imposed limitations. They may serve also as a basis for referring individuals to available psychiatrists and as a safeguard against overambitious attempts at direct treatment.

Finally, it is as we understand the purpose served by the delinquent behavior as well as the meaning of the correctional experience in relation to that behavior, that we may see possibilities for that more effective use of the authority, the discipline, the limiting realities—in short, the use of the "social will" expressed in the institutional regime and parole procedure.

We are indebted to Mr. Pray for a thought-provoking discussion, one which should stimulate us to careful evaluation of our casework efforts and of our correctional programs. He has reinforced our long-standing conviction as to the importance of good institutions and of adequate parole supervision as a framework for effective social casework in the treatment of delinquency.

Social Casework
in Modern Society

THE SOCIAL CONTEXT in which this article was written was the aftermath of World War II with all its shifts, uncertainties, dislocations, turbulence, and the long-awaited breathing-space that could, at last, be used to take measure of where we had been and where we were going. Thus, this article is in a sense an overloaded one because in it Charlotte Towle tries to take stock not only of social casework but of social work and of the society in which it is one institution. It is an effort at synthesis, at putting pieces together into some coherent pattern to reveal relationships. In it one sees her constant conflict between the saddened recognition of how things are and the stubborn affirmation that they can and must be bettered.

Reprinted from *Social Service Review*, vol. 20, no. 2 (June 1946).

Some of the social measures Charlotte Towle identifies and calls for have, indeed, come into being. But the problem —if "problem" is the designation—is that a rising level of expectation and sense of need obliterates the sense of accomplishment. Many of the unmet needs that Charlotte Towle points to here are as ubiquitous today as they were twenty years ago.

For today's reader some major points of interest thrust themselves into attention. One is the clear recognition that social casework is only one part, one process in social work, and that its effectiveness or limitations are heavily determined by the presence or absence of adequate social resources and opportunities. Charlotte Towle is realistic and direct about the conditions under which help to people on a case-by-case basis can work. She protests the unsound administrative policies in which "the right hand keeps the left hand busy"; the thin spread of casework to cover too many problems unfeasibly; "The social caseworker has labored all too long in futile attempts at helping the individual feel better on an empty stomach. She has slaved all too long at easing secondary problems while primary ones persist. . . ."

But Charlotte Towle had no question about the value and necessity of individualized help to individuals because she understood that even in the best of all worlds there will be individual human dilemmas. So she recapitulates herein the underlying knowledge and know-how that characterize good helping along with the potential contributions that casework's knowledge can make to administration, to social policy change, and to other associated professions. It is with her recognition of casework's unrealized potentials that Charlotte Towle looks forward with hope.

                                                              H. H. P.

Today want, fear, and hostile feelings give promise of reproducing themselves in an ascending and widening spiral. When and if they again pit man against man, he has at hand for malignant use scientific knowledge and technical devices far beyond those of yesterday. Confronted with the inescapable realization that, as never before, he holds his destiny in the hollow of his hand, man stands on the brink of an abyss. Beyond the chasm he can see that better life for all peoples for which he long has been striving. It stands forth in bold relief. Furthermore, the knowledge and materials for bridging the gap are at hand. What, if anything, is lacking? What—except a clear and confident purpose? Self-distrust and fear bring a yearning for the now idealized past, a flight backward into the conviction that what has been always must be. This way lies self-betrayal and self-destruction. . . . Perhaps this present period of transition is unique in that man must not permit the marked repetition of the past which throughout history has characterized transition periods. Civilization is not at another crossroad in which it may again select the familiar, even though the tortuous road, ahead. It is at a jumping-off place. A bridge, a one-way bridge, must be flung quickly and surely across the chasm.

At this decisive time I can discuss one aspect of the profession of social work only on the assumption that this bridge will be built in part through measures implicit in comprehensive and integrated governmental action. Such action must include active participation of the United States in the United Nations to promote social and economic measures that will remove the causes of war and thus check any threat of aggression; a program that will establish a system in which business management, labor, agriculture, and government together provide full employment, full production, and fair employment practices. In this framework it is inevitable that social services and social welfare measures should be brought up to date to assure, when adversity strikes, adequate financial and medical assistance, vocational and educational opportunity to every citizen regardless of race, color, and creed. This would involve many developments such as: the establishment within the federal government of a department of welfare and security under the direction of a cabinet officer; the extension of the coverage of the Social Security program and a substantial liberalization and broadening of unemployment compensation and public assistance; an adequate health program as proposed in the new Wagner-Murray-Dingell Bill; and a broadened long-range program of federal aid in the field of education. Unless these events, among others, occur, there will be no profession of social work, and social casework in modern society will be engrossed in sitting with its thumbs and fingers helplessly pressed against the weak spots in a crumbling dike. There would be nothing to say about it beyond what it has been, and that has been said. . . .

It is necessary that we look at social casework in the context of the profession of which it is a part. The profession of social work is concerned with the creation and development of a democratic society which will afford every individual opportunity for the maximum development of which he is capable. In achieving this purpose, the profession has worked toward two objectives: (1) the reshaping of social and economic institutions which are failing to fulfil their functions and (2) the creating of special services for groups of individuals where needs are not being met. Appropriate measures in the attainment of both these aims long have been the active concern of social work, but those that have fulfilled the second objective have been more peculiarly its province.

During the last fifty years, a period during which the social and economic structure gradually has become vestigal, there has been much unmet need. Accordingly social work has developed in the very process of assuming an overwhelming responsibility for the provision of special services for all kinds and conditions of men. Many agencies, varied in nature, have been flung up, sometimes as emergency measures, to become permanent because of continuing need for their function or because they got frozen into community life. Since unmet need presented itself in the form of innumerable individuals urgently asking for help and since basic social and economic change could not be wrought overnight in times unreceptive to that change, it was a natural development that social casework became a very prevalent and a dominant avenue for the promotion of the welfare of the individual, even though without essential social support it was at times a meager and palliative one. In view also of the dire need on every hand it is not surprising that social caseworkers, together with many other social workers and philanthropic citizens, became absorbed in the development of more and more programs to administer casework services or to incorporate these services into other institutions. Today we recognize the limitations of casework; but wherever there are individuals who are unhappy, ineffective, or troublesome—and they are everywhere without reference to class, color, or creed—there is still an urgent demand for "that something" that social casework has to offer to help the individual in need. . . .

What has social casework to offer, first, to the people whom it serves directly, individual by individual, and, second, to the profession as a whole, which in the last analysis also serves the individual? In social casework we deal with people who are experiencing some breakdown in their capacity to cope unaided with their own affairs. This breakdown may be due primarily to social factors beyond the control of the individual, that is, he is a victim of circumstance such as unemployment, poverty, physical handicap, or illness. The breakdown may, however, be partially, largely, or wholly due to emotional disturbance, interpsychic conflicts, or mental ineptitude within the individual. He may himself have created his social dilemma, whether it be unemployment, poverty, physical illness, or infringements against the law. In either instance we deal with people who are in trouble, who are having to ask for and take help, and who, regardless of the source of their difficulty, are prone to have disturbed feelings about it.

Furthermore, each individual in his own particular struggle for mental and physical survival has developed characteristic ways of handling his discomfort to the end of diminishing it so that he may live comfortably with it. We have learned that it is how the individual feels about his problem which will determine what he will do about it or what he will permit anyone to help him do about it. We have learned also that his way of handling his discomfort, his way of responding to his problem, will be a decisive factor in his use of help. We know, too, that, even in those instances in which the individual's problem stems primarily from within himself, the social circumstances of his life not only have had a part in creating his difficulty but now will play a significant role in fashioning his response and in determining its present usefulness or futility. This leads us invariably to focus on understanding what purpose an individual's behavior now is serving him in relation to a combination of factors and forces in his life-situation. We who are trained and experienced *know* that we cannot help him deal more competently with his problem unless we render our service differentially in the light of its meaning to him and in relation to the emotional and practical values, in terms of futility or usefulness, of his own solution. This implies a basic understanding of the individual—a penetrating insight into the meaning of his behavior.

In spite of the fact that each individual situation is unique, this understanding is aided by knowledge of the meaning which certain social circumstances commonly have for people. In understanding the personality, the social caseworker today considers types of experience in relation to common human needs and common ways of responding. How may malnutrition affect personality development? What may be the effects of physical handicap? What may the impact of war mean at different age levels? There is involved here a knowledge derived not only through psychiatry, psychology, and medicine but also through study of the import for the individual of family life, of cultural backgrounds, and of community life. In helping people there is involved not only a knowledge of skills in working with people but also acquaintance with all types of community resources; knowledge of the function of social agencies; knowledge of the individual's rights and recourse under the law; and, finally, skill derived from knowledge and practice in bringing to the service of the individual the resources indicated by the nature of his problem as well as his capacity to use help.

The effective use of these general bodies of knowledge and kinds of skill presupposes the acquisition of a way of thinking and a way of feeling. We long have struggled for an orderly way of thinking which approximates scientific method. The pressure of the client's problem, his urgent need for help, may make necessary action on the basis of a minimum knowledge of the facts. Once embarked, however, there is a continuous attempt to sustain disciplined feeling and hence orderly thinking. This entails a continuous selective exploration of each case situation for relevant facts; the formulation of significant questions and tentative hypotheses, that is, interpretative statements; the testing of the facts against the interpretation and against the client's response to the help given, to determine need for further inquiry and need for changing treatment emphasis; and the recognition of bias and a continuous awareness of the possibility that our own feelings, prejudices, and convictions may distort what we see, influence our thinking, and dominate our action. There is general recognition of the fact that the social caseworker's professional effectiveness cannot be based on an absence of emotional need but instead on self-knowledge and on both an innate and an acquired capacity to control it. In what she has learned in coming to understand herself and to deal objectively with her own response to the impact of the client's demands, needs, and pressures, the social caseworker has a contribution to make to the profession as a whole.[1]

Our knowledge and skill in understanding and in helping the individual operates within the context of a consciously controlled professional relationship which also requires both knowledge and skill for proper management. In return this relationship contributes to a deeper understanding of the client as well as to his use of help. It facilitates both the diagnostic and the treatment processes. The essential characteristics of this relationship have been described vari-

---

1. For discussion of scientific method in social casework see Charlotte Towle, "Underlying Skills of Case Work Today," *Social Service Review*, 15 (September, 1941): 456–71 (also in *Proceedings of National Conference of Social Work, 1941*, pp. 254–66), and "Some Basic Principles of Social Research in Social Case Work," *Social Service Review*, 15 (March, 1941): 66–80.

ously, somewhat as follows: It is a warm relationship in which the worker "feels into" and with the client without feeling like him. . . . The worker affords the client a relatively neutral but understanding response. Theoretically this neutrality . . . for many individuals is unique and gives him a feeling of freedom. What freedom? Supposedly it brings freedom to express what he cannot bring out elsewhere, his hopes which others might ridicule, his aspirations which others might oppose, his unsocial impulses which others might condemn, his hostile impulses which others might taboo or to which they might retaliate. Presumably, then, . . . certain gains may occur, notably:

1. As he gains freedom to bring out negative feelings toward others or fears or aspirations formerly repressed, there may be a release of tension, of the blocking that formerly prevented action in coping with his problem.

2. As he experiences the worker's understanding and acceptance of his complaints, blame of others, frustrated strivings, he may gain courage to face his own part in the problem or to acknowledge his own formerly repressed wishes. *This person to whom he is talking does not condemn wrongdoing, and therefore he can admit to wrongdoing.*

3. As he experiences the worker's understanding of his limitations or his part in the problem, that is, his wrongdoing, he may develop the capacity to understand and to endure the limitations of other people. He may endure the denials implicit in adverse circumstances with less impoverishment of the personality. *As he is given to, he gives, and, having received understanding, he now can give it.*

4. Insofar as in these first three steps he has experienced a change in feeling, he begins to *think* differently. At this point he gains insight or is ready to receive it. *Since feelings influence thinking, a change in feeling will bring a change in thinking and hence in action.*

5. As he grows better able to deal realistically with the adverse social circumstances in his life, *one counts on the modifiability of these environmental factors to intrench his gains.* As his behavior toward others changes, *one again counts on the capacity of others to react positively to the*

change in him. When this occurs, there may be a quick intrenchment of therapeutic gains.

There has been depicted here the theoretical formula of
what has happened sometimes through the talking-through
of difficulties in a relationship in which the worker affords
the client a neutral but understanding response. Experienced workers know that the relationship must be subject
to continual modification in endless variation depending
upon the needs of the individual with each changing
response. . . .

We have learned how to be supportive—that is, how to
use authority, meet dependency, impose demands, and
convey moral judgments in a sustaining way so that the
individual may become more self-determining or, at least,
less self-destructive in his behavior.[2] Experience has made
indisputable the fact that the relationship afforded the
client is a decisive component in casework treatment. We
have made considerable headway during the past decade
both in the understanding and in the management of this
relationship. We have much to learn, and one can expect
accelerated process in this area in the years ahead if casework is practiced under more favorable conditions. But the
therapeutic benefits possible through this relationship cannot be realized when the social situation operates against
the intrenchment of gains.

In the process of becoming what it is today, social casework has developed certain characteristics and working
principles which bespeak its philosophy. . . . The following
notable concepts are part and parcel of the feeling, thinking, and doing of every worker who truly represents this
field of practice:

First, a deep conviction as to the individual worth of man,
which implies that he has a right to survive on satisfying
terms with himself and the world. What are satisfying
terms? Granted individual difference, by and large his
normal wants are: the right to manage his own affairs,
which implies the opportunity to learn, the chance to work,

2. Thomas M. French and Ralph Ormsby, *Psychoanalytic Orientation in Case Work*
(New York: Family Welfare Association of America, 1944).

the desire to marry and to establish a family. He wants, furthermore, a participating and contributing part in the life of the community. These wants are basic needs; and, when he is denied the requisite opportunities for normal life, he is deeply frustrated, with resultant damage to his personality growth. . . . We know that unmodifiable adverse social circumstances are decisive and that the tender ministrations of an understanding relationship cannot compensate for basic environment lacks, meager services, and restrictive agency policies.

Second, a conviction that social casework has much to offer in using the strengths of the individual but little to offer in overcoming basic personality weaknesses dedicates us to helping efforts which engage the individual's participation and to rendering services in such a way that he is enabled to make more productive use of his powers in relation to his social situation.

Third, the social caseworker emphatically contests the traditional concept that taking help in any form should be made painful in order that pauperization may not ensue and instead maintains that humiliation and pauperization go hand in hand. This principle holds not merely in the rendering of financial assistance but in giving help of all kinds. Impoverishment of the personality must not occur, and this demands that the recipient must not experience humiliation in taking help. We can work most effectively, therefore, in an agency framework in which the policies and procedures enable us to enact our own feeling of respect for the individual we serve.

Fourth, a full acceptance of the importance of the concept of individual difference enables us to separate one individual from another and ourselves from any one of them. Thus in helping we do not impose our wishes, needs, standards, sense of values, but instead we try to understand the individual's wishes and strivings to help him solve his problem in the light of them. We know that social justice implies treating "unequal things unequally," and we find it difficult to be helpful when this is not possible.

Fifth, we understand that, no matter how unusual an

individual's behavior or attitudes may seem, they have a rational foundation, a logic. They are something to be understood in the light of his past experience, his present circumstances, and his future aspirations. We turn with him to the past insofar as it is necessary to help him understand the present and plan for the future. Frequently, the individual is so caught in an untenable present and so blocked in his future prospects that he resorts to the past. We know all too well from frustrating experience the limitations of social casework to help the individual who has solved his problem through a deep and satisfying regression.

We know also the limitations of social casework in the lives of those people whose social realities prevent them from looking and planning beyond their immediate struggle for survival. We feel a keen sense of inadequacy when often, as we offer help, we cannot bring adequate resources to help them surmount the adverse present. It has been said that helping people plan realistically for the future can serve as a balm for past hurts and as a stabilizing influence amid the difficulties of the present. The social caseworker of the past has had too little experience in helping her clients look beyond the present to the future. This is attested by the fact that, as social workers reach out to understand the meaning of a problem to an individual, they explore the past and the pressures of the present but seldom take into account what the social difficulty has done to those aspirations for the future by which man is motivated and strengthened in the present. If modern society attains conditions essential for life, the social caseworker can well rejoice that those whom she helps will no longer be committed to an infantile state of mind, implicit in living precariously from day to day.

Sixth, and finally, we have a professional responsibility to bring the protective resources of our agencies or of the community to the assistance of the person whose basic ineptitudes made it impossible for him to use help resourcefully and to gain the capacity to manage his own affairs. Support and protection instead of rehabilitation are frequently the function of social casework even though wherever possible we aim toward rehabilitation of people rather than merely toward protection. . . .

It is not a simple matter to summarize the content of "that something" which social casework has to offer which places it in high demand, but perhaps this thumbnail sketch will suffice: A disciplined way of thinking and a disciplined way of feeling derived through knowledge and experience which enables its practitioners to understand the individual in all walks of life at those times when he is not getting along and when his disturbed responses make him least understandable to himself and to his fellowmen. A knowledge of what to do and how to do it so that the resources within both the individual and his environment may be used to help him either solve more satisfactorily his human relationship problems or overcome to some extent other difficulties. A knowledge of protective resources and a readiness to serve supportively the individual who is incapable of self-help. An understanding of the individual in relation to his environment, including those agencies and institutions which exist to serve him, which could well be useful to the profession as a whole, and notably to social welfare planning, social welfare administration and social research.

It is clear today that social casework, insofar as it has been used to help individuals in trouble, has made, in spite of gigantic odds operating against any full realization of its aims, a place for itself in the minds if not always in the hearts of administrators of agencies and of institutions both within and without the field of social work. It is equally clear that its contribution to social welfare planning and social welfare administration still is to be made. Because this is so, many demands for its service have not been realistic. There is small recognition of the conditions under which social casework can function and of its limitations, particularly when it is not an integral part of the program, institution, or agency which it serves.

In the past social caseworkers, almost without question, have answered any and every demand for their services. Whenever there were individuals under the care of an institution or welfare agency of almost any type and there came a request for casework to assist the individual in his adjustment or to help him use the agency's service more productively, there casework has gone like a fireman to a fire. We have learned the hard way that these requests have not always been realistically oriented to what social casework had to offer. We know, too, that it is not always possible to help people in every setting—in fact, that certain conditions are essential for effective service.

A school system establishes a social work service. Many children are not fitting in; they are failing in their work, and/or they present behavior problems of many sorts. This problem may be due to adverse circumstances at home, disturbed relationships in the family, unfavorable influences in the community, ineptitude of teachers in teaching or in child management, or often to the lack of essential educational facilities for certain groups of children. Any one or several of these factors may be operating in a given instance. So great is the need for the kind of understanding which casework can offer the individual child, as well as the teacher or school officials, in understanding him that soon the service is swamped with children referred.

The school official may assume erroneously that his responsibility has ended when he has procured a good social service staff. We social workers, too often overwhelmed with pressures, have struggled along, giving a bit of help here and there. Too pressed with the impact of many difficulties and beguiled by the fact that in almost every instance there is some need which we can meet and thus ease a situation or demonstrate our usefulness to the system, we get absorbed in a "pinch-hit" emergency service. This way lies defeat of our professional aims and the waste of an invaluable service.

Some of these staffs have learned that they must limit intake. . . . They painstakingly try to discover the primary difficulty and then realistically to assume the responsibility of enlisting the co-operation of others in its solution. Often this involves making known lacks in educational facilities and obstructive measures in the school regime. In such instances the social worker's responsibility lies in making casework limitations known and in revealing the educational treatment issue. Fear of admitting casework limitations has led to much misguided leadership. It takes the security afforded through genuine competence and professional conviction to withdraw from service in those instances in which our contribution is not of decisive importance. Instead, out of our humanitarian readiness to help in small ineffectual ways, often we continue to assume responsibility for the case, thus making it possible for others to evade basic issues. As long as we are *doing something,* others comfortably may evade doing *the things that matter.*

If we could have been more realistically oriented to our own limitations, there might *now* be more social workers in schools. In this setting social workers are in a strategic position to render preventative help to children in making known unmet needs not only within the schools but also within the community. Engaged in collaborative work with educators, we have the opportunity to learn much about the child as well as to contribute to the educator's understanding of the part played by family life and social conditions in his learning response. During the years of the great depression, social work was discarded as a "frill" because it had not become an integral part of the educational systems which it served. Today we are being wanted anew. There is no more important place for the preventative contribution of the social caseworker in modern society than in public schools. It is essential that we do not repeat the past but, instead, that we become an integral part of the educational program. This implies that, in order to fulfil our own important function, we place elsewhere, squarely and decisively, the responsibility that belongs elsewhere.

There has been a long history of the use of social casework in correctional agencies. That there is a need for what casework has to offer on the part of the individuals concerned is clear. When casework is administered within the framework of an authoritative system, it is obvious that it must use that system. We cannot escape it by identifying with the client against the correctional agency. Instead we must help him in such a way that the demands of society, as conveyed through a correctional agency, may become sufficiently desirable that he himself regulates his behavior. When these regimes are destructively restrictive, when they are administered by people who are harshly punitive and who lack respect for the individuals they serve, that is, when everything is done to defeat the aims of a rehabilitation program, then caseworkers are driven either to reject the agency or to defend it blindly. In either instance confident, resourceful, and creative service is obstructed. Until many correctional institutions are changed, caseworkers will find it difficult if not impossible to give what casework has to offer within their authoritative framework.

Social casework belongs in public assistance programs both as a preventative and as a remedial measure. Economic need is both cause and effect of a whole gamut of human ills. In a money economy loss of financial resources and application for assistance can immediately affect the individual's capacity to deal with his everyday affairs. It can modify drastically his opportunities for physical, intellectual, and emotional development. Changes implicit in his need for financial assistance may alter his status and role in the family group as well as in the community. The catastrophes of life which bring people under the care of these agencies inevitably cause emotional disturbance. How the person feels about the difficulty created, as well as how he feels about the help given, will determine his use of the assistance. Frequently rehabilitation or pauperization are at stake, not only in the adequacy of the services rendered but also in the way they are rendered. It is for this reason that the knowledge, understanding, and skills of the social caseworker are needed throughout the administration of these programs—from the initial service of helping the applicant establish eligibility through all the other services indicated in individual instances.

On the assumption that in modern society there will be a substantial liberalization and broadening of public assistance together with a more adequate health program and extended educational opportunities, social casework should have a greater opportunity than in the past to make real the purposes of these programs. In this premodern era in which we await important changes, it can be said only that trained caseworkers in public assistance have been nourished largely by their stirring conviction rather than by the realization of their aims. Many factors have negated what casework has to offer, notably: inadequate financial assistance, grossly deficient in many areas; case loads so large that individualization based on knowing the person and understanding the differential factors in his situation has been impossible; statutory provisions inherited from the past and agency policies colored by outmoded conceptions of what is good for individuals and for society; reliance on such devices as unrestricted money payments to enact respect for human right without respect for the human personality. All these factors combine against social casework. For example, in many instances there is a lack of realization that a person who is granted his statutory rights to far less than he needs will feel that his rights as a human being have been violated. Also there has been oversight of the fact that the aged and disabled person who needs help in management may be failed by a ritualistic adherence to the concept of "right to be self-determining."

It is clear that many administrators have not used the understanding available to them through their casework staffs for guidance on what administrative provisions and policies are doing to people as well as failing to do for them. There has been a tendency in some administrators to let the recipient bear the brunt of the community's ill-grounded fears and expensive superstitions rather than to deal with those attitudes through interpretation of the cost of unmet human need to the community. These factors among others have starved many well-qualified social caseworkers out of the public assistance services, and they will continue to do so as long as agency provisions and policies are shaped by the ambivalent attitudes of society rather than by the needs of the recipient. Many examples could be given wherein the administration with its right hand obstructs or undermines the efforts of its own left hand occupied in casework services. Examples could be given also of situations in which the right hand keeps the left hand busy. Unsound administrative policies can grind grist for the mill of the caseworker.

In response to extensive demand casework has been blown to the four winds in the past several years. Well-established social services have been deserted by workers who have scattered to a great variety of new settings. We have been spread as thin as human need is widespread. Can we serve individuals best in a few focal points or should we try to meet their need wherever it presents itself? It seems clear that we cannot function competently everywhere and that the time has come for deciding where we shall serve. In making these decisions, we may find the following considerations useful.

First, the function of the agency is important. Does it exist in order to promote the welfare of the individual whom it serves, as in the case of social agencies, schools, and hospitals? Or does it exist to serve other ends? If so, is casework wanted primarily for the good of the administration rather than for the good of the recipient of the service? In the latter instance, can the setting sustain work oriented to the needs of the individual, i.e., respect for his right to be self-determining; protection where rehabilitation is not possible; maintenance of the confidential relationship so that his confidences are not used against him? For example, in the light of these questions is industry a setting in which social casework can be practiced or should industries use extramural social agencies?

Second, the structure of the agency is a decisive factor. Granted an avowed social welfare purpose, are the agency's policies, regulations, and provisions so constituted as to express respect for the worth of the individual, that is, understanding, acceptance of individual difference, and a desire to help him help himself or to protect him against himself? Do they instead belie the social welfare purpose and express disregard for the worth of the individual in harsh judgment and an inclination to humiliate, deprive, or punish him? In the latter instance, how ready is the administrative staff to work for change in agency structure? Is casework wanted to compensate the individual, to make amends, and to ease hurts inflicted by the service, or is it wanted for what it can contribute to the total agency's understanding of how to realign its services in the interests of the recipient? The social caseworker has labored all too long in futile attempts at helping the individual feel better on an empty stomach. She has slaved all too long at easing secondary problems while primary ones persist and are aggravated further by a depriving or authoritative regime whose care or supervision necessity drives the individual to endure.

. . . Just as it is the caseworker's responsibility to convey widespread need which is not being met to those at the agency's helm, so it is the administrator's responsibility to make it possible for her not to be wholly absorbed in case situations. This implies not merely a manageable case load, but also that administrators expect casework staffs to habituate themselves to inquiring of their case loads: What do these cases say in terms of common needs in relation to agency function? Wherein have we failed to fulfill our function or wherein should our function be changed? Wherein do our procedures and routines fulfill our function or obstruct it? Caseworkers are in a position to test out and observe the ways in which the agency works or fails to work. In modern society the attainment of this kind of integration of casework and administration will mean that caseworkers will be trained to become competent administrators of casework programs.[3]

Implicit in this discussion is the relationship between social casework, social research, and community organization. We long have been criticized for not having systematically made known our findings in order that new community resources might be developed and existent ones co-ordinated for more effective service. Social casework and community organization are interdependent. This implies systematic records designed in advance for social research and oriented to community welfare needs.[4] It implies also

3. Charlotte Towle, "Professional Skill in Administration," *Newsletter of the American Association of Psychiatric Social Workers*, vol. 10, no. 1 (May 1940).
4. Wayne McMillen, *Community Organization for Social Welfare* (Chicago: University of Chicago Press, 1945).

that salary scales and prestige values be adjusted so that experienced caseworkers remain in practice rather than move on to supervisory and administrative positions. Whether the social caseworker in modern society assumes this important responsibility will depend in the last analysis on administrative conviction and policy. Only through leadership at the administrative level and the provisions of means to this end can it be attained and the caseworker's understanding of individual needs used in community welfare planning.

The continuous attempt to sustain orderly thinking and disciplined feeling demanded in social casework should make it essential groundwork for social research. The social caseworker's way of thinking through a case *ideally* in all instances and *actually* in many instances is essentially the same as the research worker's method in studying a situation. Furthermore, the caseworker's training and experience in the management of professional relationships in which she has learned to understand and to deal objectively with her own response as well as to help the client express his thinking and feeling would seem to have a direct carry-over to interviewing in the research situation. One cannot teach research workers interviewing techniques with which to extract *valid* information from people whom they do not understand or to draw valid inferences from the data thus obtained. The informant's response speaks a language of its own, which should be meaningful to the worker well grounded in the knowledge, understanding, and skill which the social caseworker possesses.

In spite of this fact, casework has not made a significant contribution in social research. Many factors have operated against this contribution, notably: absorption in service; the emphasis in casework on the uniqueness of each individual situation; professional education which in many instances has been highly specialized and fragmentary; and, finally, operating as a deterrent, the caseworker's awareness of subjective factors in her work. Today there is wider recognition at the administrative level of the importance of research as a basis for intelligent service. There is recognition also of the absolute necessity for broad professional education rather than for narrow specialization. Through knowledge acquired gradually and applied painstakingly over the years, we social caseworkers are better prepared than formerly to think comparatively from case to case and to formulate general concepts with which to view specific instances. We are now more ready to raise significant questions. Furthermore, our fear of subjective factors can be expected to diminish as we become more competent in the management of professional relationship.[5]

In modern society there will be important problems to solve in our working relationship with other professions. In the past the great proportion of work in which caseworkers have been engaged has been in helping people with social problems. Since all these problems have been disturbing to the individual emotionally, we have had a rich experience in understanding feelings and in helping individuals modify their attitudes. The focus of our work has been largely, however, on those feelings immediately operative in the solution of the problem. Gradually over the years we have increasingly been dealing with people whose emotional difficulties have not centered around external problems so much as within themselves. Accordingly, a good many social workers have had considerable experience in direct treatment of psychological problems. There has been a close working relationship with psychiatrists. During the depression years there was a marked increase in this activity, owing in part to internalization of emotional disturbance that occurred when the individual could not cope with adverse social circumstances. The increase was due also to a tendency on our part to resort to this treatment because the usual social-treatment resources had broken down. In such instances our efforts often were futile in terms of the client's good. Out of the experience, however, we have learned a great deal.

During these same years there was a marked widening of

5. For the place of social casework in social research see Robert T. Lansdale, "Research as a Major Function of a Private Social Agency," *Social Service Review*, 16 (December, 1942): 641–49; Richard C. Cabot, M.D., "Treatment in Social Case Work and the Need of Criteria and of Tests of Its Success or Failure," *Proceedings of the National Conference of Social Work, 1931;* Gordon Hamilton, *Theory and Practice of Social Case Work* (New York: Columbia University Press, 1940), p. 371.

the client group. Starting prior to World War I, at the point where social casework moved out from relief-giving agencies to hospitals, clinics, and schools, there has been an upward trend in the number of individuals and families served who were not in the economically dependent group. . . . The present trend toward fee charging for social casework services in some agencies and clinics is indicative of the change in economic status of the group served.

The recent war, just as World War I, has brought large numbers of people from all walks of life into social casework services. The number of individuals who are in need of help because of emotional difficulties which produce social problems presumably has mounted not only through wider recognition but also through higher incidence. The work of the social caseworker in this area closely approximates that of the psychiatrist. With the marked shortage of psychiatrists to meet present demands, there is a definite trend toward extending to the social caseworker much responsibility for treatment which formerly would have fallen to the psychiatrist both in public and in private practice. There are many problems which await solution.

First, there is the consideration of the demands of this work. Does the caseworker have less to offer than the psychiatrist, and is she being drawn in primarily because of the shortage of well-trained psychiatrists? Or does casework training and experience fit her admirably for this responsibility? Does she have something to offer not brought to the situation by the psychiatrist? If so, this is a valid field of endeavor for social caseworkers. It should follow that she will be accorded a legitimate place in this aspect of practice. If, however, she is used to fill a gap in "pinch-hit" fashion, then it is important that her function be clearly differentiated from the psychiatrist and that the profession of social work continue to assume responsibility only for her social work function. It should not assume responsibility through schools of social work for the training of makeshift psychiatrists.

Second, it is important that training requisite for competent performance in this area be formulated if this responsibility is assumed. Training should not be left to *chance* association with a psychiatrist who is willing to assume responsibility for teaching the social worker. Third, there should be avoidance of recourse to psychotherapy when other measures are indicated. . . .

In modern society there will be many important problems to solve in order to effect the change depicted here as essential. Were conditions previously described as being essential for life to become a reality overnight, it might be concluded that there would be little if any need for social casework. Actually there still would be great need. First, because, under the most favorable social-economic system, disaster often is not timed to the person's readiness to meet it practically or to assimilate it emotionally. Second, because it can be expected that the new world of social security and opportunity will be lived in and used by people who may not immediately make the most of it. When people attain a new way of life, they do not cut off abruptly from the past. They bring the past into the present, and, therefore, the new conditions favorable to growth will be used slowly.

One might say that the major difference between yesterday and today probably will lie in the fact that, for the first time in its history, social casework may begin to serve people with some chance of enacting its ideology and realizing its aims. . . . Preventative work rather than remedial measures increasingly must be our aim. This will make necessary deliberate efforts of many kinds, among which there could well be careful selection of strategic settings and public programs which offer casework services apart from financial assistance. To some extent this development may occur naturally, for a deepened social conscience can be anticipated as a logical outgrowth of a more socialized system. We can anticipate a wider and a more genuine acceptance of help for disadvantaged groups and for *all* individuals who need it. As our cultural resistance to obtaining help is lowered, individuals may seek it early rather than late because social attitudes will permit them to regard it as evidence of strength rather than of weakness.

In considering the place of social casework in modern society, I have emphasized its contribution to the field of social work as a whole because of a deep conviction that it cannot go forward alone. It is only as it becomes an integral part of the profession of social work, serving and being served by social welfare administration, community organization, and social research, that it will attain its own aims in decent measure. . . . It is clear that social casework must have a vital place in a comprehensive curriculum for all social workers.[6]

There is general recognition of the fact that man's mastery of nature, in the form of scientific discoveries and technological achievement, "has proved a curse rather than a blessing in the hands of men ignorant of their own personalities and of human relationships." . . .[7] As we move into an area in which the gap between the natural and the social sciences will be bridged, it can be expected that the profession of social work will have a decisive contribution to make and that it will therefore become an integral part of the social structure rather than the adjunct it has been in the past. Social casework must find its responsible place within the profession, in relation to other professional fields, and within society.

Casework Methods of Helping the Client to Make Maximum Use of His Capacities and Resources

MANY READERS about to scan this article were scarcely toddlers when it was written. It stands today as solid and

---

6. Edith Abbott, *Social Welfare and Professional Education*, rev. and enl. ed. (Chicago: University of Chicago Press, 1942) and *Twenty-one Years of University Education for Social Service, 1920–41* (Chicago: University of Chicago Press, 1941); Gordon Hamilton, "Planning for the Future in Schools of Social Work," *Social Service Review*, 18 (June 1944): 145–51.

7. Franz Alexander, *Our Age of Unreason* (New York: J. B. Lippincott Co., 1942). "Casework Methods of Helping the Client . . ." is reprinted from *Proceedings: National Conference of Social Work, 1948* (New York: Columbia University Press, 1949), where it appeared as "Helping the Client to Use His Capacities and Resources." Copyright 1949 by The National Conference of Social Work. Also in *Social Service Review*, vol. 22, no. 4 (December 1948).

useful a presentation of certain major ideas that govern helping as it did twenty years ago.

Within this article Charlotte Towle deals with a number of treatment considerations that she had touched on before (notably in "Factors in Treatment" and "Underlying Skills of Casework Today"), but with the surer touch of longer experience. One sees here, too, the nascent stages of ideas that were to come to full development in the Chicago faculty's perspectives on casework. (A few high spots of this theory development are recounted in her 1956 article "Some Aspects of Modern Casework.") Here, in 1948, she writes of these considerations, which still hold import for practitioners: the client's *motivation* as the well spring from which his change and coping will flow; and the client's *capacity*, particularly his capacity to form and utilize relationship.

(*Motivation* and *capacity*, combined with *opportunity*, became working concepts of a cohesive faculty group under Charlotte Towle's leadership and support. The problem-solving model of casework practice utilizes this triad concept as an area of major diagnostic focus, as seen in my *Social Casework: A Problem-solving Process* [Chicago, 1957]. The Chicago research on client utilization of casework services was also based on this m-c-o construct: see Lilian Ripple and others, *Motivation, Capacity and Opportunity: Studies in Casework Theory and Practice*, University of Chicago, Social Service Monographs, School of Social Service Administration [1964].)

The principles of casework treatment set down herein mark the necessity that social study inquiry be a *selective* one; that exploration of facts should be shaped by consideration of the nature of the problem and the function of the agency; that there should be help "to focalize on part of a problematic situation when over-all exploration is too involving of the total personality." These guides, perhaps familiar to today's caseworkers, were particularly vital when they were set down by Charlotte Towle because it was a period when a large segment of casework practice was still floundering about in the labyrinths of the client's background history in the search for an explanation of his present problems. In the same period, when "catharsis" was still thought to cleanse the soul, and when the cognitive functions of the ego were scarcely recognized, Charlotte Towle makes clear both the limits and the potential problems in catharsis, and sets forth the conviction that "new intellectual orientation may produce a change in feeling." Further in this article one finds a classification of persons-with-problems. Whether the categories suggested are fully valid is less important than that they offer an organizing mode of viewing the too varied persons and circumstances encountered in casework.

This article is a rich lode to be mined by the attentive reader.

H. H. P.

Social work as a profession is one of society's instruments for enabling the social conscience to find expression. The very core of social work is social reform. The very core of social casework is the rehabilitation of the individual. The stigmatized reformer is one who needfully attempts to impose himself on others, to re-create the individual in his own wishful image of himself, or to mold the world to his own liking without realistic reference to needs, capacities, and motivations of individuals and groups.

In social casework it is realized that one cannot rehabilitate another. Motivation and remotivation come from within the individual and his family group. As the individual and his family seek help, however, it is the responsibiilty of the social worker to maintain an unswerving identification with the social conscience. This means that he will bring his professional knowledge and skill, the authority which he carries as representative of a social agency, to bear upon the community to create conditions favorable for the individual's development and to provide opportunities for his growth. It means, also, that he will use his powers to help the individual become socially competent. The social worker continuously will understand the individual, but he will not necessarily affirm his feelings, his thinking, or his acts. A basic acceptance of the social reform motive, that is, the rehabilitative goal in social casework, is occurring as social workers increasingly see it as meeting human need rather than fear it as a violation of man's right to self-determination.

To bring this subject within limits, I am excluding two groups of clients: those who come under care against their will in response to community pressure and those who are physically, mentally, and emotionally incapacitated for self-help. I am confining my discussion to those who are seeking help in some form and who it is reasonable, *tentatively*, to assume bring a certain wherewithal to the solution of their difficulties. What wherewithal? First, there is some motivation to seek and presumably to use help. Second, there is some capacity to tolerate limits and to face reality. Third, in so far as these qualities prevail, there is some capacity for relationship and consequently a propensity for change if not for growth.

It might seem that I am selecting a small group of those clients who least need help. These are the people, however, who constitute a large proportion of the load of social agencies and social services within other institutions. They come with troubled feelings from all walks of life, seeking specific services and help with problems of personal or interpersonal adjustment. These include disturbed parent-child relationships, marital difficulties, and general unhappiness due to maladaptation to various situations. The high incidence of individuals disturbed by relationship problems needing and often requesting help is a dramatic feature of our times.

While there has been a slow but steady upward trend in the number of clients who are not in the economically dependent group, the majority of applicants are those who have lived marginally. By and large, they have been the people who have been in an uncushioned position in a competitive society, the people whose struggle for survival through war, depression, and inflation has been a precarious one. Throughout this period in all economic groups, family life has been maintained under stress, so that normal family conflicts have been increased and intensified. Emerging from insecure families into a precarious world, many individuals have shown resilience and capacity for growth in spite of odds. Many, however, have attained an uneven growth, while in some instances impoverishment of the personality has occurred. They bring to the complexities of life a development more precocious than mature, while frequently their strengths are those of aggression and defense. Unmet need in many forms has produced basic want which has engendered that response sequence so familiar to social workers—want, fear, hatred, aggression (wishful or enacted), guilt, and anxiety over retaliation resulting in confusion, indecision, submission, fragmentary aggression, and many other reactions which obstruct growth and effective living. This constitutes the soil in which defenses essential for a man's survival have been reared, defenses which may hold or break under the pressure of the circumstances or problems which bring a given individual into an agency.

Whether they serve him well or crumble will depend on several factors: (1) the nature and extent of the present pressures; (2) the nature of his early life-relationships, whether they met his need to sufficient extent to make possible enduring sublimations and socially constructive defenses; (3) the adequacy of the agency service as he turns for help in his quest for a solution to his present problem.

These, then, are *not* people who least need help. In the interests of prevention of further difficulty they need it urgently. Turning to a social agency for help commonly is a decisive episode in the life of an individual. It is therefore imperative that social workers increasingly help him affirm, through use, the strengths that he brings to the experience. It is important also that they understand the purposes served by defenses. These must be seen as a resource to be conserved in many instances. This implies an investigative focus which seeks to discover actual and potential strengths rather than merely the pathology of the individual, one which, however, does not wishfully ignore pathology.

These ends will be attained in so far as throughout the life of a helping relationship the worker's practice is governed by four general principles: (1) *The dependency of the client has been met freely* on the assumption that normally unmet dependency produces helplessness, resentment, anxiety, and confusion, which in turn beget further dependency and social incompetence. (2) *The caseworker has affirmed and helped the client use his strengths* through making it possible for him to talk freely, participate in thinking, planning, and doing throughout. (3) *The client has not been threatened or put to rout by unrealistic demands* as the imposition of the worker's standards and goals, by pressure for information beyond that essential in order to help, by premature interpretation, or by the worker's need for relationship beyond that sought by the client. This implies also that effort will be made to relieve adverse circumstances operating against the attainment of self-dependence. (4) *Certain demands of the reality situation have not been ignored.* Instead these have been focused on, and the client helped to meet them.

Specifically, the worker's initial mode of working is to bring a positive attitude to the interview—an attitude that an applicant for help is eligible to an agency's service until proved ineligible, that he is competent until proved incompetent, that he has a capacity for self-dependence until he convincingly reveals inability to use his right to self-determination. The unprejudiced social worker who does not equate a need for help with ineptitude will not relate to the client with a narrow focus on what is the problem and what is wrong with the person, but, instead, his approach continuously will be shaped by an intent to discern what help is wanted, needed, and can be used; why the need has arisen; and what this person brings to the situation which he can be enabled to use in his own behalf. Not what is the problem per se but what needs is the person revealing is the concern which gives depth to our understanding of people who are seeking help. Disturbed feelings such as anxiety and resentment with resultant manifestations of dependency and confusion are prone to be in the foreground when people in time of trouble turn to an agency for help. The seeming pathology which emerges under stress is readily discerned. In contrast at such times strengths may be obscure, these strengths which stem from mature readiness to cope with adverse circumstance or with one's self, as well as from relatively constructive defenses.

As a worker focuses on determination of need with readiness to meet it, the client experiences social acceptance of his need. Instead of engendering greater needfulness, the worker's attitude will tend to ease feelings of humiliation and restore self-respect, at which point seemingly pathological projections, rationalizations, and defenses may subside. Instead of being driven defensively to exaggerate his problem or to minimize it, the client is thus encouraged to present it realistically. Because of a change in feeling about himself he may be able to view it more realistically, which often is the first step in taking action in its solution.

The first step in treatment is to provide favorable conditions for the client to talk productively. The social study, or what habitually has been termed the history-taking or investigatory process, is one of the major measures whereby the client may be helped to use his own capacities and resources. It also is a means whereby the worker may come to know not only his needs but one through which his capacities and limitations may be differentiated. A selective history may enlighten the present problem for both worker and client.[1] Furthermore, it becomes the means to several other ends: first, in so far as the client talks spontaneously, participates in exploration, and assumes responsibility for making his needs known, it can early set the pattern of self-activity in his relationship with the agency.

1. For elaboration of social study as a scientific inquiry and also as a treatment process, see Charlotte Towle, "Underlying Skills of Case Work Today," *Social Service Review*, 15 (September 1941): 45–71. Also in *Proceedings of National Conference of Social Work, 1941*.

Second, in so far as both worker and client participate in the process so that it is a "thinking and feeling together to some purpose,"[2] a working relationship is established. There has been an erroneous concept that one delays securing anything but minimum information until "a good relationship is established." There is no better way to obstruct the development of relationship. If one secures information to understand in order to help, it must be secured *early;* and, if the purpose has been shared with the client, the history process becomes a vital part of the working-together toward the solution of the problem.

Third, there frequently will have been certain benefits for the client in so far as he has been free to bring out what the problem means to him and to others close to him; insofar as he has recounted its onset as well as what he has done up to now about it and with what results; insofar as he has been able also to express his wishes and aspirations, that is, what he would do if he could, together with a formulation of the present obstacles to his plan. The following gains repeatedly have been noted: change in feeling about the problem and about himself in relation to it, which may imply perspective, resolution of conflict, gain in understanding, in short, a general clarification or reorientation to his problematic situation. In instances of acute emotional upset over a situational difficulty wherein the individual's basic personality conflicts have not been activated and the total personality involved, the social study may constitute the treatment process, and the individual move immediately into the solution of his problem.

In the social study process there are certain principles of practice to which experienced workers adhere conditionally. First, there is general agreement that a client cannot talk productively alone to a monosyllabic, nondirective worker. It is recognized that the client will not know what the agency and he himself need to know in order to help him. Hence, it is the worker's responsibility explicitly to convey their

2. Unpublished statement, "The Process of Making Tentative Diagnosis in Social Case Work," by Florence Sytz, to the Curriculum Committee of the American Association of Schools of Social Work.

joint need for information and to direct the inquiry in accordance with the client's need for help in talking relevantly and productively. This meets a certain reality dependency which every client brings into a situation in which "he does not know the ropes." It enables him to feel secure, to function competently. It prevents him from a feeling of being lost, entangled, and hence frustrated and confused in talking to no end. It helps him to use his capacities in coming to grips with the reality of the helping situation. The individual who is unable to participate under these conditions with a professionally mature worker leads one to question his motivation in seeking help, his readiness to use it, his capacity to tolerate limits and to meet reality demands, and his capacity for relationship.

We do not seek information beyond what we need to know in order to help. The variation in amount and kind of information sought and whether the study focus is oriented entirely to the present or also to the past obviously will vary in accordance with the nature of the problem and the function of the agency. Thus varying lengths of time will be involved in social study, for worker and client proceed together in the exploration of the problem at the client's pace. Furthermore, a more intense relationship will be engendered in the process in some situations than in others. Likewise, there will be great variation in the amount of emotion engaged and the extent of feeling provoked. An experienced worker will help the client deal with his anxiety, resentment, guilt, and other feelings in various ways, notably through acknowledgment and understanding of the feeling shown; through interpretation which stresses the helping purpose or his own therapeutic goal, through interpretation which universalizes, through setting time limits, and through helping him focalize on the exploration of a part of a problematic situation when over-all exploration is too involving of the total personality. When guilt is preventing movement into the helping relationship, the worker guided by general knowledge and by what understanding he has attained of a specific situation will help the client deal with it in various ways. . . .

The problem of the release of hostility presents itself early in the exploration of a situation. Often it is essential that hostility be expressed in order that the need out of which it arises may be understood and met. We have continued to gain a deepened understanding of its import both as it affects the personality adjustment of the individual and as it affects the treatment relationship. I can only repeat what I have said elsewhere some years ago: "The skilled worker has learned to move slowly in this area and to observe intently the individual's response in relation to all that he has learned about him as a person so that hostility and anxiety may not be released beyond the capacity of the individual to deal with it, or beyond the circumstances of his situation to afford opportunities for the redirection of hostile impulses and the constructive utilization of anxiety."[3]

There is no better way to weaken the client's capacity than through breaking down that inner resource—his socially constructive defenses. There is no better way to precipitate hostile dependency than to elicit the expression of hostility beyond the controls of the situation. Workers must learn "ways of limiting the person. . . . He may set time limits or help the person handle his guilt through bringing out positive feelings to offset negative ones; he may interpret, reassure, permit, or even help the person maintain some of his rationalizations and defenses; he may direct the individual to activity in the social setting or to activity comprised in steps in agency procedure through which the hostile impulses may be atoned and the anxiety eased."[4]

I have envisaged the worker as playing an active role. When the client's emotional pressure is the basis for the precipitous response, this is necessary. He will need the worker's help because he momentarily is unable to limit himself. Often, however, the worker's active role is self-begotten. Because he has elicited more hostility than the traffic will bear, he is forced into action. The individual sometimes cannot use his inner capacities or the helping resources until hostility is released through the worker's ac-

3. Towle, *op. cit.*
4. *Ibid.*

ceptance and recognition of the unmet need out of which his feeling arises. When the client uses the worker's understanding as permission to enact his feelings, his response must be limited. This frequently is done through focus on reality consequences and through conveying that it matters what happens to the client. Thus love and fear inhibit his unsocial impulses.

I think it is clear that trained workers have moved beyond that blind worship of the unburdening process which prevailed some years ago. The vague impression that in some mysterious way it was therapeutic for a client to unburden has been corrected through knowledge and experience. With intelligent use of this measure, the worker helps the client keep his feeling directed toward the reality situation and his focus on his present problem and on his purpose in seeking help.

In the early stage of the case, preceding the first formulation of the problem, the initial plan, and working agreement, the worker's understanding of the client often is limited. The client's early production and responses, however, are made meaningful through the worker's knowledge and experience. He knows the client in the light of a basic understanding of the ego, its needs, its defenses, its adjustive mechanisms, as it operates in a helping process and as it operates in certain problems and life-situations. "Certain vital life-experiences which create common problems in relation to common human needs, age, prior life-experience, and present circumstance are known to him, i.e., asking for and taking help, illness, physical and mental handicap, failure in school, work, marriage, relationship loss through death, separation, or sharing. These significant experiences have constituted a repetitive refrain in human maladjustment throughout the worker's experience. Likewise, certain kinds of life-situations have been repetitive, as the state of poverty, being an immigrant, being an orphan, the state of unmarried motherhood, being a prisoner, being a soldier. Each of these situations again in relation to common human needs, age, and prior life-experience has created a special state of being inducing common problems in personality development and social adjustment with which an experienced worker has become familiar."[5]

Hence, the worker's early formulation has been shaped in large part by the import which the client's verbal production and initial response have had for the worker in the light of certain generalizations at which he has arrived. *Quick and accurate diagnostic insight frequently is thus made possible. Decisive misunderstanding of the client as a particular entity, however, may result unless the worker continuously reaches out to know the client as an individual and to check impressions against early assumptions.* It is as worker and client proceed together in the solution of his difficulties that early impressions are corrected and understanding is deepened. It is thus that a worker may come to a more precise knowledge of his personality structure in relation to his difficulties. It is thus that the individuality of the client will become more clear, so that it will be possible not only to differentiate characteristic ways of responding from situational responses but also to gauge his strengths and capacity for change. Precise understanding of the ego structure, of its adaptive mechanisms with differentiation of strengths from precarious or flimsy defenses, is decisively important in some forms of help. Therefore, it is around this knowledge that helping methods become more precisely differential and are used with a surer touch and a more predictable outcome.

The clients selected for this discussion probably would fall roughly into four groups.

1. *People who might be characterized as victims of circumstance.*—They need concrete help and seek a specific service with a minimum of emotional disturbance about their problem and about the agency relationship. A service adequate to meet the reality need, rendered in such a way as not to humiliate or to undermine the individual's morale and with understanding of the feeling involved, will constitute the helping process.

---

5. Unpublished "Report of the Case Work Curriculum Committee, School of Social Administration, University of Chicago (Charlotte Towle, Chairman) to the Curriculum Committee of the American Association of Schools of Social Work, November, 1947."

2. *Those individuals who may or may not be victims of circumstance.*—They have social problems calling for specific services, but their problems may be to considerable extent self-induced. Whether this is true or not, the problem has involved them so as to produce considerable emotional disturbance and conflict. Not only must services be rendered with understanding of the emotional difficulties but often help with these difficulties will be necessary for productive use of the services.

3. *Those individuals who come for help with a problematic relationship.*—They do not seek any of the other social services available in the agency. They may attribute their relationship difficulty in part to social stresses and to other people, but they place it or feel it placed partially within themselves. Direct treatment through the interview is the major measure used. The help, however, frequently can be focused on the relationship rather than wholly on the person. The helping process often will involve other people and make use of community resources.

There is variation in the extent to which these individuals have placed the difficulty within themselves. If a person has placed it rigidly outside self, there will be a strong defense against the helping relationship, because to enter it would involve some inclusion of self in the problem. Consequently, he may need to keep the relationship superficial but repetitive of a former relationship in which he was done to and for. He may seek only the reassurance of having his projections and denials approved. He may experience only release from responsibility afforded through the punitive value which realistic judgments have for him. Insofar, however, as he can permit himself to acknowledge his feeling of responsibility for the problem, his urge to enter and to use the helping relationships will be strong, but at the same time his feeling about help and about his difficulty may be more intense than in many specific service situations. He may be more deeply humiliated because of the conviction, "Something is wrong with me." Because help will imply change in self, he may be more deeply fearful. Because he feels more responsible for his behavior than for what happens to him through adverse circumstances, he may suffer feelings of guilt and hense anticipate disdain, condemnation punishment.

As help is experienced, fear of change may persist. The sense of guilt over sins of omission or commission may compel intimate confidences, while the impulse to tell all may be reacted against with fear and resistance. Hence a worker may expect, on the one hand, more marked escape reactions, more bizarre uses of the problem, or, on the other hand, a stronger urge to face the problem realistically. In short, anxiety may be handled through escape, through compensatory strivings, through a strong impulse to get help and to use it productively. The implications of this for the worker-client relationship are obvious. A worker can expect to encounter more extreme responses, stronger impulses toward dependency, deeper fear of succumbing, more stubborn resistance, fear of the relationship in terms of having the inner self exposed, more marked resentment, hostility, guilt, anxiety. Furthermore, the deeper emotional import re-creates more vividly the parent-child relationship, often leading at an early point to a more intense transference situation than may obtain in casework relationships where external factors constitute a part of the social problem.

4. *Those individuals, and frequently they emerge from the third group, who seek help with a personality problem per se.*—The problem may be placed wholly within themselves. They need and at least ambivalently want help with their own inner difficulties. Direct treatment through the interview will be the major and perhaps the sole measure used. The helping process often will not involve other people or make use of community resources. By reason of these factors and also because of the fact that the treatment process involves a direct focus on the inner self by a worker who is prepared in knowledge and skill to proceed in accordance with the client's need or to limit treatment procedure with close reference to his incapacity at a given moment, this group of cases constitutes the controversial area of practice. It is considered by many social workers to belong to psychiatry.

It is obvious that each of these four groupings would demand difference in mode of working and extent to which certain measures are used. Each would require difference in use of such treatment measures as specific social services and community resources; providing the client the opportunity to unburden; advice or guidance; interpretation and the relationship. Progressively these groups from the first to the fourth require an increasing degree of knowing the individual precisely in terms of personality structure, psychopathology, characteristic ways of responding and differentiation of ego strengths. In all four groups the working principles previously defined would be in operation in varying degrees throughout the use of all treatment measures.

It is beyond the scope of this paper to discuss treatment differentially in relation to these case categories. I have presented the major implications of catharsis. I shall present briefly the general import of the following helping measures: specific services, advice, interpretation, and the relationship.

Clients come to agencies largely for specific assistance as money, help in procuring medical care, help with employment, facilities for the care of children, household management, etc. The specific request represents an unmet need, but it may not be the basis of their social difficulty. To them, however, as unmet need, it is actually and psychologically vital in a stress situation which they are unable to carry alone. Almost invariably there are complicated feelings about not being self-sufficient. Hence, with each client, the request involves a small or a large part of himself. Though the individual is not seeking help with an emotional disturbance, he is disturbed, and the help given must take this factor into account.

Clients are disturbed not only about the problem which has brought them to the agency but also about the agency itself. On the one hand, they may feel relieved, even gratified, that there is a helping resource in time of need. On the other hand, they may resent the helping hand, fearful that their need will not be met or that, if met, they will be unduly obligated to pay an exorbitant price in terms of gratitude and submission. Or, resenting their predicament, they may feel hostile toward those with whom they must share it. Feelings of fear, humiliation, and rage in the helping relationship obstruct productive use of help. It is demoralizing to be the recipient in a relationship in which one feels deprived, humiliated, and hostile. Feelings of humiliation, of despair, and of being discriminated against, over being unemployed, out of money, ill, handicapped, a failure as a parent, or the victim of circumstance in one way or another *must give way* to feelings of adequacy, self-respect, and hope. Feelings of being victimized frequently must be replaced by some realistic understanding of the factors and forces which have operated against him and by the reconditioning effect of an experience in which he is not victimized.

Hence, the specific services which we render will strengthen the client's capacities and inner resources in so far as they *meet his realistic need* and in so far as they are oriented to a sound understanding of him as an individual and are given in the context of a relationship in which the meaning of the experience is understood and the disturbed feelings dealt with indirectly or directly. When they are administered without reference to his feelings and in ways which make him feel deprived and hostile, they may demoralize him. In such practice lies the history of pauperization. It is for this reason that the administering of the so-called "practical services" calls for casework knowledge, understanding, and skill.

Advice, guidance, educational service have been termed the "counseling component" in social casework. There was a time when social workers assumed erroneously that the difficulties which brought clients to social agencies stemmed largely from ignorance—a lack of knowing what, where, and why. Hence, they torrentially handed out advice. Then came the day when they reacted against the practice rather than against their own lack of discrimination. Rejection of the guidance role was reinforced by the stereotyped use of a number of prevailing concepts, i.e., the client's right to self-determination; skepticism as to an intellectual approach; the client must struggle through to his own solutions even though he struggle in the dark; if there is anything wrong, it must be a basic conflict to be righted. Treat the total personality but tell it nothing almost was a creed social workers lived by a few years back.

Today the principles of progressive education operate within casework in the matter of counseling or advising the client. The giving must be oriented to felt need and readiness for it. Insofar as advice provokes feeling, the feeling which interferes with learning is something to be released, understood, and sometimes interpreted. Under these conditions this measure can be a vital one in helping the client become more competent and more resourceful in dealing with related problems as well as with the major problem which brought him to the agency.

Today we are not so blindly worshipful of interpretation as a means to insight for the client as we were some years ago. Today we are not so fearful of it as a means to disturb him as we were only yesterday. This obviously is because we are prepared for more discriminative use of it. We know also that insight often will be gained spontaneously by the client as he experiences change in feeling through other measures than interpretation. We know, too, that change in feeling may bring a change in action so that the problem is solved without insight gains. Interpretation as a means to understanding and insight, however, sometimes is essential for the client's maximum use of his capacities.

The principle that a new intellectual orientation may produce a change in feeling and thus facilitate learning and contribute to greater competence in doing is a familiar one to educators. Hence, interpretation which produces understanding and insight may ease disturbed feelings with a threefold result for the client: energy previously tied up unproductively may be released for productive purposes; the client gains the intellectual wherewithal for realistic self-direction; and the client gains a sense of mastery over self in relation to people and circumstance. Thus, as he copes with his social situation more competently, he becomes progressively more confident and resourceful.

Certain well-recognized principles in the use of interpretation are worth noting. Commonly it should be a mutual process with the client participating actively and the worker affirming and supplementing his self-interpretation. There are valid variations here, and in some instances it will be indicated for the worker to be more active than in others. Since clients commonly bring only a part of their life-situation and a part of themselves into the casework relationship, care is taken that interpretation is partialized and does not involve the total personality. The total personality will be engaged only as the client incorporates interpretation and uses it. By and large, interpretation will deal with the client's response in present relationships and circumstances relevant to the immediate problem. It does not often deal with remote origins of present responses and difficulties. There are valid variations, however, in the extent to which causes and the past are explored and interpreted.

All helping measures operate within the context of a relationship. It is both an outgrowth of all these measures and has been a determinant both of their use and of their usefulness. For example, the giving of advice, the timing and content of interpretation, and the limiting or the extending of the opportunity to unburden frequently are decided by the stage of development of the relationship. In addition, the professional relationship is in and of itself a treatment measure. Its characteristics are: its confidential nature, its respectful nature, its dispassionate quality. On the part of the worker it involves a feeling with but not like the client. Between client and worker it is a feeling, thinking, and doing together to some purpose, the client's need and purpose being the lodestar. Help for the client frequently derives through the fact that he has the opportunity, in time of trouble when he is disturbed and confused and in conflict, to experience the response of a worker who sees his problem differently, who feels it differently, but who sympathetically understands.

Clients will react to the relationship realistically or unrealistically in accordance with their need. To some extent the relationship repeats an old relationship, that is, meets a need met by a former relationship, out of which the individual's present conflicts arise. It repeats with a difference, and that difference is decisive, for it constitutes the corrective element which makes treatment possible. For example, the corrective element may lie in a worker's permissive attitude which eases guilt or in an authoritative one through which the client's conscience is strengthened.[6] Insofar as the worker has knowledge, skill, and emotional capacity to assume responsibility for its management to productive ends, the relationship element in the helping process will have benefited the client in various ways to varying degrees. Through the relationship he may have experienced change in feeling and thinking as an easing of guilt or reinforcement of conscience. He may have gained perspective, a new feeling of security, a modified identity through which he makes more vital use of the agency's several helping measures and deals with his social situation more effectively. As this occurs, his capacities and inner resources are strengthened, so that gradually the relationship with the worker and the help of the agency are needed no longer.

The client's response in terminating is a natural outgrowth of what the total agency service and the relationship have meant to him. Consequently, termination may be self-initiated and moved into without a struggle. In other instances it will be resisted so that the client will need help in understanding his response, in clarifying disturbed feeling about termination, and in appraising himself and his situation realistically so that he can proceed strengthened rather than threatened. Life-circumstances and the response of others to the client often will be a factor in its timing in that they effect his use of help in his social situation. The client's need will guide the worker in this final aspect of the helping process.

In summary it may be said that the worker is responsible to conduct the helping process. Because he exerts, for the client's welfare, those controls implicit in professional responsibility, it does not follow that the relationship is a controlling one. It is essential that the worker bring a posi-

6. Franz Alexander, M.D., and Thomas Morton French, M.D., *Psychoanalytic Therapy: Principles and Application* (New York: Ronald Press Co., 1946), pp. 66–95.

tive attitude to the helping situation, for it is through experiencing acceptance and understanding that the client
becomes self-understanding and self-directive. Emotional
acceptance of the helping process is sought rather than submission to it. Submission implies "being done to and for,"
whereas acceptance involves taking something and making
it one's own—"doing rather than being done to."

Methods must be oriented continuously to the client's
need in relation to his purpose in seeking help. Agency function and community resources will determine not only what
he can be helped to do but also the mode of working. . . .
Enduring sublimations and constructive defenses stem
largely from gratification rather than from deprivation. If
energy now used to maintain precarious defenses is to be
redirected toward socialized living, every individual must
have sufficient security to be assured not merely survival
but also opportunity for realization of his capacities. Social
casework can play a small but important part in the lives
of many individuals at a decisive time. The modern social
caseworker cherishes no illusions. He looks beyond social
casework with deep concern for the greater participation of
his profession in welfare programs and social planning to
effect that social and economic change essential for the
attainment of the aims of democracy.

Notes on
Interdisciplinary
Collaboration

TWO EXCERPTS ARE PRESENTED here: one on the collaborative
work between psychiatry, psychology, and social work in
clinic settings; the other on social worker–nurse relationships, particularly on the use of social workers to teach
members of the nursing profession.

The psychiatrist and psychologist whose joint paper Charlotte Towle discusses had observed that in the current (1950) practices in child-guidance clinics, social workers were likely to be "handmaidens" to the other professions. Their proposal was that social workers ought to develop their own area of special competence: that of the psychosocial aspects of child development. With this fully developed knowledge, they proposed, the psychiatric social worker would be the one member of the team to see the child as a whole. She would be at the center, not the periphery, of the team—the coordinator, not the willing but limited servant.

This position was fully congruous with that held by Charlotte Towle. But she was realist enough to know the obstacles both within social work training and within the hierarchy of professions that could stand in the way of achieving an equal but different position of social work within clinical teams. So she sets these forth, undefensively, realistically, practically, with no need either to assign blame nor to avoid responsibility.

Today's clinics are perhaps characterized less by hard-drawn hierarchal lines than by blurred identities and the denial of differences in some anxious press for "equality" among the professions. When this is so, the result may be the loss of the special knowledge and the special responsibilities of the several teamed professions and a consequent loss of expertness and precision. For this situation, as well as for the one described in the article she discussed, Charlotte Towle's comments offer food for thought.

The discussion of social worker–nurse relationships in public health activities is focused chiefly upon consultation and teaching. Based upon her belief that sound professional learning occurs in large part from sound identifications with the learner's professional models, Charlotte Towle was dubious about the use of one profession to teach another.

If and when this had to occur, she argued, it must be safe-guarded by the teacher's clear understanding of the differ-ence between his profession's use of the knowledge he con-veyed and that of the particular learners he was addressing. She held this to be the case in consultation, too—that a con-sultant from another profession must know precisely the particular context and conditions under which his offerings are to be used.

In this regard it is worth noting that out of her firm con-viction about the learner's sense of professional identity growing upon his identification with models within his own profession, and about the necessity for selection of relevant knowledge for social work's use, Charlotte Towle became the pioneer in undertaking to teach the year-long course in normal human development given at the School of Social Service Administration, University of Chicago. Until she did so, this course in schools of social work had almost always been taught by psychiatrists, or, at least, was held to be "respectable" only under such tutelage.

H. H. P.

I

On the Psychiatrist-Social Caseworker Team

. . . When social work as a profession has matured, in the sense of accepting its responsibilities and its limitations, in the sense also of finding its own identity, all social workers will be psychosocial specialists. For example, a so-called welfare worker in a public assistance program or other social agency will have that psychological understanding and social insight with which to administer programs and to render services in ways that are pyschotherapeutic.

"On the Psychiatrist-Social Worker Team" is excerpted from discussion of "The Significance for Social Workers of the Multidiscipline Approach to Child Development," a paper by Peter B. Neubauer, M.D., and Joseph Steinert, reprinted in *Social Service Review*, vol. 24, no. 4 (December 1950).

Recognition of and a demand for the knowledge and skill involved in work of this nature within the profession and in collaborating professions should enable social workers to use their education more appropriately. . . .

There will be no handmaiden problem in multidiscipline programs where trained social workers are granted their appropriate function. In these instances social workers will participate in staff deliberations with the right to define and to decide their responsibility. They will make social work recommendations rather than accept social work prescriptions. They may take issue with the dictates of other specialists. There will be no menial tasks, because certain social services commonly regarded as "hack work" will be done differentially rather than routinely or ill-advisedly. In such a situation not only will they participate in decisions affecting those policies which influence practice but they may well be given a leadership role in this area.

The social worker has been trained to focus on external pressures, on the conditions of the individual's life in relation to his needs, responses, and capacities. The current agency experience is a vital life-experience for the patient or client, and it is the social worker's province to remove the social reality obstacles which may become psychological deterrents to his productive use of the service. Hence when social workers are free to put first things first, they may initiate action toward the modification of procedures and practices. In an institution, an agency, and a community where there are multiple services available, the social caseworker is prepared to play an integrative role in bringing services together in an economical and appropriate treatment procedure. There is evidence of this in the effective multidiscipline work which is being done today within social agencies where social workers are administrators. In how many multidiscipline programs under administrative auspices other than social work is the social worker's education in administration being used to the utmost? In some his overtures in this area have been opposed. And because sometimes the psychiatrist is so engrossed in everything but psychotherapy, the social worker has become the psychotherapist. The result in some instances has been poor administration and poor psychotherapy.

I affirm the opinion that the social worker should find his own area of research in multidiscipline programs rather than take over the psychiatrist's focus or wholly play a subordinate part in the research of another profession. That social workers have not done so is due to two factors. First, there are definite educational lacks in their own professional training. In the two-year Master's degree program it is not possible for social caseworkers to attain that competence in social research which will enable them to initiate and conduct research without supervisory help. It is only as more social workers are trained beyond the Master's degree level that leadership in social research can be brought into multidiscipline programs. Second, the research orientation they do bring or that eventually they may bring will not be used to the utmost until the administrators of these programs recognize and value research of a nature which is appropriately the responsibility of social work. . . . The social worker might be concerned to discover what the regime of a particular institution or agency is doing to facilitate or defeat its treatment aims. What are the intake procedures of this clinic or agency doing to obstruct psychotherapy or to make intake an initial therapeutic experience? How may the regulations, politics, and procedures of this health or welfare program become an integral part of treatment? . . . It is the social worker's natural province to evaluate and make known not only what services people need but also what existent services are doing *to* people in doing something *for* them.

The several disciplines in a multidiscipline program will make productive use of one another . . . when each profession has respect for the individuality of the other. This implies that each must have knowledge and understanding of the nature of the other's training, function, and general approach. This knowledge is easy to impart, but understanding involves the elimination of certain traditional hierarchies and power and prestige strivings. . . . When education in these professions gives attention to the emotional growth of the learner as well as to his acquisition of knowledge and skill, concern for the recipient of the professional service will surpass self-concern, so that collaboration in the full sense of the word may replace the competitive struggle which under-lies some of our present efforts. . . .

In the present scene competition and distorted use of one another have been heightened, not by the differences in training and function of the several disciplines, but by their likeness. For example, in the psychiatrist-social worker relationship some psychiatrists fear social workers because of the element of common knowledge and skill. They may then begrudge the social worker his valid psychosocial function and relegate him to a routine service function. Others overevaluate and misuse this likeness. When fearful, some seemingly handle their rivalry through identification as a defense, and the defense is to absorb the social worker as an assistant. The social worker becomes the psychotherapist of a lesser order who must forever work under his tutelage. The current shortage of psychiatrists has made this solution a readily justified one. He has been able to "make do" with the social worker in this capacity on the basis of the social worker's understanding of human behavior, some knowledge of psychopathology, and understanding of the helping relationship and its management and interviewing skills.

Social workers have been responsive to this use of their professional training for many reasons. A notable one is that their identification with the psychiatrist as a mentor from whom and through whom they have learned often has aligned them with his profession. This propensity often has been reinforced by social casework educators who through their vital educational and psychoanalytic relationships with psychiatrists have lost or subordinated their identification with social work. Since social work always will need to depend upon psychiatry for its educational . . . contribution, this problem will be solved only as the members of both professions recognize it and deal with it in the context of the teacher-pupil, doctor-patient relationships. It

must be recognized and accepted among the several collaborating professions engaged in the promotion of human
welfare that there is a common need for a core content of
knowledge, understanding, and skill which each must have
for different use. No one profession should have a corner
on it, doling it out to others as the donor's fears and defenses permit, or as service exigencies dictate.

II
On Consultation and Teaching of Nurses

Certain professions long have been concerned with the
development of the individual and accordingly they have
had certain orientations now considered basic to all human
welfare work. The members of these professions have been
conscripted to become teachers of colleagues in other disciplines, often imparting what they know without necessary
references to decisive differences in the other disciplines' use
of their orientation. The current scene abounds in extra-
professional "in service" teaching, well intentioned, but of
varying quality and often of confused purpose.

As we look to the future when present lags in professional
education are taken up, it would seem that there always will
be a valid place for exchange, for collaborative work. The
"in service" teaching to be eliminated is that wherein the
members of one discipline teach the members of another
discipline certain knowledges and skills, unmodified for use
in the performance of their own work. For instance, social
workers are in demand in some school systems not primarily to render social services but to convey to teachers
their understanding of human behavior and their skills in
working with people. Since the social worker is not competent in the classroom, this content would be taught more
effectively in the teachers college where it can be closely related to the learning process in children, to learning difficulties and to the management of discipline problems in the

"On Consultation and Teaching of Nurses" is excerpted from discussion of "Why a
Nurse Mental Health Consultant in Public Health?" a paper by Katherine Oettinger,
Journal of Psychiatric Social Work, 19, no. 4 (Spring, 1950).

classroom. Likewise in nursing, social workers have been conscripted to teach nurses not only what they know of human behavior, but also interviewing skills in the management of the helping relationship. Since the social worker is not competent in the nurse's function and since her skills in interviewing are fashioned by several factors peculiar to her profession, it would seem that what she has which nurses want could be taught better to educators in schools of nursing and subsequently through nurse consultants, rather than through the use of consultants from other disciplines.

The arguments for the indigenous consultant in any discipline follow.

1. When the knowledge, insights and skills of one discipline are needed for use in another profession they are useful only insofar as they are deeply incorporated. The learner must do the integrating but for sound selection and for better integration the nurse will need the nursing educator's help in applying learning from another field to his own. Social workers in drawing on psychiatry slowly learned this the hard way.

2. The authority of the knowledge of a person in one's own field may not carry more weight than that of an authority in another field, particularly if the other field is highly respected, but it is more deeply influential for several reasons. The element of identification plays a vital role in professional education. Learners in a given profession identify more closely with their own leaders. Professional education as a reeducative process has to fulfill a task which is essentially equivalent to a change in culture.

Since the individual's original attitudes have been formed through his dependence on relationships and through his response to authority pressures within the family and other organized groups, Kurt Lewin holds that one of the outstanding means for bringing about reeducation is the establishment of an "in group" in which the members feel belongingness. A profession is an "in group" to which new members are motivated to belong and where common knowledge, sentiments, convictions and practice prevail. A strong "we feeling" can be created so that as students in a very real sense enter a new culture they can put forth roots and grow into it through identification with mentors and colleagues as together they learn.

The limitation of a consultant from another discipline is that professional identification may be fostered with the other discipline. Or the consultant being an "auslander" whose authority of knowledge is imposed, the learners may identify as a defense. This is particularly prone to occur when the consultant comes from a rivaled field, so that he is a threatening opponent. When this occurs the learning may remain a foreign body within the ego always to be reacted to with ambivalence and never to be deeply incorporated. In this connection there is a very real problem in social workers serving as consultants to public health nurses. . . .

In interprofessional consultation roughly two types of help are sought by one profession from another.

1. Knowledge of the profession, what it does, its ways of working, its resources for intelligent comprehension in order that disciplines associated in health and welfare programs may collaborate intelligently. Thus knowledge of social work, its services, its methods in general, its resources should be conveyed to nurses to promote intelligent collaboration and discriminative referrals.

2. Knowledge of some of the insights and skills of one profession for use in another, for incorporation into their practice. This is teaching which we hope eventually will be done in the several professional schools. But not having been done in the past, it now will have to occur in practice. Also there always will be a certain amount of it, as associated professions keep abreast of advancing knowledge in related fields. In these situations the consultant should be clear as to what content is desired and what use the content is to be put to; in short the other profession's purpose in seeking help. If social workers are drawn into teaching nurses, for example, interviewing skills in the management of their helping relationship, it preferably should be on the learner's own case materials and in relation to his function

rather than through social work materials which demonstrate social work function. This is essential if pseudopsychiatric social workers are not to be coined. Otherwise identification as a defense will be prone to result, and the nurses' ambivalent alliance with two disciplines fostered.

It is essential that educators in any one discipline be aware that their teaching, helping, administering relationship with the learner is the core of his preparation for professional relationship. There is growing recognition that it determines in large measure his capacity to work purposefully with people in ways *appropriate to the profession*, whether in the helping relationship between practitioner and recipient, in collaborative work with colleagues or in his relationship with subordinates and persons in authority within his own profession's hierarchy. In the report of the proceedings of the Interprofessions Conference on Education for Professional Responsibility, Dr. John Romano describes the physician-patient relationship as having its own peculiar demands. Mr. Lon L. Fuller holds law schools responsible not only to help students gain knowledge and skill in basic legal processes, but also to implant the peculiar characteristics of the lawyer-client relationship.[1]

In social work we long have been conscious of the relationship between our educational process and the development of the learner as a professional person. Only nursing educators can be responsible for the process through which nurses are prepared to conduct their own helping relationship. Is the nurse-patient relationship identical with that of social worker-client? May she perhaps validly carry a different authority than a social worker? Are these differences determined in part by the authority accorded the two professions in society? This I do not know. The decisive point is that as social workers teach nurses interviewing, . . . it should be taught with reference to the nurse's function and with an attempt to understand the nature of the helping relationship as determined by the nature of the service and

---

1. See Education For Professional Responsibility. Report of the Proceedings of the Interprofessions Conference on Education for Professional Responsibility. Pittsburgh: Carnegie Press, 1948. See papers by Dr. John Romano and Lon J. Fuller.

by its meaning to the recipient of help. This principle should apply in all interprofessional consultation which involves imparting one's own knowledge and skill for use elsewhere. . . .

Evaluating Motives
of Foster Parents

THE PROBABILITY IS that Charlotte Towle was chosen as discussant for this topic because of her early practice experience in placement and adoptions. But, retrospectively, a better reason for choosing her was that she was deeply involved in considerations of motivation.

Her special contributions on this subject are manifestly clear here: that motivation has many facets; that it is often unknown to its possessor until it is channeled and given specific form by behavior-in-a-situation; and that it cannot be accurately known and diagnosed by a caseworker except as it is viewed in relation to specific circumstances and events.

One further note of special interest today, when the family is central to the caseworker's interest: Charlotte Towle saw a foster family as a *family*, not just as a mother. She recognized the role and relationship reorganizations that occur when one member is added or taken away. She implies, thus, that the entry of a child into even the best-motivated of foster families may cause problems and bring changes that call for the social caseworker's immediate attention.

H. H. P.

Discussion of paper by Irene Josselyn, M.D., reprinted from *Child Welfare*, vol. 31, no. 2 (February 1952).

The gist of Dr. Josselyn's message is that selecting foster parents is not simple. Professed motives often are partial masks so that basic motives are not readily known either through words or action. And when they are known, this insight does not necessarily solve the problem of determining whether a family can assimilate a child and meet his needs in ways which promote his development. Dr. Josselyn stresses a common fallacy in current thinking—that to know the motive is to know the outcome of the course of action. When I was on a recent vacation the mountains so recreated the past for me that I was strongly motivated to climb to their very tops. My motivation, however, was not supported by my wind. The motivation was rendered useless because I did not have what it takes to master the incline. The implications are obvious in relation to many a strongly and desirably motivated foster parent. . . .

Our observations support Dr. Josselyn's contention that even though some motives are promising and some suspect, there is no such thing as a good or bad motive in and of itself. Motives cannot be lifted out of context and evaluated. They are relevant only in relation to other factors and forces in the life of the applicant and in the lives of those in close relationship to him. Basic motivation is rendered useful or useless insofar as it is sustained by or united with conditions essential for the attainment of the goal which has incited the individual or group to action. [There is a] current tendency to focus narrowly on motives as an index to outcome. . . . One suspects that social workers comprehend the complexity of the task which confronts them in predicting the outcome of human relationships. Weighted with the difficulty of the task and charged with concern for the welfare of those whom they serve, they seek simplification. The human mind in a complex learning situation fraught with anxiety tends to become somewhat obsessive and thus to seek generalizations and to center on one aspect of human development and response to the exclusion of others. As Dr.

Josselyn has shown, this monolithic tendency can but lead us astray in the selection of foster parents.

Even though we cannot reduce the complexity, it seems important that we reduce the anxiety in this situation. A profession makes the emotional demand of enduring denial and frustration in not knowing. This implies capacity to labor and to await the lessons of one's labors. The fact of the matter is that there are limits to our understanding. Our present knowledge and our means to understanding do not permit infallible prediction of human responses in prospective experiences. When we overrate the efficiency of our tools, we are most prone to misuse them, and short cuts to understanding represent one form of misuse. Eminent psychiatrists have emphasized that a patient's capacity to use treatment is best known through treatment. Social caseworkers long have stressed the fact that the helping process is their best diagnostic tool. Social work educators concerned with the selection of students admit humbly that while they have criteria which permit them to make some sound selections, in many instances the individual's potentialities can be known only through his response to the learning situation.

It is not initial motivation that matters as much as capacity for remotivation. The meeting of need, the nurture afforded through a desired experience, may contribute to the individual's growth so that remotivation occurs. It would seem to follow that in some instances an individual's capacity for foster parenthood can be known only through his experience in that role. This is a harsh fact to accept, knowing as we do the high cost to children of experimentation. Acceptance of this reality, however, may reduce the homefinder's anxiety. Excessive anxiety begets a search for easy solutions which sometimes take the form of stereotypes with which to form judgments. Lowered anxiety will not necessarily . . . be expressed in laissez faire experimentation. Instead, it is hoped, the social worker will be freed to work creatively within limits with an intent gradually to reduce them.

Because I have argued against an overemphasis on the

motive as an index to outcome, this does not mean that I believe that motivation should be disregarded. Because I have claimed that one cannot always know an individual's capacity for parenthood in advance of placement, this does does not mean that one should not continue to attempt to know him in order to evaluate and to predict as reliably as is possible. Motives, Dr. Josselyn has shown, often are multiple. I repeat that they should be evaluated in relation to many factors and forces. It is beyond the scope of this discussion to detail them comprehensively or to depict fully the social worker's means of understanding prospective foster parents. It is possible merely to note some of the learning which the social worker could well put to use systematically. . . . I know that it is not necessary for me to stress to the members of this group the need for and importance of research in this area.

A social worker in homefinding will need to use all he has learned of human behavior in his professional training and that he has of self-knowledge to attain further understanding and insight. Knowledge and understanding of the needs and strivings of the individual, and of the purposes served by defenses and adaptations, will be essential not only in order to help a given applicant make himself known, but also for the evaluation of the applicant's potentialities to render the service, that is, to perform the work which he wants or thinks he wants to undertake.

The foster parent applicant, unlike the client of a social agency, is not seeking help. To be sure, he is asking to be given a child, but his feeling often is that he is giving himself and his resources more than that he is asking. His concept may be that he is proffering a service and being evaluated for a job. In understanding the applicant as a person, the focus must be on him as a potential parent useful to the agency, rather than as a client or patient with a problem to solve, who is primarily a recipient of the agency's service.

Nevertheless, there is a problem to solve, that of mutually determining whether the need he brings will be met through becoming a foster parent and whether he has the capacity and can offer the conditions of life essential for his success in our mutual undertaking. The social worker will need to use his knowledge of the relationship as the basis for interviewing and to use all he has learned for conducting problem-solving investigation interviews. In this situation, this implies interest in and concern with what the applicant brings from his past experience which qualifies him for this undertaking, as well as an attitude that presumably he has something to offer.

It implies also making clear the agency's expectation of a close working relationship, making known its procedures and demands, one of which is use of the help implicit in supervision. There is an imposed helping relationship in this situation which is akin to that of the supervisor-caseworker relationship, in which some of the principles of casework supervision obtain for clarifying the relationship and for dealing with resistance to help. A prospective foster parent may be prone to talk for approval. Just as any other job applicant, he may talk to conceal rather than to reveal. A relevant focus which engages his participation in measuring the demands of the job, and in gauging whether it is an undertaking which will meet his current interest and need, may lower his defenses and free him to be more revealing of himself and of his family situation. It has been said that a foster parent's potentialities are best known after he becomes one. The first step in becoming a foster parent is in the application and investigating process. Hence the applicant's participation in and response to this experience often is revealing if the worker lends a knowing ear to the language which it speaks. The social worker will need to use all that he knows to establish a productive working relationship. The outcome of many a foster home is determined at this stage. Often a foster parent has failed the agency because it has not been conveyed at the start (as well as later) that the agency will be with him in his service, intent upon helping him succeed as a foster parent, rather than aligned with the anxious dependent child who, as the insecure recipient of his care, almost invariably places him on probation.

In addition to knowing the dynamics of the individual personality, the homefinder needs depth of understanding of the dynamics of family life. To appraise the family is as important as to evaluate the individual who has been motivated to apply for a child. A family is an interdependent group of individuals, each needing one or more of the other family members and each needing to preserve his own identity in the group. The dependency alignments and the responsibility roles vary from family to family, and within any one family they vary from time to time. Likewise the striving for place varies. Insofar as family life has solidarity, stability and relative harmony, it can be compared to an organism, growing, changing but maintaining a kind of equilibrium through the balance of the relationships, and the relatedness of the parts to the whole life of the group.

When a new member is added, it is not just this family plus a new part. The new part may exert considerable change in the whole so that new interrelationships are set up, which may again attain equilibrium or which may not. Likewise, when a member of the family leaves, reorganization occurs and different alignments and change in responsibility roles may occur. Very frequently parents apply for a child at a time of some change in family life which creates a lack and a feeling of need: they may be seeking to restore a former equilibrium. Hence it is important to know the nature and the extent of the change which has occurred, the need which one or more members expect to meet through a child; that is, the extent of the disequilibrium which has occurred.

The decisive point is that foster parents seek children out of some unmet need, but that this does not necessarily have sinister implications. This factor operates in the large problem of motivating people to become foster parents, the aim of recruitment programs. Motivation comes from within and often arises out of some unmet need to give and to receive. Many families with much to offer children, whom we seek to interest in becoming foster parents, are unresponsive to our plea. The very equilibrium of their family life, the implied satisfaction in their relationships, may make for lack of motive for foster parenthood.

The P family applied at a time of family reorganization. One daughter had married, another was on the verge of breaking away through becoming economically independent. The parents obviously were reaching out to fill the gap, restore the equilibrium through recapturing, in some measure, the past. Hence it was desirable to understand what the old interdependencies were, what the old alignments were, what the responsibility roles were, what the children meant to the parents, what need the parents together and individually were trying to fulfill. The picture of solidarity, harmony, and equilibrium presented by the P family which had resulted in successful child-rearing led the agency to bank on the principle that this family would have a capacity for restoration of equilibrium. The outcome did not fulfill this expectation. The child placed was a problematic child, unlike their children. He was a boy, and the father, who had always longed for a son, had a closer relationship with him than he had had with his daughters. The child placed had had a family experience which made him slow to relate to the foster mother and receptive to the foster father's kindly companionship. The foster mother felt excluded. She had not recaptured the past in which she and the girls were aligned, and in which she had carried the major child-rearing responsibility while the father went his self-sufficient way as the lone male in a female household, harmoniously related to them but not deeply engaged in bringing up his daughters. These alignments and responsibility roles were not ascertained in the foster home study. . . .

Furthermore, the agency's supervision was characterized by a strong alignment with the child, rather than by an understanding and supportive relationship with the foster mother. Had they been younger, these parents might have been helped to handle the discord which resulted. They did not know until they repeated the experience of child-rearing that they were not as young as they once were. Their motivation broke down when they found they hadn't the wind to master the incline. The extent to which age operated, however, is obscured by the nature of the placement and of the supervision.

The importance of understanding and respecting the interplay of family life cannot be overemphasized. It is essential in determining the potentialities of a home for a child, in selecting the child for the home, and in helping the parents with the responsibility which they have undertaken. The motivation in applying for a child is best understood in the light of the dynamics of family life. Dr. Josselyn has made clear that it is not easy to know the basic motivations. Individuals present their rationale for wanting a child rather than the underlying reasons. Family alignments, responsibility roles, in short, the behavior of the family, individually and collectively, as it handles its ordinary affairs, is fairly readily made known; in fact, it is seldom deeply concealed. The observer with the trained eye to see will often discern the deeper purposes being served in the quest for a child. Furthermore, through his use of his understanding of the dynamics of family life, the worker will be in a position to venture to gauge whether or not the family situation sustains the individual's motivation to become a foster parent, and whether the family can be the solution of a child's need and strivings, as well as a child the solution of their needs.

I support Dr. Josselyn's position that the motives of foster parents do not lend themselves to easy generalization. In spite of the real limits to our understanding of motives, we should make a systematic attempt to evaluate them and to predict their outcome. . . . Social research is needed as a means to learning in order that we may have greater skills tomorrow than we have today.

Some Aspects
of Modern Casework

THE ORIGINAL PAPER from which "some aspects" have been excerpted was delivered in London to acquaint British social workers with "generic trends in education for social work."

Excerpted from "Generic Trends in Education for Social Work," in *Some Reflections on Social Work Education* (London: Family Welfare Association, 1956).

The educational sections of that paper have been deleted. Lifted out and presented here are the sections that deal with casework theory and practice, especially those given prominence in the thinking and teaching of the casework faculty at the University of Chicago.

Social Casework: A Problem-solving Process had been written and was in press when this paper was given. Charlotte Towle's earlier writings and our colleagueship had deeply influenced much of my thinking about casework, and in turn, my thinking in our on-going dialogues had influenced her. Thus some of her major points herein highlight some of the basic ideas set forth in *Social Casework;* yet they are, at the same time, outgrowths of, or congruent with, Charlotte Towle's own thinking.

Lifted up for special consideration because she regarded them as vital to good casework practice were these ideas: the import (again) of motivation-capacity-opportunity as central elements in the diagnostic and treatment considerations of casework; the client as a person with an identified problem-to-be-solved (in some difference from the client as a total personality); the necessity to engage this person with his problem-solving motivations before exploration of the problem is embarked upon; the current life situation as cause, not merely as consequence of earlier causes; the present problem as a begetter of new problems and, reversing the vicious circle, the present (small) solution as mitigating the sense of stress; the necessity—and a persuasive argument— for focus; and, again, the support of casework that involves not only the treatment of emotional difficulties but the provision of necessary services and such helping as may be involved in getting the client to use them well.

One sees demonstrated here once again the growth and development of Charlotte Towle's own ideas and also her capacity to continue as a learner, not by annexation but by continuous integrated weaving of new ideas into her firm but elastic fabric of knowledge.

                                                            H. H. P.

. . . There are four components in every casework situation, "the Four P's": the person with his problem, the place, that is the social agency or social service department in which he is served, and the process through which he is helped.[1] Person-with-problem is always central in our consideration.

Modern casework strives to be client centred rather than procedure centred, just as modern progressive education aims to be student centred rather than centred solely on the subject. Thus in casework today we consider that the outcome of our activity in every instance is contingent on three factors—the client's motivation, that is, his needs and wants; his capacity, physical, mental, emotional and environmental; and the opportunity for help afforded to him. We face the fact that we cannot motivate him, or provide capacity, but we can provide an opportunity which either uses and strengthens motivation or breaks it down, one which also either uses and reinforces capacity or ignores or undermines it. Social casework therefore is client centred in the sense of according the individual the right to self-determination within social limits. The extent and nature of the caseworker's activities are determined not only by the agency's function and resources but also by the individual's need, want, capacity, and resources. It is determined also by the significance of his behaviour responses as we engage him in problem-solving at the point of breakdown in his self-dependence, which has made him unable to function alone, so that he has sought help. Hence casework activity is client centred in that it is guided by what the individual can or cannot do now and it moves in an ongoing way toward what he increasingly can do. I have stressed this concept of client centred activity and of professional responsibility to understand individuals in order to strengthen motivation and capacity because of a current tendency to depreciate social casework as a measure which violates individuals' rights through taking over the management of their affairs and

1. My colleague at the University of Chicago, Professor Helen Harris Perlman, uses this designation for graphic teaching.

which thereby pauperises the personality, making individuals dependent and less able to function on their own. This may have occurred but it need not occur and it definitely is not implicit in the nature of the casework helping process.

Social work at all operating levels is continuously concerned with defining and solving problems. In working with a client in casework there is always a problem in order that it may be solved and an early determination reached as to whether or not it lends itself to solution. The nature of the problem is not the decisive factor—but instead the nature of the person and the meaning of the problem to him. The meaning of the problem to him throws light on his nature. Our aim continuously is that of engaging the client's participation in both defining and solving problems. It is as we do this from the start that we are able to appraise his motivation and capacity in the interest of well oriented rather than disoriented helping efforts which squander the time and resources of client, worker and agency.

A *first* and *foremost* learning experience is how to explore a problem situation so that we engage the client. Only as he is engaged can we see and feel and appraise his involvement in it and his capacity to cope with it. This first step in the helping process is a treatment measure as well as a means to diagnosis. Originally seen as a study-diagnostic stage we have come to know its therapeutic import to the client through the fact that sometimes defining and clarifying the problem has been all the help a person needed. Whether this is the case or not the client's movement in this process not only constitutes the beginning of treatment but also throws light on his motivation and tests his capacity to use help.

Our ways of helping a client explore his problems, our means for enlisting his participation do not vary by agency setting. The worker's conduct of this initial aspect of the helping process varies from individual to individual in that it must be oriented to the client's physical, mental, emotional condition, hence related to his behaviour, to the in-out movement which he shows as he responds to and/or retreats from the worker's efforts to help. The criterion of progression and of resistance however do not vary markedly either with place or person. They must, however, take into account the worker's activity, the age of the client (child or adult) and the conditions of the interview which affect a client's response, i.e., pressure of time, interruptions, privacy or lack of it and the like. . . .

. . . A person in applying to an agency for help brings a problem to be solved. He seldom sees and feels his total self as a problem, and rightly, because often people have problems which do not involve them totally, nor are they necessarily highly problematic people. But whether they are or not, they often do not seek help for themselves apart from some situation with which they now are unable to cope alone.

In any instance, however, whether the individual be a victim of circumstance or the creator of his own adversity, he is in trouble and is having to ask for and take help. Regardless of the source of the difficulty he is sure to have disturbed feelings about it and problematic responses to it. Therefore, in social casework wherever practised, in understanding the individual we are intent upon understanding him *with a focus* on the meaning of the problem to him and to those in close relationship to him. We are intent upon understanding also the meaning of the helping relationship to the individual and to those in close relationship to him. Therefore, in working with people we start with the assumption that what this individual feels and how strongly he feels about his problem and the helping hand is going to determine what he thinks, how he acts and what use he makes of his agency's service. It is well known that feelings may motivate or impede problem solving. It is known also that massive affect predominantly of a negative nature lowers or breaks down motivation and ability to use capacity more than does positive affect. With strong negative feelings one tends to find deeper dependency, greater hostility towards self and others and often more involving guilt, all of which lead to defences which operate against smooth use of help and ready participation in problem solving. An initial task therefore is to help the individual feel more positively about himself, while retaining that dissatisfaction with his problem which has motivated him to get help. This implies helping him feel adequate rather than inadequate in having sought help. It implies helping him feel positively about the helping hand. At the start in an agency experience his ambivalence about help must be lowered. This will occur to the extent that self respect is restored and hope and confidence replace despair.

The fact of the matter is that people tend to feel two ways about an agency experience. There is gratification in finding a port in a storm, there is reassurance that other people must also have problems, "I am not alone in my suffering or in my inadequacy," there is renewed hope at the prospect of finding a solution. On the other hand, simultaneously, there is for the adult a feeling of inadequacy in not being able to manage alone, a fear that in taking help he may be expected to give up the management of his affairs, anxiety as to what he will pay, since he cannot pay money for the help, discomfort over confiding private affairs and feelings of obligation even in advance of receiving. These negative feelings may well stem from ego strengths, but even so they may lead to defences which inhibit self activity and the resumption of self dependence. Each type of service has its peculiar stigma and the feelings of stigma come to be recognised as commonplace by those functioning in a given field. In applying or being referred for financial assistance, for the placement of a child, for psychiatric care, for medical care, for supervision of one's behaviour, as in probation work, in each and all of these situations, apologies and protests, denials of problem, or exaggeration of it as justification, claims of past adequacy, rejection of responsibility or self blame, anxious enquiries or avoidance of them, make known the individual's discomfort as well as his effort to find where he stands in this new experience. Absorption in relating to the agency can impede or obstruct his use of it.

The decisive point is that the individual must find himself in the eyes of those who are to help him, as something other than his problem, if he is to participate in dealing with it. Until this occurs he is there to be dealt with ambivalently reaching out toward and retreating from our activity on his behalf. . . .

. . . In the social worker's focus on the meaning of a problem it is essential that he ever bear in mind this common aspect of all problems—that every problem that affects a person enough so that he seeks help with it has its subjective as well as its objective significance. Somewhat engulfed by psychiatry social workers today need to be reminded more often of the objective aspect of problems than of the subjective. When the psychological reality of the client fills the horizon to the exclusion of his social actuality one may not appraise his emotional response correctly. He may seem more neurotic than he is. We thus do not appraise his capacity correctly or orient our help to his social need. Furthermore as social workers we have a professional commitment both to rule out social pathology before assuming personality pathology and to deal promptly with social stresses as a means to psychological treatment. I say promptly because otherwise one may have a personality problem to treat. It is important to emphasise that "all personality problems were once spontaneous reactions to an experience on the outside, with which the individual was unable to cope."[2] When adverse circumstances beset and bedevil an individual chronically and when, imperilled for a prolonged period, he is engaged in struggling against them, the behaviour reactions which those circumstances evoke may become internalised and structured into the personality. Time therefore is not to be regarded as an ally when social stresses attack an individual or family.

The concept of mutual interaction and impact between the person and his living situation and the concept that the primary cause of a problem in social living may be inside the person or outside of him are of great importance to social casework wherever practised. Whether responses are situational or neurotic, whether the client *has* a problem or *is* a problem or both will heavily determine what we do and how we do it.

It is a common observation that problems beget prob-

2. Professor Helen H. Perlman. Unpublished lecture notes.

lems. This is because a problem may create or arouse a latent difficulty in contingent aspects of living; for example, a marital problem may be at the root of a man's job inefficiency, resulting in unemployment. Or a new problem may activate old latent problems or unresolved conflicts, hence loss of a job may activate old feelings of inadequacy and latent sexual conflicts. This proclivity of problems to beget problems has defeated many a social worker in his super-human attempts to direct work on all of them at once. It has also defeated many a client in his use of help because he has not been able to keep afoot under the barrage of help, let alone abreast of the social worker as a participant in problem solving.

The following mitigating factors can operate to shape this overwhelming situation to manageable size.[3] Just as a number of aspects of a person's life can be thrown askew by the maladjustment of one, so may a number of aspects right themselves by the adjustment of one part or another. Often we have seen a brief or prolonged service focused on one aspect of an individual's life restore his balance, and in turn affect his relationship to others, thus lowering family conflicts and solving problems which were recognised but not tackled at the start. Also we have seen an individual gain sufficient confidence through mastery of one problem to proceed in mastering others. Since a human being's problems in social living are interrelated and interacting and the solution of one will have an effect on others, the caseworker can be most helpful by identifying and centreing help on the one problem which appears to be most crucial, or is a problem the individual is ready to face. If in the latter instance this is not a central or basic problem, the worker may help the client with several less vital concerns preliminarily to moving toward them as he gains confidence. It may be necessary for the worker to help the client move from the problem as he sees it, to the problem as it realistically is. This ability to move or not to move often is the test of his ability to use help.

---

3. Professor Helen H. Perlman, my colleague at the University of Chicago, has greatly emphasized focalization in social casework. She has contributed much to this discussion of the means to partialize the client's and the worker's integrative tasks.

Focalisation is necessary throughout casework practice not only because of this chain reaction of problems but because all the problems of surviving as a human being in physical and emotional terms come to the door of the social agency. The performance of our function implies many time limited, relationship limited contacts, which demand that we focalise purposefully rather than relate diffusely. Focalisation is implicit in our intermediary role, that of effecting change in the interaction of individual and situation. The values of focalisation are many. First and foremost, early focalisation enables us to test a client's motivation and capacity to use help. It in turn affords him an opportunity to test this experience, which often he has been doing when he has brought us one problem and withheld himself until he has measured what we will do to him in helping him with a problem. Secondly, focalisation makes for economy of time and effort in a sustained contact. It may prevent loss of direction, circular or blind alley discussion and the resultant confusion which comes to both worker and client when they work to no end on many concerns. Thirdly and very important, it helps the client work productively, thus allaying the feelings of impotence which he brings when he is bogged down by a welter of difficulties. Tackling one problem, or one problematic sector instills hope and confidence. At least something can be done about something and anxiety may be allayed through activity in taking hold of what seems most important or most disturbing. Progressive focalisation has been found to bring a happier outcome and earlier termination than the barrage approach which merits its name in that it serves as a barrier to movement. The longstanding case noted for its length in terms of case record, the like of which encumbers the files of many agencies, termed "chronic case" in America and the "problem family" in England, could well be reviewed from this standpoint.

For effective focalisation we are guided by a number of factors. Primarily what the agency is for and can often do quickly focuses a ramified situation, and may lead to referral elsewhere for help. Also the needs and wants of the client figure prominently. Since we can help with a problem only through the person who has it we must begin with the troubled person's concern. He may come to feel a need for other help as we work with him. The client's capacity to work on a problem or to work in certain ways and not others, may determine the focus. And finally, the worker's appraisal of the situation will determine what he can lend himself to helping the client do.

. . . The social worker is committed first and foremost to environment as treatment, and to meeting reality need. In rendering the so-called practical services, material aid in one form or another, he will strengthen the client's motivation toward self dependence and his capacity to cope with adversity to the extent that these services meet his realistic need and engage his participation in the context of a relationship in which the meaning of the experience is understood and the disturbed feelings dealt with directly or indirectly. This may involve use of interpretation and guidance. When services are rendered without reference to the client's feelings and in ways which make him feel managed, deprived, humiliated and hostile they may demoralise him. . . .

We are intent today on correcting the attitude that rendering services is not casework and that only direct treatment of emotional difficulties, through the interview is casework. The psychotherapy of a better life situation and the therapy implicit in the client's participation are important matters that social work has learnt.

The Place
of Help
in Supervision

ONE MIGHT QUESTION the place of an article on supervision in a series of papers on casework. My rationale is this:

Reprinted from *Social Service Review*, vol. 37, no. 4 (December 1963). Copyright 1963 by the University of Chicago.

The developers of supervisory processes in social work took the casework process as their model—or was it the other way round? When casework in its early years was a kindly, paternalistic, overseeing process, so was supervision. When casework became nurturant-therapeutic, so did supervision—and it was sometimes hard to tell where student or worker role merged into that of client or patient in the blurred perceptions of supervisor. When casework, more recently, took hold of the ideas of ego strengths and problem-solving capacities and responsibilities in its clients so, simultaneously, did supervision begin to speak of administrative accountability and of cognitive competences and comprehensions that affected feeling. Indeed, Charlotte Towle was one of the outstanding articulators of this latter idea.

But Charlotte Towle, firm and clear about the administrative and teaching components of supervision, never lost sight of its helping aspects—the enabling means by which learning is facilitated. These means are direct derivatives of the casework method. The purpose and goals of supervisor-supervisee are quite different from those of caseworker-client and so, therefore, are the conditions and expectations of behavior and tasks to be accomplished. But the principles of tapping and engaging motivation and of stimulating and exercising ego capacities are basic both to casework and to teaching.

What this article shows is the skilled transfer by a knowledgeable caseworker of basic principles from one to another form and focus of helping.

H. H. P.

This paper was prepared for presentation at the Simmons College School of Social Work, suggested by members of Boston and Philadelphia audiences who had heard the paper, "The Role of Supervision in the Union of Cause and

Function."[1] *For coherence, the author has repeated some passages from the earlier paper.*

Supervision in social agencies has been defined as an administrative process in the conduct of which staff development is a major concern. Supervision is a process in the conduct of which the supervisor has three functions—administration, teaching, and helping. . . .

The supervisor in the full-fledged performance of his functions as administrator and teacher helps the student learn. Why specify the helping function separately rather than leaving it as implicit in the other two? Some educators do not specify separately.[2] I have done so because I think we should be aware of activity which is not implicit in all teaching and in all administration to the extent that it has been in social work education and practice. There is a need for the learner to receive help, a need engendered by the nature of professional learning and perhaps peculiarly by the nature of social work. In this paper I have chosen to concentrate on the young adult who is having his first experience in social work. . . .

The social work student begins practice before he has knowledge essential for competent performance. Even when he has knowledge, practice begins before he has assimilated it. The need for help, therefore, is created by the discrepancy between demands and capacity to perform. Furthermore, it is created by the discrepancy between demands and personality development implicit in performance capacity. When the integrative task exceeds integrative capacity, the learner often erects defenses against anxiety which impede rather than support learning. Hence there arises the need

1. *Social Service Review*, 36 (December 1962): 396–406.
2. In recent years, student supervisors have been designated "field work instructors," a practice which had the purpose of confronting them with their responsibility to teach through emphasizing their identity as educators. The author has chosen to retain the title "supervisor" because it follows through on a previous paper (ibid.), in which the administrative identity of the supervisor is emphasized. It is the pressure of this identity which often precipitates students' need for help. Also, the full-fledged performance of this function often is a means to help students accept and use the supervisor as teacher and helper. Therefore, the term "supervisor" gives prominence to the interplay of the three functions rather than to one.

for individualized help to safeguard the potential for emotional-intellectual integration essential for the mastery of knowledge. When knowledge possesses the learner rather than being possessed by him, it bedevils him, producing uncertainty and confusion. Knowledge relevant to social work practice is amassed at rapid tempo so that inevitably there is a problem in integration. Until he can make the new knowledge his own, the student is not free to use it effectively.

Social work educators became attentive to the part played by the emotions in professional learning and to social work education as a means to personality growth and change essential for the conduct of social work's helping processes. They attempted to teach in ways that would help the learner hold together his knowing, thinking, feeling, and doing as he moved through the educational experience. Such teaching called for attention to the individual differences in learners. The problem of fostering emotional-intellectual integration led to wide swings in emphasis on the priority of knowledge versus the priority of fostering emotional readiness to learn. The push to individualize led to individualization of a kind and degree which did not prepare the student for demands of practice. Some of us recall the period of passivity, when we awaited the student's psychological readiness. Supervisors, in soft-pedaling their administrative function, withheld criticism and in many ways did not hold the student as strictly accountable as was desirable for the welfare of the client or for his own development. In so doing, they provoked an ascending spiral of frustration, resentment, and anxiety and thus fostered defenses needlessly.

Supervisors, having depreciated their teaching and administering functions, thereby became overworked helpers. They were pushed into becoming therapists, and the line between help appropriate to the educational situation and therapy was crashed. Perhaps because the student's need for help was heavy, a transference neurosis occurred because the relationship was felt as repetitive of earlier relationships in which one was helpless. We no longer have the cult of passivity to create this problem, but one still does find supervisors who operate this way, perhaps because they experienced this kind of supervision, or because for varied reasons they are not secure in their responsibility roles of teacher and subadministrator.

It is clear today that individualization fails of its aims when it waives the reality demands of practice. Yesterday we were caught in the long-standing educational controversy about whether one emphasizes maturation and awaits readiness or whether one emphasizes nurture and anticipates maturation to stimulate readiness. It has become clear that the profession's demands, rather than the student's stage of maturation, must dictate our timing. Herein lies some of the stress of social work education. These demands force us to postulate readiness, or at least a potential within the student to master, with help, the stress created by discrepancy. While the demands of professional education cannot be individualized, the student can and must be individualized throughout the educational process. When an educational system processes its students without individualizing them, it becomes mechanistic and fails to afford a humanizing experience. . . . Briefly, we emphasize nurture and anticipate maturation to stimulate readiness. What nurture? The nurture implicit in meeting valid dependency freely through teaching and helping the student find what he needs to know in order to be competent in a given situation, the nurture implicit in holding him accountable and in helping him hold himself accountable. The therapeutic attitude is to regard a student as educable until we learn that he is not. One therefore assumes a potential to cope with the reality principle—the welfare of the client. One does not waive demands, but helps the student meet them to the extent possible. We afford him a relationship oriented to current reality on the assumption that he can use it.

We must be clear about the essential difference between re-educational help in social work education and therapy. A teaching situation differs from a psychotherapeutic session, a class from a group therapy session, in its heavy reliance upon the student's capacity to experience change in feeling and thereby change in thinking through an intellectual approach. In professional education, both in classroom and in fieldwork, the initial approach is to the intellect. Although the feelings provoked are of primary importance in determining what the person learns and whether or not he is able to learn, feelings are given a secondary place, in the sense that our concern is with the student's responses to educational content and to the demands of practice. In short, we teach, we administer, and we deal with the responses of the learner. The demand to think cannot be nicely timed to the individual's psychological readiness, as it may be in therapy, in which thinking is fostered as feelings are expressed, released, understood, and changed.

In a professional school, a student is assumed to be educable if he is admitted. An educable student is one who can stand up to a reality confrontation at the start, as implied in an intellectual approach and in the presentation of content without reference to his emotional or psychological readiness of the moment. One expects that the feeling provoked will not be so great and so involving of the total personality and basic conflicts that the student will be unable to deal with his feelings if given such individualized help as depicted in this paper. Today this help is supported by educational methods which facilitate integration. . . .

The student's stage of maturation is often a basic factor. What are the ascendant needs of early adulthood, the common conflicts, the traits and abilities to be expected which have significance for the demands of social work? The individual is becoming more self-determining because he has the wherewithal for the management of his own affairs and because society has this expectancy of him and accords him this right within social limits. Furthermore, he has this expectancy of himself. Self-dependence and autonomy are valued goals in which he has so much at stake emotionally that frustration in the attainment of them readily gives rise to defenses.

There is a high potential for the assumption of profes-

sional responsibility, along with a readiness to respond to
the maturation push which these responsibilities entail.
Now is the time to affirm and use these propensities to the
extent that the profession's social limits permit. But often,
newly emancipated as the student is, authority-dependency
conflicts persist or their residuals are readily activated.
Moreover, the individual sessions to which he is subjected
through a mandatory supervisory system frequently activate these conflicts, to produce resistance to supervision.
The student's responses suggest such questioning protests
as: "Why am I not accorded the freedom I had in college,
and in other jobs, to do as I see fit and to risk myself? Why
am I not treated as an adult, with freedom to use my own
head, to be a free-lancer, to experiment? Why is my intelligence mistrusted, and why must I do as others do rather
than find my own ways of doing? Their tried and trusted
ways are accomplishing no great results. I could not do
much worse, and I might be less pedestrian in getting the
client into action in solving his problems." Out of the common tendency at this stage to project one's self onto the
client, the novice is restive when his goals, felt, however, as
the client's goals, are not attained promptly. The restiveness
of the beginner with the slow movement and meager results
in many cases is well known.

The student, perceiving the implications in skilled helping, may feel inadequate and fearful of risking himself, but
he feels even more inadequate and more fearful under the
close scrutiny of that expert, the supervisor, who will see
what a "goofer" he is. And so, blocked in risking himself,
he may anxiously withhold himself. Without help he would
become a protective learner, one who would exact meticu-
lous instruction and use it warily with the aim of self-
protection. As his frustration engenders hostility toward
the supervisor whom he fears, he may distort his instruc-
tions. In so doing he is risking what the supervisor gave
him, not himself, with the unconscious purpose of defeating the supervisor.

Resistance stemming from dependency-authority conflicts takes innumerable forms, but the fact remains that

the social limits of the profession dictate that the client's welfare be put first. Therefore the student must come to peace with supervision, whatever his initial feelings about it. His concept of himself as supervisee and his concept of the supervisor must undergo change. The supervisor's helping function frequently comes into play in enabling the student to effect the change in feeling about supervision essential for modification of thinking and doing.

Miss A, aged 22, a trainee in an in-service training program, during her first month in training had bungled two cases through not seeking supervisory help, despite the fact that her obligation to use supervision had been made known. Following the first episode, she had been confronted with the demand that she seek instruction. She had remorsefully acknowledged her sin of omission, but shortly thereafter had repeated it. She was quick to condemn herself and seemed truly concerned about her behavior.

In the supervisory session that followed, she was tense but characteristically took responsibility for opening the interview. In a challenging manner, she said, "Well, I certainly messed up that case." The supervisor, acknowledging that the consequences had not been helpful to the client, commented also that the student had seemed so concerned about these consequences that she had immediately sought help as she recognized her mistakes. The student interrupted to exclaim, "You are about to say my timing is bad!" after which the supervisor asked her what she thought. She replied that she just did not understand it herself. Supervisor said she wondered whether she had been as helpful to the student as she might have been. Perhaps there was some reason why the student had felt the need to proceed alone, even though she must have recognized that she was on unfamiliar ground. Student's apprehensive manner gave way to a look of relief, and she talked freely. [The student had anticipated condemnation; instead, the supervisor conveyed her intent to understand—and in proffering a dispassionate appraisal of what was wrong, she engaged the student in problem-solving.]

The student said she had just seemed to barge in. She described the pressure that the client had brought on her for an immediate solution to her problem. She had felt she must do something quickly because the client was upset and unhappy. The supervisor acknowledged that it was good that she wanted to help the client—that this desire is fundamental in all social work—but added that sometimes in our eagerness to be helpful one gives in to pressure and then cannot be helpful without help. [The supervisor affirmed that which can well be cherished —the helping impulse—but pointed out its limitations and the student's need for help.] The student said quickly: "That's what I did—failed to help. I kept thinking last night about how I really got that woman into trouble, and I could not sleep."

The supervisor commented that some mistakes are inevitable; we expect them. Furthermore, we probably could learn the hard way out of our mistakes—they can be steps in learning—but whenever possible we should avoid them. The agency's responsibility for the welfare of the client does not permit us to let students or workers learn through mistakes that can be prevented by use of supervision. [The supervisor confronted the student with the reality demands of professional education and conveyed the basic reason for supervision.]

The student was silent. She did not respond with a prompt "Yes, yes," to the supervisor's rational approach in making known agency demands. Some students might have assented, thus conveying the readiness to conform not yet attained through facing one's feelings and misbehavior. The student shortly volunteered that she was used to assuming responsibility. She spoke of having lost her mother at an early age, and of her father's placing responsibility upon her. Emphatically and zestfully she added, "I like it—I like to make decisions and get things done." [Note that she is implying "You do not understand *me* and my ways—the kind of person I am." Also note the self-assertion, "Let me be as I am."] The supervisor commented, "I can see you do," and again pointed out the limitation of what she brings in this respect. In response to this, the student inquired, "Why do you think I did as I did in that last case?" This self-inquiry was raised not provocatively, but showing concern. [A bid for understanding in order to understand herself?]

The supervisor asked her to try to reconstruct what her reasoning had been. [Note that she omits what her feeling had been.] The student replied that she knew she had been dealing with material on which she had no information. She knew that the supervisor was just across the hall, that she had always been generous with her time. The supervisor suggested that it was something other than reluctance to bother the supervisor that had prevented her from seeking help. The student nodded her head in affirmation, but said, "I just don't understand it, that's all." She lapsed into silence.

The supervisor broke the silence with the comment that perhaps the student had some negative feelings about asking for help, that she was made uncomfortable by asking, that she felt she should know all the answers herself even though she was a beginner. The student reflected on this, then said, slowly, "I've always made good grades in school." The supervisor explored the relevance of this. The student appeared puzzled, then added: "I was just thinking about what you said, and then I remembered how important it has always been for me to be the outstanding student. My father was superintendent of schools, and everyone expected me to know all the answers. I was in agony at school if I was called on and couldn't come up with the right answer." The supervisor commented that these feelings must have been burdensome to her and that this perhaps was something to think about further if they persisted, adding that no one expected her to have all the answers in her work here for some time. She pointed out that in both cases on which she had had difficulty there were procedures not covered in the orientation sessions or in supervisory sessions. [Note that the supervisor proffered her a departure from her past and thereby opened the door to a corrective experience.]

The student commented that if the supervisor had washed her hands of her today she would have had it coming, adding, with a sigh of relief, "I just couldn't stand to fail in my work." The supervisor replied that her work showed promise. The session closed with the reassurance that the next session would be devoted to an appraisal of wherein it did and wherein she needed help.

The sequel.—After this conference the student engaged in overuse of the supervisor, asking help repetitively. [Note the reaction formation against her impulses—for equilibrium and for the mastery of a problem.] As her unnecessary use of the supervisor was identified, this response tapered off, and she progressively showed ability to differentiate between matters which she could handle independently and those which she could not. In the course of the year there was still question about her ability to control her impatience for results. This was not so extreme that the supervisor questioned her potential for casework. [One notes here the projection of her life-situation into her work—a repetition of the past in that what has been demanded of her she demands of others, a propensity with which she may need further help or which she may outgrow.]

Appraisal and prognosis.—In this instance, the supervisor encountered a student with authority-dependency conflicts typical of the young adult. She brought to the educational experience a high expectancy of success and a high expectancy of herself with anxiety about measuring-up. She suffered the burden of competing, not only with others, but also with herself. Lacking knowledge and skill for independent functioning, she handled her feelings of inadequacy by doing on her own, by denying the dependency implicit in learning. In this behavior she used an established pattern determined by demands made on her in the past and by self-inflicted demands—namely, that she as her father's daughter must know all the answers, must succeed, and perhaps also must equal her mother, whom she to some extent replaced in the life of the father. . . . One suspects transference elements here, therefore resistance to help from the supervisor. If this had been a profound problem, the student might have continued to need to rival the supervisor and to be able to get along without her. Her response to help probably would not have been as ready.

It is noteworthy that the supervisor did not explore the past familial situation thrust at her by the student. Had she confused the role of educator with that of therapist, she probably would have done so. Instead, she proffered a helping relationship corrective of the past, and relied on this to enable the student to use help. The student's response does not negate the possibility of deeper psychological implications, but it does argue that the student is sufficiently unentangled in the past to use current relationships realistically and to regulate her own behavior.

As one looks to the future one sees the following dynamic determinants which may enable the student to become a helper rather than a pusher: Her desire to succeed may motivate identification with the profession so that as she acts professionally she may mature, through being nutured for growth. But the vital dynamics in change will be her concern for the consequences to the client. The unanswered question still is the extent of her capacity for object-love as compared with self-love, her capacity to meet the needs of others as compared with need for self-maximation and the meeting of her own need. To the extent that these capacities outweigh her self-centered needs, there will be a potential for growth through her experience in social work.

Should the reverse be the case—and her propensity to push clients constitute a problem for them and for her professional development—she will need further help. In that event the supervisor would continue to focus on the consequence to the client as the means to motivate change. If the student cannot respond to this, her past's rigidly persisting in the present would be defined as a problem requiring help other than what the supervisor can give—i.e., therapy.

This situation has been cited in illustration of authority-dependency conflicts as a source of difficulty in professional education. It illustrates also two other problems often implicit in the student's stage of maturation. The first of these has to do with giving and taking.

Adult responsibilities are not shouldered lightly by mature young adults. The stress of preparation for life-work is frequently accompanied by other stresses implicit in becoming adult. Normally this is a somewhat anxious, self-centered period when the individual is absorbed in getting his own life under way. In entering social work he concurrently is drawn into helping others set their lives straight.

A major struggle confronts him in the central conflict of this period—that of "intimacy versus isolation." Erik Erikson holds that the mastery of intimacy is a major struggle now.[3] This implies mastery of the fear of ego loss so that relationships may be not only sustained but experienced fully and freely without erection of defenses which constrict or distort them. Fear of ego loss occurs in situations that call for self-abandon. The social worker comes up against many a personal and social situation which cries out to him—to give fully, freely, and with depth of feeling. It may be difficult to do so without getting lost, confused, and entangled in the giving. Who am I, myself or my client? The threat of loss of self-identity compels self-questioning and, in some instances, the defense of retreat into self.

Experienced supervisors perceive that the problem is that of overidentification versus repudiation. Self-abandon alternates with self-restraint. Caught in this conflict, students cope with themselves variously. Some swing back and forth

3. *Childhood and Society* (New York: W. W. Norton & Co., 1950).

between these extremes; others are more consistently inclined to one or the other—overidentification, with aban-
donment of self, or weak identification out of self-restraint.
A common defense against loss of self-identity in the helping relationship is to try to make the client over in one's
own image through projection of one's own values and
goals onto him. Or there may be the reverse of this self-
assertion: self-negation may occur. Empathy may push the
worker to permit the client to project his values, his problematic concerns, upon the worker to an extent that the
worker is helpless because he feels like the client rather
than with him. A reaction against this propensity may
follow as the student tries to extricate himself. He may retaliate through self-assertive projection of himself onto the
client or may repudiate him through withdrawal. His motivation to help breaks down in the face of discouraging outcome, and he gives up the struggle. Students who invest
themselves deeply out of strong feeling for troubled people
are prone to let the client engulf them. The potential for
object-love, the strong motivation to serve, often implies
an ability to put the client's welfare first, once the student
is helped to regulate his own feelings and needs in the give-
and-take of the helping relationship. Sometimes the self-
assertive student is more difficult to help, as his own need
for self-identity and self-maximation may engender defenses
against identification with troubled people. He cannot risk
finding himself in losing himself. In these instances, nar-
cissistic ego and constricted personality sometimes operate
against the making of a full-fledged social worker, in whom
the motivation to serve must outweigh self-centered aims.

The problem of overidentification occurs with high frequency in the educable social worker. Supervisors will find
the reading of Virginia Robinson's portrayal of Jessie Taft
a rewarding experience as a study of the growth and development of a true learner.[4] In her early years she was prone
to overidentification and self-abandon in giving. What moti-

    4. Virginia P. Robinson, *Jessie Taft—Therapist and Social Work Educator: A Pro-
fessional Biography* (Philadelphia: University of Pennsylvania Press, 1962), part 2,
pp. 41–63, specifically p. 48.

vated her to regulate this propensity? The same qualities of heart and mind which motivate students today to use the supervisor's help in the regulation of their needs—her readiness to look at what she was doing to her clients, her discomfort over failing them. The student who is self-centered and self-concerned will be more defensive about the use of this help. He will be more prone to project his failure. He will find it difficult to make learning a conscious process. He may become a self-conscious worker rather than one ever ready to become conscious of self in the sense of looking objectively at himself in the client's response to him.

In early adulthood, as the individual enters social work, his problem commonly and normally is that of giving and taking, of giving and withholding. The mature individual gives all that he has to give on occasion, but discriminative giving rather than giving which protects the giver must become a pattern. Many students will need individualized help in making the need and capacity of others the measure of their giving and of their withholding.

Other problems stem from the persistence of the past in the present. At this stage of life the student is more vulnerable than he may be later to experiences which activate his past. He may still cling to cherished values as he evaluates others. Specific incidents or demands or knowledge may revive past painful experiences or ineptitudes. The latter may become repetitive trauma, provoking emotional response that may be exceptionally stressful and may call for help that the supervisor cannot give. Whether he needs help may be contingent on the extent to which he survived the earlier stress—that is, whether it impeded growth or contributed to growth. Of decisive importance is the extent to which the individual is accessible to experiences and relationships that correct the past. For example:

A student may reveal marked anxiety in trying to help a client who rejects her child. Her hostility toward this mother causes her to swing back and forth between the expression of punitive attitudes in the withholding of help, to opposite behavior in which she must correct her professional misdemeanors through permissive attitudes and giving excessive help. From all this student says and does, the supervisor is reasonably certain that she is undergoing a repetitive experience that is painful and confusing. He does not explore the student's early experience in her relationship with her own mother. He focuses instead on eliciting and understanding the student's feelings about his mother. He shows understanding of her anger and dislike. He directs her to consider how this woman came to feel and act as she does, and he holds the student accountable to try to understand and to meet this woman's need, regardless of whether or not she feels kindly toward her. He grants that the woman's behavior is unacceptable, but he holds that the woman herself is to be accepted and understood and helped. As the student sees and feels that this mother fails her child out of having been failed in her own relationships, the student becomes less aligned with the child versus the mother. She begins to feel with the mother and, as the mother responds positively, making more productive use of help, the student is able to fulfil her professional responsibility.

In this instance the student subsequently made brief comments which showed insight gains—to the effect that she had a hard time not projecting her own experience, but she was working at it. The supervisor did not explore to elicit the specific in her own past. Since she was able to be confronted and to confront herself with her learning problem and achieve mastery of it, the supervisor relied on the therapy implicit in the educational experience progressively to correct the past. An important clue to her probable ability to use help lay in her ambivalent behavior toward this woman—out of strong motivation to behave professionally, and her discomfort over failing her. As guilt and hostility were lowered through the supervisor's help, she could permit herself insight.

I cite one more supervisory situation, one in which a complex of problems and more total involvement of the personality might have made the line between re-education and therapy difficult to hold, had the supervisor not had the skill he brought into helping.

Mr. J, age 24, was admitted to second-year fieldwork conditionally, when it was difficult to assess his unsatisfactory performance the first year because of objective factors which had made for an unrealistic demand. His first-year placement had been in an experimental group in a psychiatric hospital where he had a difficult caseload of seriously disturbed patients whose relatives posed a large task for a beginner. There had been a change in supervisors at the end of seven weeks from an experienced woman supervisor to whom, however, he could not talk freely because he found it difficult to talk to women, to a young man with no previous supervisory experience, with less casework experience, and with no experience in this setting. It was clear that the supervisor had been insecure in his role as teacher and helper and seemingly therefore overactive as a didactic teacher and hesitant as a helper. The student saw himself, retrospectively, as having overidentified with his patients when he felt the supervisor's limitations and could not turn to him for help. At the time, he attributed his own poor performance to his own problems, and he suffered much anxiety in feeling that he, like his patients, was mentally or emotionally ill.

Academically his work had been satisfactory, but he had become increasingly withdrawn in class discussion. He used his faculty adviser only when she initiated conferences, and he denied any difficulty in fieldwork. The assessment at the end of the first year was that the persistence of his past in the present indicated a neurosis. In his work with clients, the student revealed a fear of hostility, a fear of relationships with women, and an inner absorption which depleted his energy and limited his ability to relate to the needs of others. He personalized his clients' initial resistance and withdrew rather than helping them express their anxiety. He pervasively recreated his family's conflict in his work with clients. This appraisal confronted the school with a discouraging picture suggestive of pathology. The question remained: To what extent was this a situational neurosis or a character neurosis? Not to be ignored was the fact that in his retreat from helping and being helped the student was repeating his supervisor's retreat from that function.

To his second-year supervisor in a family agency, it was clear that the student from the start must separate the two experiences, must have a new beginning. In the initial conference the supervisor functioned as follows:

The supervisor encouraged Mr. J to talk about past experiences that had been successful and gratifying. This interview provided data for tentative evaluation of his initial motivation and enabled the supervisor to help him reclarify and assert his wish for professional achievement. It enabled the student to share his feelings of discouragement and afforded the supervisor information about what had been emotionally disturbing.

The supervisor made known some of the demands in his first-year caseload which required more skill than might be expected of a first-year student. The discussion relieved the student's feeling of failure and prompted him to volunteer that his difficulties were heightened by problems in supervision. He described in some detail what he felt had happened to him to effect his use of supervision. Although there was some bitterness and rationalization, there was not excessive projection. The supervisor used this discussion to make known that he would be working differently with him and that he was ready to accept responsibility to help him in areas in which he had felt deprived. As the student blamed himself inordinately, the supervisor tried to reverse the pattern of self-recrimination by injecting the realities he was ignoring. Reality was also introduced to correct his distorted fears of the faculty.

No attempt was made to discourage personal remarks about his parents. These were not explored in depth, but the supervisor indicated that they had interest in relation to his motivation for social work. He attempted to enhance the student's wish to learn, by clarifying that, in spite of difficulties, he seemed determined to become a social worker. When he asserted his wish, the supervisor clarified mutual expectancies in the supervisory relationship.

The supervisor explored the student's feeling about agency assignment, because of the feelings students have about lack of choice. There was opportunity for him to consider his motivation in relation to a family agency. This was not clarified until later, when he revealed his unrealistic expectation that he would be dealing largely with requests for concrete services and less with problems in relationships having emotional content.

At the close of the initial conference, the supervisor focused on immediate tasks by outlining the kinds of cases the student would be expected to carry and selecting the specifics of the policy manual that would be of immediate concern to him. The supervisor also suggested questions to focus the study of two cases assigned. In this he was attempting to partialize the task in order to protect the student from feeling overwhelmed with the complexities of the new situation.

In this introduction to the second year, the new beginning was marked by the prominence given to the supervisor's helping function, the performance of which the previous supervisor had abdicated. The administrative function was highlighted in making known demands, in the assignment of responsibilities, and in making known certain expectations.

Subsequently the supervisor for a period gave time freely to convey interest and direction in learning. However, he maintained a task-centered focus. Consequently, when the student described his personal problems and expressed a feeling of hopelessness, the supervisor heard him out and accepted his feelings but then related these discussions to case situations. Discussion of case situations involved considerable clarification of what was inherent in the case and what Mr. J was projecting into it. This sorting out of the objective and subjective sharpened his perception of his own anxieties. Accompanying this there was open discussion of his problems in case management as they emerged more clearly, in his fear of hostility and rejection, his anger toward clients. In these discussions the student related his learning problems to personal fears and life-patterns. At the close of a month the student reported with elation that he had arranged for psychiatric treatment.

The supervisor had some anxiety that his tempo had been too fast, that he might have precipitated Mr. J's treatment. If so, he feared that the precipitous decision might mean a retreat from learning, but the student did not use his treatment defensively. In fact, his social work performance improved progressively. The supervisor recalled that before this self-referral to a psychiatrist there had been several discussions in which he had attempted to enhance the student's respect for the courage and potential maturity involved in the client's seeking help. Apparently this discussion was incorporated and used by the student in his own behalf. At the close of the year he showed promise as a social worker, so that the school had no reservations in recommending him for employment.

One sees here a situation in which a supervisor in the context of a supportive relationship oriented his threefold function of teaching, helping, and administering to the student's need without waiving reality demands. Because the supervisor gave him help in seeing himself in his work, the student saw much that simultaneously heightened both his discomfort and his ability to cope with himself. Undeniably the supervisor's activity pushed the student into therapy. The student needed and wanted more relief from his discomfort over his problematic professional performance than he could obtain from the supervisor. Thus he became motivated to get help elsewhere, but, because the supervisor had helped him, he had hope and confidence that he could be helped. This hope the supervisor affirmed in making "taking help" ego-challenging rather than ego-deflating. This is a good example of an educational relationship which served as a therapeutic one.

Whether his difficulties are rooted in unresolved authority-dependency conflicts, in intimacy-versus-isolation conflicts, in attachments to the past, or in other sources, it is probable that the student is feeling stress. The nature and extent of his feeling, as well as both his capacity to cope with his feeling and his ways of coping, will determine the size of his integrative task. These factors will determine also the nature and extent of the help he needs and his response to it. It is common for students under stress to deny their feelings out of discomfort and out of fear. Reared in a scientific age, students may draw on their misconception of the scientist's schooled feeling. The protective ego often whispers, "To be objective professionally one must not feel." This is an unhappy solution for many reasons. Denial of feeling will desensitize the student. It will constrict him in relating to people and lead to emotional shallowness. It will impede his identification with social work as a helping profession. It is as the student's relationships gain emotional depth that acculturation to the mores and demands of social work occurs. Furthermore, it is to be remembered that freedom to feel makes for play of the mind and thereby contributes to creative intellectual functioning. His mentors in classroom and field can well be concerned to free him to feel warmly and deeply. It is as he is free to feel that he becomes able to face and to regulate his feeling. He thereby is enabled to make conscious use of his feeling, that is, to express disagreement or withhold it with appropriate reference to time, place, and person. It is as his feelings are expressed and respected that he will be able to respect the feelings of others and come to see that "as a man thinketh in his heart, so is he." The dignity of man, his individuality, is contingent on the fusion of his feeling and his thinking.[5]

Space limitations have driven me to focus narrowly on the beginning stage of young adults. We encounter many older students, some with social work experience and all with more work experience. In some instances the authority-dependency conflicts, the problems in giving and taking, have been outgrown, but often these problems are there, more masked now by the individual's defenses against them. These defenses may or may not be useful in social work. The demand for change therefore may be more threatening because it involves acceptance of the dependency and authority implicit in learning at an age when it may be even more difficult to be dependent and to be subjected to professional discipline. It may involve also the unlearning implicit in modification of well-entrenched behavior and of social work practices in which the student has felt competent. Supervisory help is essential, however, even though in some ways and at times it is difficult for the supervisor and the student. The principles and means of helping are essentially the same.

Summary

It is clear that the helping function of the supervisor is lowered when educational and administrative methods bear the imprint of psychological understanding—understanding of the learning process and of the stress implicit in the demands of social work education. Helpful methods aim to support the ego's adaptive capacity and to prevent the individual's overuse of its protective function. This summary will not include these methods. It will instead focus on methods and principles of helping when teaching and administrative methods have not fulfilled their aim, either be-

5. I recommend to all social workers the paper entitled "Living and Feeling," by Jessie Taft, first published in *Child Study* in 1953 and now reprinted in her professional biography (Robinson, *Jessie Taft*, pp. 140–53).

cause the student is unable to respond to them or because they have fallen short of good educational practice. . . .

1. The supervisor helps the student identify the problem or confronts him with it. Confrontation may precede the student's readiness; the needs of the client dictate the tempo.

2. The supervisor gives the student ample opportunity to delineate the problem as he sees it and feels it. The supervisor encourages and explores, so that he may explain the student's part in it and the part played by circumstance or other persons. He helps the student sort out both the subjective and the objective factors and forces.

3. The situation is then set up as a problem-solving one. What can the student do about it, and what can the supervisor do to help him perform more competently in the interest of the client?

4. In the process of reaching this point, the supervisor affirms what is acceptable and useful in the student's behavior in the problematic situation but makes known the what and the why of that which is inappropriate. This may imply clarifying agency demands and the demands of professional learning. Often it involves clarifying the supervisory relationship, if use of it is part of the problem.

5. In evoking and exploring feelings, the supervisor acknowledges and understands the student's feeling. He thus accepts the student himself but not necessarily his behavior. The limitations of it are made known again with inclusion of why the behavior is not useful or appropriate.

6. When, in exploring the problematic situation, the student blocks in recognizing the import of his part in it, the supervisor tentatively postulates probabilities—presenting them as what the import may be, what it seems to him, the supervisor, to be out of his experience with other students and workers with comparable difficulties. This may provoke resistance which will then have to be dealt with. If blocking persists, the student is charged with the responsibility of trying to figure out for himself the import of his behavior. Whether or not he is able to do this, the behavior will have to change. Students at times have to be pushed to

act in a way they do not feel. In so doing, they may come to feel differently. Furthermore, as they cope with themselves with some success, defenses are lowered, thus permitting insight gains. Sometimes, contingent on the seriousness of the implications for the client, the student's inability to change will lead to consideration of his educability for social work and/or his need to get help elsewhere.

7. If the student is appraised negatively, he may feel threatened by the resultant deflated concept of himself, how he looks both to himself and to the supervisor. It is important to use "norms" of development in appraisal of lacks in performance and inappropriate attitudes and behavior. Unrealistic expectancy of self or of others is unjust and ego-deflating. It can lower motivation. If he feels that he has not fallen below realistic expectancy, the student's sense of failure is diminished so that he may be enabled to work on the problem. False reassurance is not helpful. When a student is not coming up to norms, the reasons should be ascertained to the extent possible and efforts should be made to assess what he can do about it or what the supervisor can help him do.

8. When the student places his difficulties in the past, the supervisor does not immediately explore the past, but makes known the difference, with the hope that the student may be able to use the current experience to correct the past through being able to separate the two. But if his use of the past to explain his difficulties persists, the supervisor may explore it, though not deeply or extensively. Some exploration is important in order to see its relevance to the present for use in helping the student relate to his current work performance.

9. . . . A good deal inevitably happens to make learning a conscious process and to help the student become conscious of himself in order to regulate his use of himself as a social worker. Normally, students gain insight as anxieties are lowered and defenses relax. They often will spontaneously verbalize insight and often use it, whether or not they put it into words.

10. Finally, the student-supervisor relationship should

not be a one-to-one relationship but a twosome in which the two as one are continuously related to the agency and the client. This relationship has been set up to serve the agency on behalf of the client; therefore, these are kept in focus—as the reality principle. As this occurs, student and supervisor do not become absorbed to an entangling degree in one another. The issue of controlling and being controlled disappears. As they work together, the student's capacity to put the client's needs and wants before his own and to use the agency and supervision for the client rather than for self-maximation will become the dynamic factor in his use of help. If the student is not motivated by concern for the client, it is probable that his personal needs call for a help of a kind beyond the scope of agency supervision. Concern for the client's welfare and concern for his own professional competence motivate change, given the capacity to change. They therefore are the major criteria of a student's educability.

Brief Excerpts

WHAT TO DO WITH some choice bits that remain? Three of them are from the 1930's—all the more precious because they are old; all of them are as up-to-date as anything in current journals. So I have decided to put them here despite their breaking up a careful chronology.

Notes on Treating Parents and Children. "Treatment cannot be given to any member of a family without affecting the group." This is the theme excerpted here. How many years it was before this was translated into the legitimized practice of casework! "The parent who fails frequently is the parent who has been failed." How long it has taken us to grasp the meaning of this for our practice!

On Selection of Foster Homes. Two notes: First, the

recognition that "ideal marriage" is illusory and that the focus for casework diagnosis should be upon how the marital pair *cope* with their problems. (This is one of the frequent "throw-aways" one finds in the works of original thinkers like Charlotte Towle—and one wonders always why it was not picked up at the time by someone and examined in all its potential imports.) Second, and of the same nature, the idea that for some children a one-parent foster home might be better than none. Only recently has this idea recurred in foster-home practice, and, happily this time, been tried out.

Casework and Social Work.   This is a clear and unequivocal statement of casework's limitations, of its dependence for effectiveness upon the presence of certain social provisions, and of the responsibility of social caseworkers to make those provisions known and secured. In today's attacks upon casework for what it has not done and the counterdefenses these attacks call forth, this simple statement may offer some firm footing for ponder and planned change.

Notes on Treating Parents and Children

When a problem is presented to a social agency by a family or one individual of a family group, it is essential that the social examination depict not only the life experiences of each individual, but also the emotional values of these experiences for the entire group; just as it should consider the interrelationships and interdependencies of the entire group if an adequate social diagnosis is to be made, so must treatment be planned with careful consideration of the emotional interplay of all the individuals concerned, if it is to be effective.

Treatment cannot be given to any member of a family

"Notes on Treating Parents and Children" is excerpted from "The Treatment of Behavior and Personality Problems in Children: The Social Worker," *American Journal of Orthopsychiatry*, vol. 1, no. 1 (October 1930); the final paragraph is from "Reinforcing Family Security Today," *Social Casework*, vol. 32, no. 2 (February 1951). Copyright 1951 by the Family Service Association of America.

without affecting the group. In some cases the entire family must be drawn into treatment. Furthermore the approach of this or that member as well as the centering of treatment on certain individuals cannot be a random thing. In fact there must be a discriminative approach and a selective treatment emphasis in accordance with the peculiar needs of the case. Which parent shall we see first, is a vital question even at the stage of history getting, for it is frequently then that we arouse certain reaction patterns which make for a positive or negative treatment response on the basis of attention given or not given this or that parent. It is therefore important at the time that a problem is referred that as many clues as possible be secured, such as, which parent referred the problem, the parental attitudes toward the problem and its referral, in order that at the very start the parental emotional interactions may be taken into account—rather than opposed.

It is generally agreed that fathers have been left too much out of the picture. This has occurred largely through the inconvenience involved in reaching them, and because of the scarcity of their time. They are now generally interviewed at least once during the social examination and occasionally during the treatment process. The fine point of sometimes seeing the father first during the social examination and of making him the focus of treatment, if the case indicates this need, is not a very general practice due to inconvenience, in spite of a realization of his significance in the situation. . . .

It is necessary to recognize that [an] overprotective mother is strongly identified with her child and that the worker will only threaten her if she identifies with the child without including the mother. A mistake frequently made in the past, on recognizing that the child was too tied to mother, and having the child's development at heart, and feeling perhaps a bit irritated at so foolish and destructive a parent, was that the worker frequently launched into an intensive therapeutic program for the youngster, such as getting him into clubs, sending him to camp, seeing that he got sex instruction, etc. She therefore displeased the mother through a too sudden removal of her source of satisfaction, so that the need to clutch the child was accentuated and her need to reject the worker so profound that all hope of getting her cooperation was immediately lost. Frequently, too, the child was not ready for the sudden weaning, so that, intimidated by the camp experience or other stimuli offered, he returned to the mother, to cling all the more tenaciously. So the purpose of treatment was not only defeated but the dependency situation increased. Repeated failure due to such procedures has made these mothers loom large as overwhelming obstacles in treatment.

Progress has been made in some cases, however, by recognizing at the start the mother's emotional needs. It is very important that the worker treat the mother, that she interest her in the child's need for certain changes in handling, and that the first treatment steps be taken by the mother, rather than by outsiders for the patient. As the child is subjected to new growth experiences, the worker should see that the mother is kept in close touch with what is going on, that she be given approval for patient's improvement, that she be given new growth experiences akin to his, as substitute satisfaction for any release of him. For example, if possible, when he is sent to a club, some such interest should be injected into her life. If sex instruction is given to him by a psychiatrist, it should be with her permission. The worker might parallel his experience with her by giving her books to read or by covering the same ground with her that the psychiatrist covers with the child so that she may meet his questions and share the experience with him. All of this may seem to not be separating the child from the mother, and having the child's development at heart, and mate objective, the immediate objective is to induce some growth in both individuals . . . in order to prepare them for the ultimate weaning. In a number of cases it has been observed . . . that the child himself begins to throw the mother off and when this point comes the mother is sometimes more ready to release him than previously. It is very necessary, however, that the worker be in close touch with her at this time in order to fortify her with approval, to give substitute satisfactions and to give her an appreciation of the possibilities of satisfaction in a growing child as well as in a baby.

To help children we frequently must first help parents. A deprived parent who receives understanding and help may gain in capacity to give understanding and help. The parent who fails frequently is the parent who has been failed, hence a corrective relationship will imply that the social worker and agency should not repeat his unloving parent through aligning with the children versus him, through condemning him, and through restrictive services given begrudgingly, without understanding his frustration at the limits of the giving.

On Selection of Foster Homes

It might be asked—is there a well-adjusted marriage? If every marriage were thoroughly evaluated, would there be any homes that would not seem too precarious to use? It must be remembered that every marital relationship has its precarious elements. Every individual brings to marriage certain deep-rooted emotional determinants which frequently by fortunate chance neutralize or complement one another. When these drives come into conflict they are frequently handled by the understanding and resourcefulness of either one or both individuals. The test question in all aspects of the history is therefore *how* are these individuals handling their conflicting drives? Their capacity to handle such factors constructively should be a gauge as to the usability of the home. Another point to consider carefully: experience shows that the placement of a child will sometimes precipitate trouble in cases where conflicting drives are somehow maintaining adjustment; also the contrary, precarious situations are sometimes stabilized through the placement of a child. One must therefore evaluate each fam-

"On Selection of Foster Homes" is excerpted from "Psychiatric Approach in Home Finding," *The Social Worker* (Boston: Simmons College of Social Work, 1931).

ily situation; study each child to be placed; and then re-evaluate the family situation in regard to the particular child to be placed.

Another point . . . for discussion is the use of the broken home. At one time the home of the single or widowed woman was rejected almost routinely, because it was not considered a normal home. The psychiatric view from one standpoint reinforces this attitude. It considers essential the presence of both mother and father persons in order that normal emotional development may be assured through identifications with the two parents. Even so, recognizing the emotional liabilities of such homes, not only because of the lack of one parent, but also because of the exaggerated emotional needs which are so often manifested by the single or widowed woman, the psychiatric viewpoint throws a new light on this type of home. There are instances in which it can be more constructive than the two-parent home. For example, in the case of the child who has a devoted father with whom he is in touch, and with whom he is strongly identified. Such a home precludes the possibility of conflicts over two father persons. Even though such a conflict is not probable, such homes can be used constructively for any child with an attached father. The adolescent who has been deprived of a satisfying mother, but who has worked out an identification with an own father, even though the father may be dead, will frequently find this type of home more constructive, because of not having to adjust the original father ideal to the reality of a foster father.

Casework and Social Work

In the past we have tended to persist indefinitely in attacking problems and in dealing with situations in which case work service was not the answer. We are coming not only to recognize the futility of persisting in situations which are beyond the scope of casework help, but to realize also our social responsibility for revealing the inadequacy of social

"Casework and Social Work" is excerpted from a discussion of "Changing Concepts in Visiting Teacher Work," a paper by Gladys E. Hall, in *Visiting Teacher Bulletin*, vol. 12, no. 1 (September 1936).

casework in these instances, in order that interest and effort may be directed toward social action.

I can imagine that the visiting teacher encounters many cases within the school, such as certain kinds of delinquent behavior, in which the total situation of the individual has now gone beyond the scope of the social caseworker. If that kind of person were recognized throughout the country as needing something other than casework care, there might be provided something other than casework facilities for his care. . . . I can imagine that within the school the visiting teacher frequently is asked to conpensate to the child for what the school lacks. Because of the absence of certain educational facilities the child's needs are not being met, and the visiting teacher may be asked to take him on as a casework problem because certain behavior has been induced by the school inadequacies. In such instances her responsibility lies in making casework limitations known, and in revealing the educational treatment issue.

As caseworkers let us cease to be the great pretenders. Casework is not a universal panacea. It cannot substitute for certain other lacks, and it is our charge not to assume misguided leadership. In such an instance let us build intellect and energy toward revealing the real needs and toward securing the necessary facilities. In this field, as elsewhere, our responsibility as caseworkers has assumed broad social implications which we cannot ignore.

Part Two
Perspectives
in Social Work

Trends
in Social Casework: 1900-1930

THERE ARE A NUMBER of historical accounts of the development of social work to be found in the profession's literature. Each is written, as is all history, within the particular reference frame of the particular historian. Each history writer can view the past only through the lenses of his conception of the present—so each account presents some different slant or new angle.

The excerpts that follow are from an ambitious article that the young Charlotte Towle undertook to write on the evolution of social work. In it she began with the ancient Hebraic-Graeco then Graeco-Roman social and economic attitudes and services, traced these through their Christian church manifestations, up into the nineteenth-century developments in this country. If only because of space limits, it was a breathless journey. The reader who would take it must go to the original article.

In the special sections presented here, Charlotte Towle was particularly attuned to the development of social *casework*, especially of the specialization of psychiatric casework of which she was one of the early and most competent practitioners. Her focus was determined by her particular

Excerpted from "Changes in the Philosophy of Social Work," reprinted from *Mental Hygiene*, vol. 14, no. 2 (April 1930). Copyright 1930 by The National Committee for Mental Health.

place in the social work scene. The excerpts here hold interest because of their particularity, because they present
the circumstances and questions of casework through the
eyes of a perceptive and knowledgeable participant-ob-
server of psychiatric casework.

But even the most prescient among us does not always
read the signs of his current history correctly. In response
to the question she raised, "Should not all social workers
be 'psychiatric'?" Charlotte Towle answered that there
would probably always need to be especially trained caseworkers to convey their special knowledge to the mass of
social workers. Yet it was she herself who, slightly more
than ten years later, was one of the prime movers in the
then American Association of Schools of Social Work to
develop "generic" casework—which is to say the inclusion
in the education of *all* caseworkers, regardless of their special field of practice, the psychodynamic principles which
explain human behavior and inform the caseworker's action. It was because of Charlotte Towle's conviction about
common human needs and common human relationships
that, under her guidance at the University of Chicago, one
of the first generic casework sequences was inaugurated.
It was not that all casework students were schooled in psychotherapy. Rather, concurrently with the upsurge of ego
psychology it was that all casework students were inducted
into the psychosocial forces and mysteries governing everyday life.

H. H. P.

A few of the outstanding precursors of significant events
and trends during the dynamic early twentieth century in
this country are:

1900.—Breakdown of Clifford Beers, and his rebirth as a
social leader and synthesizer through his organization of
The National Committee for Mental Hygiene, with the coöp-

eration of Dr. Thomas Salmon and other supporters of the psychiatric and medical profession.

1904.—The beginnings of hospital social service. Emphasis on preventive medicine, with a carry-over to preventive measures in social work.

1905.—The appointment of a social worker to the Neurological Clinic of the Massachusetts General Hospital.

1906.—The beginnings of social service in the New York State (mental) hospitals, the workers being designated "after-care" workers. Funds were provided by the State Charities Aid Association.

1909.—The founding of the Connecticut Society for Mental Hygiene, again through the work of Mr. Clifford Beers. Social service recommended in the new Boston Psychopathic Hospital. The beginning of William Healy's work in Chicago with the individual delinquent under the Institute for Juvenile Research subsequently carried on by Dr. Herman Adler. Freud's first appearance in America in a lecture on psychoanalysis.

1912.—Eugenics field worker stationed at Cold Springs Harbor.

1913.—Social workers detailed to psychiatric work at Danvers State Hospital and Boston Psychopathic Hospital. At Bedford, the establishment of the Laboratory of Social Hygiene, one of the first attempts to make a diagnostic study of every aspect of delinquency, a forerunner of the child-guidance clinic.

1914.—Several individuals termed "mental-hygiene workers" located in Boston, New York, Baltimore, and Chicago, working under psychiatrists in the social supervision of clinic or hospital patients in the community.

This period from 1900 to 1914 represented not only the formulation and furtherance of social casework techniques and the beginning of specialization—in a period in which the family, as the unit of society, was still the unit of emphasis in diagnosis and treatment, and in which there was also still considerable emphasis on economic factors—but also the rediscovery of the individual as a unit of emphasis. We say rediscovery because of the previous periods of emphasis on the individual, as in the early Christian era and in the nineteenth century. It is in comparing periods of similar emphasis that we get a sense of progress and a realization that it is evolutionary spirals and not closed circles that have been described in the process of change. To such men as Dr. E. E. Southard, Dr. Adolf Meyer, Dr. August Hoch, Dr. Thomas Salmon, Dr. William A. White, social thinking owes much, for they gave a dynamic interpretation of behavior. They were interested in relating the normal to the abnormal, and in so doing contributed to the evolution of the genetic approach which has been described as "the recognition of the continuity of mental life in relationship, not only to the organic growth of the individual, but to the experiences which he undergoes and survives".[1]

In 1917, Mary E. Richmond writes: "Social case-work consists of those processes which develop personality through adjustments consciously effected, *individual by individual*, between men and their social environment."

Nor can we pass lightly over the birth of psychiatric social work, or perhaps one should rather say the development of that specialty, since at this point particularly, it was an application of general social casework techniques to the field of psychiatry. The actual birth with formal christening took place in 1919 at the National Conference of Social Work in Atlantic City. By this time, through the utilization of casework methods, it had, with the assimilation of social, physical, psychological, and psychiatric elements, begun to achieve a *purposive* social diagnosis, which was to constitute a dynamic contribution to the entire field of social service.

In tracing the gradual intensification of the relation between psychiatry and social work, we turn to the reports of the National Conference of Social Work, from which the following outline—showing shifts in focus—is taken:

1914–15–16.—The conference includes sections on defectives and the state care of the insane and feebleminded. Mental hygiene was mentioned in connection with mental

1. Dr. Lawson G. Lowrey, director of the Institute for Child Guidance in New York in his annual report, 30 June 1928.

defect, and there was a beginning emphasis on the prevention of mental disease. Alcoholism, drug addiction, syphilis, social hygiene, and delinquency were also in the foreground. In 1914 Dr. Healy reports on his work with young offenders. Drs. Meyer, Goddard, Davenport, and Southard appeared in 1915 to talk about the prevention of mental disease and defect and a program for state care.

1917.—With the entrance of the United States into the World War, a mental-hygiene section of the conference was created. The problem of war absorbed the conference for two years. The experience of war-devastated Europe pointed to the importance of the psychiatric examination to eliminate, or to facilitate the adjustment of, enlisted and drafted men who could not withstand the strain of active warfare. New lessons had to be learned with regard to the causes and treatment of the so-called "shell-shocked." There not being enough psychiatrists to meet the need when we entered the war, an experiment was attempted in the training of a group of women to assist in treatment through psychiatric social work. Thus this critical period saw the opening at Smith College of the Training School of Psychiatric Social Work by Dr. Southard and Miss Mary Jarrett. In this, psychiatry made a definite attempt to express its contribution to training in a systematic form. In the summer of 1917 the first courses in mental hygiene were given at the New York School of Social Work.

1919.—Field-work training in mental hygiene was established at Vanderbilt Clinic by the New York School. "In Atlantic City the conference was a landslide for mental hygiene; the conference was swept off its feet . . . a note prophetic of the next step, the new focus of psychiatric and casework interest in the mental health of the child, the maladjusted school child, the delinquent child, the placed-out child."[2]

Before continuing with this account of events, it would be well to consider some of the causal elements in the shift of emphasis from the family as a unit to the individual, as

2. Data on National Conferences from Jessie Taft, "The Relation of Psychiatry to Social Work," *The Family* 7 (November 1926): 199–203.

well as the reasons for the growing realization of the necessity of preventive and remedial work with the child. A few
of the outstanding factors are as follows:

1. Specialization in medical and psychiatric social service, as well as work with the individual in courts, prisons,
and industry, led to a focusing of attention upon individuals
apart from the family setting.

2. The war brought both an extensive and an intensive
focus upon individuals from families of all levels of society.
Furthermore, it shifted emphasis from heredity and economic environment. The army service constituted a laboratory test, bringing out individual differences in response to
an experience of emotional strain, and in so doing it revealed that responses do not necessarily correlate with significant hereditary factors or material environment. That
is, men with apparently good biological inheritance and
from socially advantageous backgrounds sometimes suffered breakdowns, whereas individuals with a poor physical
inheritance and disadvantageous backgrounds frequently
endured the strain. What, then, besides physical, mental,
and material factors, determined emotional stamina in periods of stress? Psychiatric workers who had the experience
of working with disabled ex-service men gradually became
aware of the significance of early life experiences in relation
to the individual's capacity for adaptation during the war
and in the difficult post-war period. There arose mass recognition of mental breakdown induced by justifiable emotional and mental strain and affecting individuals from any
social and economic strata. This did much to change the
attitude of the medical profession and of the public toward
this group of the "inadequate," in that the stigma was removed. The result was a greater sense of responsibility for
prevention and treatment.

3. For some time prior to the war, there had been a gradual convergence of biological and sociological concepts—a
convergence that grew into an integration at about this
period. In this connection we quote from a noted biologist:[3]

3. Herbert S. Jennings, "The Biological Basis of the Family," *Family Life To-day*,
Ed. Margaret E. Rich (Boston: Houghton Mifflin Company, 1928).

"The family is a small group of individuals that share in a common stock of genes, furnished by the two parents, and that also share a common environment, of which the members of the family are themselves the most potent factors. As compared with a set of individuals taken at random, their inherited differences are less and their environmental differences are less. But it is a serious error to assume uniformity in the family in respect of either inheritance or environment. The method of shuffling, distribution, and recombining the genes of the parents insures that no child shall be like either parent in its genetic constitution, nor like any other child, with the probable exception of identical twins, derived from a single fertilized egg. In consequence of these genetic differences, the members of the family differ considerably in the way they develop; in the way they respond to a given environment; in their behavior under given conditions; in what we call temperament, mentality, character. Even if it were possible to make the environment the same for all members of the family, it is by no means to be expected that all should develop the same type of personality; there are deep-lying and far-reaching differences in their original constitutions.

"But the *effective* environment, like the genetic constitutions, is never the same for the different members of the family. . . . The differences resulting from the multiplicity of life and the change of days insure that no two members shall have the same effective environment. This diversity of environment, like the diversity in genetic constitutions, may also induce great differences in what we call temperament, mentality, and character. Particularly effective in these respects are the things that happen in early life, from birth to eighteen months, possibly also those that happen before birth."

4. Modern psychology, like biology, had gradually been contributing to our social concepts. Individual differences in mental capacity within the same family had been scientifically demonstrated.

5. Modern psychiatry advanced the point of view that "the behavior of an individual at any given point in his

career is conceived as a definite response to the demands placed upon him through the medium of his biological, physical, intellectual, and emotional equipment, plus the sum total of all his life experiences".[4] The behavior is purposeful in the sense of satisfying some need.

Thus specialization in the social-service field, the war upheaval with the resultant focus on individual differences in capacity to adjust, the assimilation of modern biological, psychological, and psychiatric concepts, all tended to build up a momentum of emphasis on the individual. By 1921 and 1922, the reports of the National Conference reveal that "all the world had discovered children."[5]

The Milwaukee conference and the Providence conference emphasized the visiting-teacher movement and the school as a center where the child must be reached. The utilization of casework in the schools is evidenced by the increase in the number of visiting teachers throughout the country. The Judge Baker Foundation and the Commonwealth Fund launched programs for psychiatric work with children. The latter, in establishing the Bureau of Children's Guidance as a five-year experimental training center for students of mental hygiene at the New York School of Social Work, took a big step in formulating scientific training for psychiatric social work. The coöperation of the Commonwealth Fund and The National Committee for Mental Hygiene in the establishment of some seven community child-guidance clinics throughout the country, by means of demonstrations in this field for five years, enlarged the scope of psychiatric work with children, which still continues to be a dominant trend. Large numbers of such clinics have since come into being. The Institute for Child Guidance, established in New York City in 1927 by the Commonwealth Fund, is a training center for psychiatric-social-work students from the Smith College School for Social Work and the New York School of Social Work, as well as for certain fellows in psychology and psychiatry working under fellowships financed by the

---

4. Marion E. Kenworthy, M.D. "Psychoanalytic Concepts in Mental Hygiene," *The Family*, 7 (November, 1926): 213–23.

5. Jessie Taft, *op. cit.*

Commonwealth Fund and administered by The National Committee for Mental Hygiene. This training aspect of its program was the result of the experience of the period of demonstration, which made it clear that specially equipped psychiatric and psychological personnel must be supplied commensurate with the increasing demands for child-guidance programs in the United States.

The need for research in the entire field is plainly indicated by the dangers of a rapid growth in a comparatively unformulated field. Several other schools for social work have organized psychiatric-social-work programs since the establishment of the first two. Mental-hygiene courses have been added to generic casework training and to other specialties. Emphasis on the importance of nurture in the early years of an individual's life has also motivated the establishment of numerous nursery schools and habit clinics throughout the country.

What of this emphasis on the individual, with its centering upon the child? It is true that there was an early period when the child, as the patient, was thrown into such bold relief for study and treatment that he was perhaps overemphasized and the family problems as a whole somewhat slighted. The very nature, however, of the social-psychiatric study of a child—in that it calls for an understanding of both parents, of the basic marital relationship, and of the siblings, as well as of the interaction of the entire group—has precluded any very complete omission of the family. Treatment has inevitably drawn us into the realities of the total situation. The centering of treatment in the child immediately brought such significant response from the other individuals in the family circle that it was not long before in some cases we were centering treatment on the parents, including this or that sibling, and sometimes so minimizing contact with the patient that there was actually very little direct treatment of him.

In the Toronto conference of 1924, parent-child relationships constituted the major refrain, and it has increased in importance ever since. While specialization, as well as the assimilation of biological, psychological, and psychiatric concepts, may have produced a momentum of emphasis toward this or that individual, which may have led to a temporary imbalance, we were aided in regaining our balance not only by our casework techniques, but also by the assimilation of psychoanalytic concepts, which have made so meaningful the interrelationships of the family circle. Whereas we might otherwise have been led to trends toward "scrapping" the family, the psychoanalytic point of view has aroused a deep-lying and far-reaching appreciation of the family as a basic need and a high potential in both causation and treatment. Our objective, therefore, has been and will continue to be not only the adjustment of the individual to the family, but also the reconciliation of the family to the individual's needs, in order that his basic parental identifications and emotional conditionings may be as constructive as possible. This facilitates his adjustment to society, which, in that it is essentially an enlarged family, will inevitably repeatedly recreate his early life experiences for him.

The number of psychiatrically trained social workers who have found a place in non-psychiatric as well as psychiatric centers is significant. The membership of the American Association of Psychiatric Social Workers, where training and experience is quite homogeneous, represents the following diverse fields of service: hospitals for mental diseases; institutions for the feebleminded; research work; educational institutions, including grade and secondary schools and colleges; institutions for delinquents; protective and probationary agencies; state societies for mental hygiene; mental-hygiene clinics; nursing and health agencies; vocational-adjustment centers; nursery schools; training schools; family social casework; children's institutions and child-placing agencies; recreation projects and settlements; and private psychiatric social work. Child-placing, temporary or permanent, in foster homes and in institutions, largely the result of broken families, has offered a fertile field for the application of mental-hygiene concepts. The transplanting of children tends to induce emotional maladjustments that call for psychiatric assistance, not only for the children, but also for the institutions and families involved.

The family casework field has also a high capacity for assimilating psychiatric techniques, for not only does it deal with many maladjusted personalities, but it is also in a position, on the basis of its expert application of casework methods, to make effective use of them. Furthermore, it is safeguarded against any tendency to overstress the individual by its ingrained appreciation of the family as a whole and by the fact that the realities of the situation necessitate an inclusive point of view. In the matter of the worker-client relationship—in terms of emotional quality—the handling of which is a vital factor in success or failure, the family caseworker, through the nature of her services, has an opportunity to make this relationship particularly dynamic, even though *relief* in itself frequently makes the situation highly problematic.[6] Similarly, casework health programs, and others are taking over the principles of psychiatry and the assimilation of this into an already existing body of knowledge is shifting the emphasis of the work. Work is, moreover, increasingly extended to include the dependent young, and progressive education and mental hygiene are joining hands in the effort not only to prevent maladjustment, but to realize more fully the potentialities of growing individualities for happiness and effectiveness. Crichton Miller, the English psychiatrist, has put it in terms of three phases of development: the first, when the teacher of Latin needed to know Latin; the second, when it was recognized that in order to teach Johnny, the teacher must know Latin and Johnny; and the third, when it was realized that the teacher must know *herself* in order to do her job. . . .

With the specialization of psychiatry there came a period of extensive referring of individuals to psychiatric sources. Two difficulties became paramount. It was recognized (1) that existing facilities could not handle all the problems referred; and (2) that, in the case of individuals and families under the supervision of other agencies, the specialties

6. As substantiated in Grace F. Marcus *Some Aspects of Relief in Family Case-work,* (New York: Charity Organization Society of New York, 1929).

could not be expected to adapt its contribution to the functions of the referring agency. As a result, two developments have taken place. The non-psychiatric agency has taken over personnel from the psychiatric field as caseworkers, or as consultants, to assist in the process of adaptation at the level of the agency's needs. In addition, the psychiatric clinics are increasingly offering their services at the level of the needs of the various agencies. They are also doing a more interpretive job. As part of this, there has developed what is generally termed coöperative work, in which the caseworker of the referring agency continues to function as a caseworker with the clinic, furnishing the social data, participating in the clinical conference on the case, and carrying out treatment on her own ground, with subsequent consultation aid from the clinic.

The permeation of the field has been so extensive that the query is already being made: Why the psychiatric social worker? Should not all social workers be psychiatric? It is agreed that all social workers should be psychiatric to the degree that the job demands, but not all jobs need an equally intensive application of psychiatric techniques. It would, therefore, seem unnecessary for all social workers to take intensive psychiatric training, but highly necessary for some to be so trained for the jobs that do require an intensive application. The eagerness of the profession to absorb mental hygiene and the effective use that caseworkers in general are making of psychiatric techniques challenge the specialized psychiatric social worker to high standards and to creative efforts, if she is to meet the need for a specialized leadership. Her response to this challenge will probably determine her future. A few of the present needs seem to be as follows:

1. Because of the scarcity of psychiatrists, and because of the fact that treatment must be largely extramural and therefore in the social worker's hands, she should be taking on more treatment on a more intensive level, which means that she must perfect her treatment techniques.

2. She should do this not only for the good of her cases, but also in order to be able to articulate social-psychiatric

treatment concepts for those who are less specialized, or whose jobs do not afford an opportunity for intensive work because of a lack of psychiatric supervision, high pressure, or some other reason.

3. If she is to formulate principles of theory and practice, she must keep in touch with the various fields, not only for an awareness of the general level of psychiatric development, but for an appreciation of the problems of the particular fields.

4. There is a need for social psychiatric research of a qualitative nature, particularly in the field of treatment.

5. The increase in training courses in social psychiatry in various schools and organizations calls for this specialization in the supervisors. In short, if psychiatric social work is to mean to the general caseworking field what psychiatry means to the general medical field, then there will probably be a permanent need for a more specialized group to act as a contributing source to the general field.

Naturally, social diagnosis seems to have an adequacy of technique that has not yet been realized in treatment. In spite of considerable adequacy in diagnosis, is it possible that we lack confidence in our diagnostic material? If not, it would seem to follow as the night the day that we would hold with assurance to our diagnostic evidence and treat with confidence. The truth of the matter possibly is that we are afraid of treatment. Our fears, moreover, are probably not due so much to insecurity in diagnosis as to personal insecurity in the handling of the worker-client relationship. With a new awareness of our personal needs in our work, we hesitate in the handling of the essential close identifications, lest we not be sufficiently detached and thus make the relationship a destructive one. Or if we do tackle treatment unhesitatingly, it is sometimes without an awareness of our own personal needs, which later block the treatment response and thus make for failure. The social worker is beginning to realize the need for handling her own problems, for working out certain adjustments apart from the job, for building in constructive satisfactions in avocations, so that she will be less dependent for emotional satisfaction upon her relationships with her patients. That she needs to face and to handle some of her own inadequacies if she is to be a source of adequacy to others, is fairly generally realized.

In looking to the future, we reflect that past and present trends toward specialization have been a maturation process. Further growth, however, demands integration, for specialization without synthesis would mean eventual disintegration. The process of synthesis is now underway, the facilitating factors having been our training schools and other organizations of leadership, such as The National Committee for Mental Hygiene and the Commonwealth Fund. Blocks preventing integration have occurred, on the basis, more frequently than otherwise, of the personal needs of the individuals identified with the organizations. Thus the handling of the inter-organization relationship, like that of the worker-client relationship, is interfused with individual need. The growing awareness of this factor, with the tendency to objectify professional relationships through the application of mental-hygiene concepts, is a hopeful note. . . .

. . . Education, the changed economic status of women, and the industrial system affecting all classes, have operated to change the point of view on personal adequacy. The state's growing assumption of responsibility for causal factors in the production of personal inadequacy militates against the former "charitable" attitude toward dependency. During and after the World War, many adequate individuals were rendered temporarily inadequate. A large group of ex-service men and their families were served through social casework methods, not only in matters of relief, but in varied types of need. With the formation of child-guidance, school, and adult psychiatric clinics, a large group from all levels of society were likewise served by social casework. There has been a growing tendency for persons with small incomes, though economically independent, to go to medical clinics where they frequently come into contact with social service. The visiting teacher is entering a wide range of homes. Thus, the general level of the assisted group is higher than formerly; in fact, there is no fixed group of the assisted. Moreover, those assisting no longer come largely from the rich; their "adequacy" lies in their equipment for the particular service to be rendered. Thus the relationship [between assisted and assisting] has been removed from a class or economic basis to an objective professional basis. . . .

The Individual
in Relation to
Social Change

THIS IS A COMPLEX, ponderous article even with the deletions that have been made. It must be viewed in the context of a complex, ponderous, and kaleidoscopic time. It carries two major themes: one, the indivisibility of social work—and casework—from the larger social order; second, the search for insights by which to understand the human dilemmas that were being highlighted at this time, both in their individual and in their societal forms. It sets down the thinking and plaints and hopes of a social worker deeply concerned with what was happening in private and public worlds, and while today's reader must inevitably see things quite differently, having the benefit of thirty years of hindsight, there remain here many insights and perspectives that deserve our further thought.

The time was 1939. The Social Security Act was not yet four years old; its implementation machinery and its applications still creaked at the hinges and failed here and there. The depression had still not lifted; this was to occur dramatically when war began in Europe, half a year later. Charlotte Towle, working with her colleague faculty members, Edith Abbott and Sophonisba Breckinridge, was

Excerpted from *Social Service Review*, vol. 13, no. 1 (March 1939).

deeply affected by their mixture of critical pessimism and militant hope about the future of income-maintenance programs. The limitations of casework as a social change factor are frankly faced—"one cannot but regard casework as a sustaining force within an imperfectly realized democracy."

Like all of us in the dark years of the thirties, Charlotte Towle was aware and wracked by the rise of totalitarianism across Europe and the bloody aggressions by which it maintained itself. Democracy and all its hopes never seemed more precarious or precious. So, like many of us, Charlotte Towle tried to find answers to what were the motives and drives in man that led to his fierce brutalities or cold indifference.

What is put forward herein must be viewed within yet another context—that of contemporary explanatory theory. Freud's *Civilization and Its Discontents,* that powerful and pessimistic view of aggression in man, was scarcely ten years old. Anna Freud's *The Ego and the Mechanisms of Defense* had come out less than two years before. Charlotte Towle immersed herself deeply in such sources. As the modern reader will detect she reflects here an early Freudianism, which was later to undergo considerable modification as she came under the influence of the newly emergent ego psychology and herself made some signal contributions to it. But at the time this article was written the "strong superego" appeared to be the bête noir in the human makeup. Today, when the cry is that the superego is all but a vestigial function, one may smile at this. Yet, Charlotte Towle was never so naive, as the article reveals, as to take a one-cause view of any human problem, and she shows very clearly, too, her doubts about whether, indeed, it is valid to try to understand group and societal behaviors by an individual-system model.

The discerning reader will find herein disconcerting echoes and some illuminations of problems that plague us today.

H. H. P.

These turbulent times prompt the individual to try to find himself. Uprooted, he gropes for footing on familiar terrain. He seeks to find where he stands today in relation to where he thought he stood yesterday. People are talking, talking, talking, in vehement, anxious tones. They no longer talk so much of the small circumstances of daily life as world affairs, broad social issues, baffling economic forces; and inevitably their anxiety centers about the effects of change upon themselves, if not as individuals, at least as members of some group.

Social workers as members of a profession that is an integral part of the social scheme are experiencing change in their relation to the social order through drastic change in their traditional sources of security. Accordingly, they too are thinking, talking, and writing on this subject, which they approach with the purpose of clarifying their own confusion as to where the profession stands today in relation to where it stood yesterday. They ponder also its present function with particular reference to the assumption of constructive leadership. . . . It would seem that only as social forces combine to enable man to resolve constructively that ever existent basic conflict between his instinctual urges and group demands have we ever worked toward the democratic ideal or can we at present do so. This leads one to reflect upon the nature of the human individual in relation to the nature of democracy, . . . of how change may occur within a democracy and to evaluate the significance of social work for that process.

In the first instance, we are limited by our present understanding of human nature and can only utilize some prevalent point of view. In presenting the nature of the individual the psychoanalytic point of view is arbitrarily chosen [here] because of its wide and deep influence not only on casework thinking but also on the literature and drama of the day. Many of those who serve people today as well as many of those who depict them bring this particular understanding to their task even though they may recognize that tomorrow their understanding may be a quite different one. Regarding man then from this standpoint we see him coming into the world as a bundle of instinctual strivings operating under the pleasure principle to achieve satisfaction for impulsive needs. At the start of life he is assumed to be almost wholly dominated by these strivings, which Freud has termed the "unconscious."[1] In adult life hopefully the unconscious becomes only one element of the personality. Freud depicts it as the dark, inaccessible part of the personality, a chaos of excitations, which is open toward the somatic through which it receives energizing impulses. It is unorganized, produces no collective will, knows no moral values, is irrational, and a purely primitive dynamic force which would soon destroy itself in its striving for instinctual gratification. Immediately in the interest of survival the unconscious begins to be modified by contact with the outer world and there develops an enlightened part known as the ego, which Freud describes as being comparable to the integument with which any living matter surrounds itself.

The ego's function is to act as a governor through receiving and preserving stimuli and interpreting them to the unconscious for its own good. Therefore, there is soon interposed between impulse and action the delay of thought processes, during which experience enters, advises, and modifies action. Specifically, then, the child soon finds its enacted instinctual strivings bringing discipline or taboo, and because he values the parent, initially as a gratifying source of food and warmth, and eventually as a love object to whom he is obligated, he modifies the primitive strivings in order to insure his security in the parents. Thus the ethical values, customs, and ways of a particular culture are assimilated and become temporarily his values and his ways. The young child insofar as he is civilized recapitulates his elders and reacts in accordance with or in revolt against the culture values of his group. [This part of the] ego is largely imposed and has therefore been designated as superego, vestiges of which remain with him throughout

1. Sigmund Freud, *The Ego and the Id*, trans. Joan Riviere (London: Hogarth, 1927).

life in varying degrees of dominance, depending upon his eventual development. Gradually as he experiments with the ways and values, and as he grows less dependent on his parents, he begins to form his own set of values, selecting from his cultural heritage those which are workable and relatively satisfying to him and rejecting those which do not serve his purpose. This development of his own ego to supplant in some measure the superego constitutes the very core of the growth process. Only as the individual struggles through and resolves the conflict between his instinctual drives and his social reality through testing out and finding his own solutions can he develop any basic inner security and thereby gain a flexible kind of stability to serve him in an ever changing world.

Much individual resistance to social change might be explained in terms of the lifelong dominance of the superego within the personality structure. Many individuals think as their parents thought and adhere rigidly, though sometimes superficially, to their ideologies without reference to a changing world. Many factors varying endlessly seem to obstruct the development of the ego. It is not strange that this occurs. When one considers the child's anxious struggle to adapt his unacceptable instinctual drives to a demanding social order, together with the prolonged period of physical and economic dependence upon his parents in whom his first security is vested, it is not surprising that deep dependence upon parental and social-group values is engendered. Furthermore, deep feelings of obligation to parents, resentment of them because of repressive or possessive handling, anxieties induced through overprotective or neglectful and punitive treatment, fears created by a hostile, too competitive, and depriving social order, all these and countless other factors may operate to defeat the individual in the development of a strong ego. It might be said that at best the human individual carries a strong superego into adult life and that inevitably many function almost wholly under its domination. Freud asserts that although the ego possesses a certain regulative power over the pleasure principle operating in the unconscious, still it leads an anguished

existence in its role as adjusting agent between the environmental demands, the instinctual wishes, and their superego
control. . . .

In turning from an exploration of individual behavior to
collective responses it is recognized that our thinking may
not be valid. The relation between the response of a group
of individuals and the individual reactions of its members
is not clear. Therefore, in this consideration of the broad
social implications of the individual's tendencies, it is
stressed that these ideas are stated as tentative possibilities
rather than as certainties. Focusing then upon the social
import of the assertion that the human individual probably
carries a strong and frequently very dominating superego into adult life, we are led to ponder upon certain
possibilities:

First, it would seem that many individuals out of their
persistent depedency go through life enacting a part projected onto them, due to complications in the emancipation
process. They are not free to live their own lives, but instead
they react in accordance with or in revolt against an imposed pattern. In such instances there is very little self-
identity, for the real self remains relatively undeveloped.
Inevitably there would be very little basic security, for such
a person would lead an uncentered life because his security
is vested in other persons. Satisfaction in reacting a certain
way would be grounded not so much on basic conviction as
on persuasion. Satisfaction would be derived not so much
in terms of what basically meets one's need as on an ap-
peasement of need. Realization throughout life must be an
infantile sort of gratification for such persons rather than
a positive and dynamic kind of pleasure in reacting in ways
which are genuinely one's own because they have been
emotionally assimilated in the struggle of resolving basic
conflicts. Conflicts must persist because, instead of having
been basically resolved, they have been only eased or even
narcotized.

When such an individual encounters social change one
might expect him to be filled with anxiety. His ideologies
would be a superstructure to which he would have to cling

tenaciously, decrying any change. Or if change, drastic and sudden, came in spite of him, he would need to adhere to the new as abjectly as he had done to the old. A Democrat yesterday, a Fascist today—and perhaps a more comfortable citizen than he ever was as a member of a democracy, for he might well be easy prey for a totalitarian state or any authoritative political system. As we look beyond the individual to the group we see democracy persisting as a kind of imposed political system rather than becoming an enacted social philosophy. Indeed, for many it means little more than a political system with a right to operate only in certain well-defined areas. A few perhaps have accepted it as a way of life. Lip service to ideologies would seem to emerge as a symptom of individuals who have inherited them through the superego rather than having accepted them through their own choice.

Second, it is clear that whereas the ego functions as a regulator with a certain power over, and capacity to direct, instinctual strivings, the superego might be described as an oppressor of these same strivings. This is a decisive point. When the individual carries a very strong superego into adult life, his primitive drives are being repressed rather than resolved. One may then expect devious solutions and explosive reactions of an unstable nature rather than socially constructive sublimations. Repression stimulates destructive unconscious reactions. There are countless ways in which repressed conflicts find devious solution; in fact, they may produce many types of asocial and uncomfortable adjustments from minor delinquencies and slight emotional disturbances to criminality and the major psychoses. The difference between repression as implied in a dominating superego and self-control as implied in a strong ego lies in the fact that in repression the individual evades the conflict without conquering it, while in self-control the conflict is redirected into some socially acceptable activity which gives the individual not only a sense of accomplishment but also a justification of self, that is a satisfaction in self as part of the social scheme.

Focusing now upon these concepts of personality formation in relation to an individual's reaction to social change, we might expect the individual with the strong superego to present certain problems as a citizen. Perhaps it is significant of a devious solution through negation that some individuals are loud in their anxious cries against any change in and by way of the democratic scheme which would interfere with their own undemocratic way of life. Perhaps it is significant of abject submission as an evasive or self-punitive solution that certain individuals endure the coercion of authoritative individual and political systems. Perhaps it is significant of a pressure outburst that others gravitate to organizations which enact hostility toward the social scheme rather than into groups which are endeavoring to think and plan constructively. These speculations lead to the assumption that the dominated and repressed individual who brings into adult life an infantile ego becomes a precarious member of society—particularly during periods of drastic change. Primitive strivings that are held in check rather than constructively resolved may prove a ready foil for primitive leadership, particularly if it emerges in the guise of a beneficently punitive parent person.

Before giving further consideration to the individual within the democratic scheme we should reflect upon the nature of democracy. Although commonly understood as a political system, there is less general recognition of its importance as a social philosophy with significance for every form of group life.

Democracy is first of all a faith in man, in his worth, his possibilities, his ultimate dependability. . . . Central for the democratic faith is the conviction as to the sacredness of human personality. Man is always to be treated as an end, never as property or tool as Kant pointed out and as the prophets and Jesus made plain long centuries before. Against all exploitations by class or vested privilege, against those ancient social ends of slavery and the assumed inferiority of women and the defenselessness of childhood, against persistent feelings of race superiority, and of contempt for others, there stands this conviction of democracy, that property and government and church are here for men and not men for these institutions, that it is man as man that counts, not man as male or white or nordic or rich or wise, and that nothing less than the well-being of all men can be the goal of social change.[2]

It is evident that this ideal will be realized only through the operation of two principles—those of freedom and obligation. Man must be free not merely to struggle for physical survival through working for food and shelter, but he must be free also to struggle for mental and emotional survival. He must be free to realize his own identity through searching for truths and faiths that serve his purpose. He must give expression to his personality in determining conditions of government and industry in order that those institutions may be dynamic in accordance with his changing needs rather than static obstacles to change. "Men and nations are no more created free than they are created equal."[3] This freedom comes not as a gift or through ruthless action but instead through the individual's struggle for insight and self-mastery in both public and private life. For individuals and nations the opportunity for self-determination, therefore, is the only way to a realization of democratic ideals. It has long been recognized that unrestrained freedom defeats itself through bringing externally imposed restrictions. Insofar as man emphasizes rights rather than obligation, license rather than liberty, he defeats democratic ideals and in so doing endangers democracy's very existence. In practicing a philosophy of "rugged individualism" he could bring upon himself imposed restrictions in the form of a totalitarian state. Democracy opposes arbitrary and irresponsible authority, but stands for authority engendered through understanding and self-responsibility.

When we envisage the ideals and principles of democracy and feel in contrast the impact of present hostile, aggrandizing, depriving, and frustrating social forces, our first impulse is to say that society is sick; and throughout the literature of social work and related fields one has recently noted statements to that effect. Certainly it is clear that a

2. Harris Franklin Rall, "Social Change," *Religion and Public Affairs* (New York: Macmillan, 1937), p. 217.
3. *Ibid.*

democratic way of life has been only very imperfectly realized, perhaps even only dimly comprehended. It has been recognized, however, that it is erroneous to explain collective problems by concepts such as "neurotic" or "normal" taken from individual psychology and therapy.[4] Society has been and always will be an ever changing combination of forces and values.

Human survival is only assured through man's acceptance of its inevitable pains and through his capacity for satisfaction in the struggle itself. Man's safety lies not in dogmatic formulas or in the rigid structure of his institutions but in the proper balance of constantly changing factors. It is recognized that circumstances such as floods, famines, drought, plagues, economic depressions, vast physical resources or the lack of them, can operate to bring a threatening degree of change. Incalculable events such as wars, discoveries, inventions, may bring unexpected cultural developments. Man has always grappled with such forces for survival, and his struggle has differed from that of other animal species only insofar as it has not been a blind struggle but a conscious one to which he has brought purposive effort. "For it is a singular thing, this human nature, and distinguished from the rest of nature by the very fact that it is has been endowed with the idea, is dominated by the idea and cannot exist without it, since human nature is what it is because of the idea."[5] Although we may be discouraged by man's present inability to fulfill the democratic ideology, such an ideology exists, in fact long has existed in one form or another. This brings conviction that the ideas of freedom, justice, obligation, and the dignity of man inherent in this philosophy are an expression of man's psychological need. Any optimism that we have today is rooted in this belief that man strives to fulfill certain psychological needs as well as physical ones and that there is a fundamental desire for those conditions of life for which democ-

4. See Otto Rank, *Modern Education* (New York: A. A. Knopf, 1932) and his "Psychology and Social Change," *News Letter* (American Association of Psychiatric Social Workers [January, 1935]). See also Jules Eisenbud, "Social Work, Psychiatry, and Social Science," *News Letter* (Autumn 1938).

5. Thomas Mann, *The Coming Victory of Democracy* (New York: A. A. Knopf, 1938), p. 16.

racy stands. Insofar as this need is conscious its realization becomes an assured rather than a haphazard eventuality.

It is clear that the ideals and principles of a democracy represent man's idea of himself as a mature being, free from the domination of an infantile ego, whose instinctual strivings are readily sublimated and who has attained a high degree of inner security which enables him to move flexibly within a changing social scheme. He no longer needs to cling so much to the old in the new because the capacity for resolving the conflict between his instinctual strivings and the social demands of the moment lies within himself. He is no longer so dependent on others that he needs to evade self-responsibility or be sustained through the approval and support or condemnation and punishment of others. What forces are obstructing this realization of self? It is apparent that man is restricted through the domination of the past over his present. . . .

Change in man is slow; change in those institutions through which man expresses collective thinking and will may be even slower. For example, headway in the re-education of teachers may be delayed by the difficulty in changing the school system so that principles of progressive education may be utilized in any thoroughgoing way. Social workers are well aware of the inhibiting effects which may occur through discrepancy between changing philosophies and unchanging agency structure. It is only as man becomes critically aware of these limitations that he will exert deliberate effort to effect structural change and that he will in the meantime function more effectively within the limitations of existing institutional structures.

It is clear that any basic change in personality development essential to a full realization of democratic ideals and principles can occur only from within through a widespread but at the same time an individualized re-educational process. Recognition of the need for a realistic struggle to secure a free and responsible life for all individuals through conscious and purposive effort expended in re-educating social and educational leaders is a basic step in effecting social change. . . .

. . . With reference to gradual change, we would like to think that the child of today is having a more democratic experience within his family than his predecessors had. We might reassure ourselves on this by citing the growing awareness on the part of parents of their responsibility to their children in the area of personality development as well as in physical care. This is evidenced in widespread attendance by parents from all social and economic groups at behavior clinics, parent-teacher meetings, and child-study groups. They turn to the doctor, minister, teacher, social agency, librarian, lay club leaders, court officials, and to others. There is evidence that the educational programs conducted over the radio and through the press are reaching parents in all walks of life. It is recognized by those who have dealt with many parents that this does not mean that all will be able to get the kind of help which they need in order to become more effective parents [but] there is evidence here of an active striving for something—perhaps in some instances comfort and affirmation of parental prerogatives, in other instances surely a desire for help in doing differently and in realizing more satisfying and constructive intrafamily relationships.

. . . One ponders upon the impacts upon traditional family structure, such as the frequent employment of both parents outside the home; the widespread unemployment of the father, with the mother sometimes assuming the role of wage-eagner; the deep insecurities which come to parents through a too competitive and hostile world. When the head of a family no longer has any security as wage-earner and is threatened not only with loss of status in the eyes of an achievement-worshiping world, but also in the eyes of his family; when the erstwhile head of the family has lost his usual means of physical survival, and with it the opportunity for release of conflict through creative activity; then one might expect reversion to primitive strivings or the assertion of those strivings to such an extent that his whole energy must go into repression of unsocial impulses or into handling the resultant anxieties. To what extent are these stresses and strains being projected onto children through punitive handling, through increased striving for self-realization in them, through overprotective tendencies, through overtly enacted rejection of responsibility for them, or through some other enactment of the anxiety and frustration which parents are experiencing. When the parent has been unable to cope with the world outside the home, when he is anxiously dependent and at the mercy of the latest relief policy, or when the work of today may be gone tomorrow—in short, when his affairs are in the hands of other people rather than in his own—then how is the child to gain any sense of security through that parent either within the home or in relation to the world? What sort of free and responsible life are such children having as preparation for democratic citizenship? Are they instead being well grounded for a regime which affords the security of efficient management, which affords work even on a conscripted labor basis, which identifies them with a militant system through which they can express their now dominant primitive inclinations? Such a system would be a persuasive opponent to the democracy which many people are experiencing today. . . .

The market is flooded with literature on social and economic questions, and there is great demand for these publications. Running a close second, one finds articles and books in the field of psychology and psychiatry. From every conceivable angle the human personality is being analyzed and surveyed. Good, bad, and indifferent, almost any publication of a psychological nature becomes a best seller, which means that many classes and conditions of people are reading with more serious intent today than yesterday. Granted that some may be reading as an escape or for comfort derived through self-centered concern in themselves, still, the significant point again is that people are seeking something; and one wonders if this is evidence that they are seeking to understand—to find themselves in relation to this strange new scheme. Again one suspects discomfort, confusion, and perhaps a distorted faith in the written word, but the hopeful note lies in the fact that they assume responsibility for informing or misinforming themselves; that they read and discuss; that interest seethes and seeks an outlet. This brings the realization that this is a strategic time not only in family life but in human life as it participates in other groups outside the family. This interest in self and, even more important, of the relation of self to other factors and forces in life is something to utilize in the interests of democracy.

The school perhaps next to the home is a strong determinant in social change in that it has the opportunity to wield prolonged influence over every educable child. Just as there is prone to be a relationship between the structure of the family and the political structure of a nation, just so there seems to be a relationship between the educational system and the political structure. Perhaps it is significant that in the age of "rugged individualism," which some of us revered as an essentially democratic period, the school was not democratically organized, the curriculum was planned with small regard for individual difference, and the teaching methods were essentially an autocratic imposition of certain knowledge with little reference to the will, the inclination, or the capacity of its subjects. Academic education, rigidly standardized around a misinterpretation of the precept that all men are created free and equal, comprised for many individuals a meaningless jungle to which they were sentenced by essential compulsory-education laws which in turn brought the need for differential educational measures. In the absence of these they endured and survived the system through erecting protections rather than through participating in an educational process.

We cannot attribute certain attitudes and ineptitudes in the present generation of adults specifically to their educational experience, but we cannot refrain from wondering about the part which the educational system has played in creating such attitudes as resistance to authority; abject worship of and dependence on the printed word; fear of new contents of knowledge with resultant indifference or submissive acquisition rather than assimilation; anxious evasion of truths, a preference for half-truths, and an inclination for myths rather than realities. We ponder also upon such responses as contentment with seeming to be rather than satisfaction in being; self-aggrandizing striving for prestige, evidencing a need to grade well in life with less concern about doing well; worship of certain walks of life rather than appreciation of all forms of occupational endeavor; unwillingness to participate in action for the common good; resignation to things as they are with disinclination to initiate change or to tolerate it. In short, the many ineffectual, uncentered, distorted responses and attitudes which bespeak man's lack of development as a social being suggest that the educational system of the past failed to assume its part within a democracy. One wonders to what extent it has operated as a repressive, regimenting force, thereby strengthening man's dependence on imposed patterns rather than as a vitalizing force through which man has been helped in finding his own solutions. . . .

It is beyond the scope of this writer and this paper to discuss the structure of the economic order, its operating principles and laws, or perhaps with Mr. Arnold we should say its rationalizing "folklore."[6] Certainly it is clear even to the layman that in this area of life man has lived out his primitive strivings with benefit of very little inward or outward restraint. Perhaps this is inevitable, when we consider that the economic life of the individual is closely and directly connected with the primitive urge for physical survival—the quest for food and shelter. The animal in man would naturally be most overtly expressed in this area. But, unlike the animal, man's strivings go beyond simple primitive needs. His ideas have created other needs, and one dominating idea seems to have been his concept of himself in relation to other men. One would assume here the origin of the drive for supremacy which may be expressed in socially constructive or socially destructive forms. As society grows more complex so that restraints increase, the need to enact primitive strivings increases, bringing greater demands upon the superego and a more precarious chance for survival to the ego, through whose development socially

6. Thurman W. Arnold, *The Folklore of Capitalism* (New Haven: Yale University, 1937).

constructive sublimations are made possible. The strengthening of the superego structure as represented by governmental forces is hopefully set through democratic procedures growing out of man's realization of his own limitations as a help to himself.

In this country it would seem that among other factors our plentiful resources made it possible for men to acquire supremacy through the acquisition of wealth without constituting too great a threat to the security of others so that in time this form of supremacy became the socially approved form; in fact, the ego ideal of the people. To be rich was to be powerful and wise. The methods of attaining wealth became a minor consideration since primitive strivings in this area now had social approval and therefore the need to repress or to sublimate was greatly diminished. A man could live untroubled in the economic world under the ideology of the jungle—though he might still need to conform to a more socialized ideology in other areas of life. Insofar as he was able to insulate the two codes he lived untroubled. But insofar as he could not quite reconcile the two within himself or in the eyes of others he has been forced to express his conflict in various ways. . . .

The ideology of the capitalistic system has become part and parcel of the thinking of many people. They have come to revere wealth and to cherish the illusion that real democratic freedom lies in the opportunity to strive for prestige and power through material gains. Personal worth is equated with financial worth. They are therefore intolerant of the very idea of government regulation of the economic order. They see it as a threat to their freedom rather than as a protection, and consequently react with anxious resistance. They have not yet faced the fact that the average man's chance for attaining this goal is growing increasingly more remote as the present system gains power. . . .

Men have not yet recognized that it is not only compatible with the democratic scheme but inherent in it that the people exert control over their own economic order through their own instrument—the government. They have instead preferred to leave its management to the unchecked personal drives of their fellow-men who, not being officially responsible, have felt little obligation to anyone but themselves. Perhaps because man has desired unrestricted freedom he has been loath to endanger his potential chance for attaining it. If the situation is left so that all are unrestrained then it becomes each man's prerogative to get this enviable privilege for himself, and for this illusion he pays. . . .

Another factor entering into the evasion of delegating authority in the economic order may have been man's fear of authority. We flee from what we fear. We fear what we have not basically accepted and utilized. Perhaps, then, it has been temporarily more comfortable for man to shed the responsibility for coming to grips with his own need for authority than to face it. It has been the line of least resistance to evade the fact that coercion was being exerted so long as it remained anonymous through being vested in parties relatively unknown and presumably unorganized. Whatever the motivation, it is clear that man's concepts of freedom and authority are a commentary on his stage of development. His response has been essentially immature and suggestive of a need to overthrow superego controls or to evade them through cherishing illusions of freedom. A need to be self-governing, as implied in strong development of the ego structure, it is believed, would have led inevitably to greater expression of a collective will and to an increased capacity to trust others, thus making some more adequate centralization of power in his own government possible. . . .

. . . People may be more ready for confident leadership than certain economically controlled sources of propaganda would have our leaders believe. There are many indications that the people are actively seeking some new source of security. We would like to believe that their strivings for something different are rooted in basic growth and readiness for more mature participation in a self-governing process. . . . Our concern today is that people will be coerced in thinking, feeling, and action. That their deepest needs could well carry them in this direction is already indicated. Their present deepest need would seem to be for security as implied in the essentials of existence and in help through democratic procedure in establishing regulations which protect them against the primitive impulses of their own kind. And where else would the members of a democracy expect to find security except through governmental action, which presumably expresses these needs for them? If their government fails to serve them it will be because in the last analysis they have intrusted their will to those who do not truly represent them. . . . The deepest need of the people, therefore, is for social and political leadership which exerts coercion for them rather than submitting to coercion with them. Therefore, the aggressive leadership of President Roosevelt, which has resulted in the passage of the Social Security Act, the Wagner Labor Relations Act, the Housing Act, the Fair Labor Standards Act, gives hope of the survival of democracy. . . .

In evaluating the significance of social work in social change one must consider first its dual motivation. Inherent in social work, as the core of its existence, is man's capacity to feel with man. Through identification the advantaged man feels with the disadvantaged one—he comprehends himself in that position and is impelled to succor him. His idea of himself is injured if he leaves his fellow-man in dire plight. Inevitably, then, if the numbers of the disadvantaged grow great they comprise a group that constitutes a threat to the happiness and security of those who otherwise could be comfortable. Around this core there has come also, as man has experienced family life, a feeling of obligation to others and a capacity to care for others insofar as he has experienced love in his relationships and sufficient emancipation to permit him to love outside of self. . . .

Operating against these more altruistic motives are the primitive strivings which would prompt man to look out only for himself and which induce no concern for the welfare of another. In group life, however, even when responding predominantly on the level of instinctual drives the unsocial individual frequently found that it paid to help another. He learned that any appreciable number of disadvantaged persons were a threat to him and to his possessions and that to appease the needs of a demanding individual or group constituted a measure of self-protection or even a source of power. That these three elements operate today in society's altruistic response is evidenced by the nature of many charity appeals. We note that they appeal to some individuals through making graphic the dire suffering of others—What if this child were yours? etc. To others, through ideas of social justice. To a third group charitable measures are presented as a practical policy with some argument such as "poverty begets sickness and crime and therefore constitutes a threat to the well-endowed." It is probable that these three points of view are closely intermingled within society today.

The Malthusian theory's wide and deep influence on relief practices in America has persisted throughout the nineteenth century into the present. This theory condemned the principle of public relief on the grounds that the poor were responsible for their own misery and would be harmed further through help readily obtained. It excluded the disadvantaged by establishing the principle that they had no rightful claim on society. Furthermore, it expressed the hope that if the more deserving destitute were saved it would be through the pity of kind benefactors to whom, therefore, they ought then "be bound by the stringent ties of gratitude." Thus the poor were denied society's sanction and placed at the mercy of and in subservient position to its advantaged members, whom Malthus believed would derive greater spiritual values from voluntary giving than from enforced giving. The influence of this thinking reached its peak in this country in the latter half of the nineteenth century when social welfare leaders took action in abolishing outdoor relief on the assumption that it could not be reformed. They at the same time exerted pressure for the extensive development of private benevolent societies which they indorsed. Thus there came a vast system of privately endowed charitable services which are still with us while the vestigial belief in their superior value as compared with public assistance persists. A prolonged depression of vast scope finally seems to have proved the inefficacy of this system, and one of the major gains of recent years has been the re-establishment of the principle that the destitute have a claim on society.

Certainly it is clear that for social work to be wholly under private control is not compatible with the ideals of a democracy. Owing to such support the ranks of professional social workers as well as many leaders were slow to function democratically since they did not see themselves or their profession as part of the democratic scheme. Being identified with the rich in the service of the poor, their attitudes too often were dominating and appeasing.

Gradually, however, the profession has shifted its focus from the supporting rich to the people whom it serves and it is beginning to function more nearly as a part of the democratic scheme. Many factors have operated in producing this change, but the contribution of those social leaders and educators in the field of professional social work, who saw beyond the times and who long ago exerted strong leadership in striving for democratic ideals in social work through emphasizing the need for reform of the poor laws rather than for their abolishment, cannot be overestimated. They not only laid the groundwork to be utilized in more receptive times, but they also set a pattern for social workers to function as leaders rather than as followers in the process of social change.

If it is true that social work reflects the thinking and feeling of the times, then one can feel encouraged about some present trends. For within the field of professional social work there is a conscious and determined emphasis upon the importance of the human individual as an individual, with rights not merely to sustenance but also to a free and responsible way of life. . . .

The field of social work is divided into two types of services —those which aim to better conditions for whole groups of people and those which help people with their individual needs. In the first group of activities social workers have always been essentially identified with the people against adverse social conditions. In striving for minimum wage laws, child labor laws, sanitary laws, workman's compensation, unemployment insurance, and such measures, they have exerted influence for social change. Likewise, in administering community health programs, in establishing and conducting social settlements and other such activities, they have worked in behalf of the physical and social welfare of many individuals and in so doing have strengthened democracy. Aside from the improved conditions and enlarged opportunities which have resulted, it is believed that there have been psychological values, intangible and unmeasurable, but inevitably inherent in these services: First, the feeling conveyed to the many people involved in these services that, amidst the impact of all the hostile and competitive forces in their lives, there are friendly and helpful forces operating in their behalf. An enhanced feeling of personal worth could come to people in realizing that they matter that much in the social scheme. The direct work with individuals in groups had the additional advantage of affording a firsthand experience in democracy, providing that the social workers who met with groups did not function authoritatively or with condescension. Now, today, when trained workers in increasing numbers are group leaders and now that this professional group sees its function as one of helping people to assimilate democratic ideology through experiencing it, this aspect of social work may exert a more potent influence in social change.[7]

The second group, those services, public and private, which help people with their individual needs through family agencies, children's agencies, medical agencies, psychiatric clinics, and which are administered through casework service, have undergone more functional change in relation to the democratic scene than have the first group of services. These are the services originally under private auspices which were permeated with a more undemocratic philosophy and whose professional authority was molded not so much in behalf of the underprivileged as in behalf of the rich for the underprivileged. Social casework services during a long period of time were probably less effective in producing social change then than we think they are now

7. Grace Coyle, *Studies in Group Behavior* (New York: Harper, 1938), pp. 1–15.

becoming. Insofar as caseworkers imposed plans, took over the client's activity in his own life-situation, moralized, exerted coercion with relief or material benefits as a tool, casework frequently was destructive, engendering dependency and lessening self-respect; it aroused resistance to authority rather than inducing acceptance of it; it contributed to lack of responsibility. Therefore, insofar as social workers functioned this way they made individuals less adequate for a democratic way of life and either more inclined to submit to the demands of an oppressive industrial system or more prone to belligerent attitudes toward the social order. In engendering dependency in relation to material benefits they may have served to appease the client so that he became a less troublesome citizen. Insofar as the competitiveness of life was eased for him he may have derived some superficial security, but insofar as his self-respect was annihilated he would derive basic feelings of insecurity. During this period social casework services, in that they cared for people materially so that large groups of individuals were not conspicuously in need, helped to sustain the economic system which supported the services through justifying it and concealing its inadequacies. . . .

Many factors have operated to bring a democratic influence to the social casework field—notably the contributions of psychiatry, psychology, and related scientific fields. When the social worker began to look at the human individual from a scientific standpoint, man as man became important, for differentiations based on social and economic status, racial, national, or sex factors, conditions of body or mind became less well defined and incidental to his identity as a person. Notable also has been the ever widening group of people in terms of social and economic level who have come to need these services.

As one examines the casework philosophy of today one finds it is essentially a democratic ideology. The basic concepts of casework practice which have been articulated in the literature for some years have been democratic concepts in that they place the center of activity in the client rather than in the agency; they recognize that unless he is mentally incompetent the ultimate responsibility for his situation should be his; they safeguard the client from the intrusion of the agency, believing he can only function effectively insofar as he is granted freedom of choice; they recognize also the agency's responsibility to the community and that insofar as the worker assumes this responsibility in her relationships with the client she may strengthen his feeling of obligation to the community. In stressing the autonomy of the individual rather than the autocracy of the agency, casework today presumably affords the client a democratic experience. In other words, casework today consciously aims to strengthen the ego of the individual and to avoid strengthening the superego structure.

We are well aware of the limitations of casework as a major factor in effecting social change. It must work slowly, individual by individual. It deals with people who have had damaging experiences and whose capacity for fundamental help frequently is meager. It may or may not be able to help the individual to become a more resourceful and adequate citizen. Its present staff may be limited in capacity to function in full accord with its present ideology. It is unable to modify many adverse social circumstances which are destroying people such as unemployment, inadequate educational opportunity, poor housing, lack of medical care, and the like. It can never serve as a substitute for social action but it can serve as an instrument of the people in revealing widespread needs calling for action. Viewed in the long run and in relation to the total social situation one cannot but regard casework as a sustaining force within an imperfectly realized democracy. In that it deals with people during times of stress and strain the values of the relationship which it affords may be deep reaching and determining as one's experiences frequently are at such times. Not all clients are able to articulate these values but occasionally they do, and in such instances one may see that the service has symbolized society's attitude toward them. . . .

The meaning of the agency relationship assumes high significance today when we consider the great number of people who are being served by public agencies, for in the minds and feelings of the people the agency is their government—society itself. It becomes particularly important then that the public agency enact the democratic ideology in its service. Operating against the fulfilment of present democratic philosophy, particularly in the field of public relief, are such factors as lack of sufficient trained personnel for efficient and objective service; inordinately large case loads [resulting in] urgent and sometimes autocratic handling of individuals; submarginal relief policies under which people are forced to endure extreme privation. Clients throughout the country have been experiencing at the hands of local authorities treatment which to them can only bespeak a hostile, depriving, and grossly indifferent government.[8] What is happening to the members of our national body in the hands of local governmental agencies is a matter of national concern. From the humanitarian standpoint and from the standpoint of the future of democracy this responsibility cannot be long ignored. How it is met could well be a potent factor determining the direction of social change while federal assumption of its responsibility in this connection could be one of the social measures promptly taken in the interests of democracy. In discussing private philanthropy it has been brought out that one purpose which it served was to sustain the economic system. Likewise, public social-work programs may serve this purpose. . . . In protecting the economic system from sudden and drastic change the security of the people is thus being sustained. Those who are not interested in seeing it permanently preserved in its present form would look to national leadership for other basic measures, such as democratic control of economic power, which would make relief and unemployment less permanent certainties.

Social change in a democratic direction is indicated in the recent Social Security Act, which provides care for the aged, the unemployed, the children in their own homes needing assistance, mothers and babies, crippled and dependent children, the blind and handicapped persons needing vocational rehabilitation. . . . While the Act has not yet included

8. See the following articles by Edith Abbott: "Public Welfare and Politics," *Social Service Review* 10 (September 1936): 395–412; "Public Assistance—Whither Bound?" *Proceedings of the National Conference of Social Work*, 1937, pp. 1–25; "Federal Relief —Sold Down the River," *Nation* 142 (18 March 1936). 346. See also Gertrude Springer, "Relief in November, 1938," *Survey* 74 (November 1938): 339–44.

all groups in need of assistance, nor provided as adequately as is desirable for those included, its provisions can be supplemented and other groups added as the method is tested and as resources are made available. It is believed that in this comprehensive plan an appropriate instrument has been established for administering to the needs of the people within a democracy. . . .

The psychological import of the Act is manifest. It implies that people in need find their security in their government, which, in the last analysis, is themselves as members of a vast self-governing body. They receive help on the basis of being eligible for it, and insofar as feelings of obligation emerge they are directed toward society as a whole rather than toward a group within the social scheme. In enacting obligation they need not feel subservient to a group but may find instead satisfaction in more resourceful citizenship. There is a popular notion that in feeling eligible for help, that is, secure in seeking aid, the individual will be readily pauperized. The modern psychological point of view inclines us to an opposite inference. While it is granted that some people, those already pauperized through deprivation and exclusion, will use any source of security regressively, it is believed that those not so damaged through previous humiliating experiences will be more prone to maintain their adequacy. Insofar as life is too competitive, hostile, and defeating, the individual reacts with infantile dependency and irrational impulses. Insofar as he has some base of security in his relationships with others and in particular with society he is free to work through his conflicts constructively and in more socialized and rational forms. Probably not until the social order is so organized as to insure every man the meeting of his primitive needs will he become much less primitive in his strivings. The Social Security Act is a step in this direction. The prompt extension of its provisions is indicated as a means of making the democratic way of life more possible. . . .

Now that we no longer feel that democracy is an assured possession we have become conscious of it and it would seem that this would be a peculiarly receptive time for persons in positions of social welfare leadership to see and feel their work in its relationship to the democratic way of life. It is only through conscious and determined effort within our various institutions that we may fulfill its ideals and principles. Basic social change toward democracy will come about slowly as the younger generation and posterity are afforded a more democratic experience within the family, the school, the social group, the social agency, the economic order, and through governmental leadership which relates itself primarily to the people and their good rather than to a group and its interests. There are signs of forward movement in almost all these areas which instill hope for democracy in the long run. In order that what we already have of democracy may be sustained pending more basic social change there is need for an immediate co-ordination of controls between local, state, and federal authorities not only in relation to the relief program but in relation to the enactment of other social measures for the common good. As society grows more complex there is need for a strengthening of the governmental structure, hopefully accomplished through democratic procedure, out of our realization that our own limitations make self-protective measures essential. It is only as the people are assured the essentials of life that we can expect them to be sufficiently rational to value a free and responsible life in the democratic sense.

The Distinctive Function and Attributes of Social Work

THE ARTICLES FROM WHICH these pieces are drawn were concerned with curriculum development in schools of social

Excerpted from "Issues and Problems in Curriculum Development," *Social Work Journal*, vol. 30, no. 2 (April 1949), and "The Distinctive Attributes of Education for Social Work," *ibid.*, vol. 33, no. 2 (April 1952).

work. To teach social work, as to teach any subject matter, it is essential to delineate its special identity and attributes and purposes. This Charlotte Towle did in the paragraphs that follow. In them she speaks succinctly of social work as a dynamic linkage system between individuals and their environment and as an enhancer of both. She is concerned with social work's finding, knowing, and demonstrating its own professional identity. And she reiterates her firm conviction that all processes in social work—casework, group work, community work, administration—have much in common that binds them together.

For the recurrent self-doubts that assail social workers and the recurrent upheavals that undermine our security, here is a simple, forthright statement of what we are and what we are for.

H. H. P.

. . . Perhaps it would simplify matters if we were to consider the function of our profession in a society in which we are aligned with the struggle for the survival of democracy. . . . What is its broad, basic function? In the last analysis all our efforts go back to the good of the individual for the survival of democracy. A democratic society is one in which the individual is assured of something more than physical survival. However, a whole complex of inimical forces endangers his welfare, interferes with his attainment of that state of mature adulthood essential for participation in democratic life. In this scene the profession of social work might be described as an expression of the conscience of the community and as having an integrative function. Its charge is to help individuals one by one and group by group make productive use of the environment. (Environment is used in the broad sense to include resources in relationship.) Its charge also is to help groups safeguard and create conditions favorable for the maximum development of the individual's potentialities.

Throughout social work practice the insistent focus is on relating the inner forces and capacities of man to the external pressures and demands in the interests of his social adaptation. This integrative role is being enacted by social workers constantly. In an institution or in a community where there are multiple services available to an individual, the social caseworker is prepared to play a definite role not only in understanding the person and his need but also in bringing services together in an economical and appropriate treatment procedure. If the social worker puts first things first, often this implies initiating action toward the modification of the services, or of the conditions of life in the institution or community. This may precede or parallel direct work with the individual to effect change in his motivations and reactions.

On the administrative or community planning level the social worker, through understanding common human needs, recognizes unmet need and attempts to provide resources; or organizes, or effects change in, existing resources to meet that need in ways which rehabilitate. He may work with groups of individuals to influence the provision and use of the resources. The social worker then, in a variety of functional roles at various operating levels, is continually focused *on the relationship of man to his environment* with the purpose of effecting a constructive interrelationship. Parents, family members, friends, associates, teachers, physicians, psychiatrists will play a more direct part than the social worker in fashioning and refashioning the individual. Other agents, such as governmental bodies, or social and economic forces will play a more direct part in shaping the conditions of his life. The social worker functions between the two using what each brings to the helping situation.

. . . First and foremost, social work has a distinctive relationship to its community. By social work's very character and function, by reason of the group it serves as well as by the nature of its relationship with its supporting public, social work education must emphasize the development of a high degree of social conscience and social consciousness. Social work is concerned with social ills. It serves a group who need to be protected and at times actively defended. It serves society which also seeks protection through social work.

Social work exists because the community has had a conscience about the disadvantaged and an altruistic impulse to protect those who need help for survival. This conscience seemingly is compounded of many elements, several of which are discernible. First is man's propensity to feel with man, so that as he comprehends himself in the position of the disadvantaged, he is impelled to succor them out of feelings of self-injury and guilt. Second, around the core of man's necessity for identification, he has developed as he has experienced satisfying and constructive group life, a feeling of obligation to others and a capacity to care for others. Inevitably, then, the disadvantaged constitute a source of anxiety and discomfort to those who are socially mature, thus motivating concerted action in behalf of the deprived and oppressed.

At the same time that social work exists because of the social conscience, it exists also because of fear. The disadvantaged, through physical and mental illness and through unsocial and antisocial behavior, become a threat to the common good, thus engendering feelings of helplessness, hostility, and guilt which may beget fear of retaliation. These feelings likewise motivate action, at times urgent and disconcerted. The profession of social work continuously operates under the impact of the mixed feelings of the community. There is fluctuating sympathy with and resentment against the groups served. These attitudes often are directed toward the profession itself. Our community feels both with us and against us. . . .

The second peculiarity of social work is that it operates wholly through agencies and institutions, largely and traditionally those established to educate, heal, and help people, individual by individual or group by group.[1] More

1. For further discussion of this, see Charlotte Towle, "Social Case Work in Modern Society," *Social Service Review* (June 1946).

recently, it has operated within certain systems where its services have been wanted primarily for the efficiency of the system rather than for the welfare of the individuals concerned, even though individual and group welfare has been a byproduct of social work's contribution to the organization—notably in selective service, the armed services, and industry. . . . To a greater extent than other professions, social work is subject to nonprofessional administration and, more often than other professions, it functions within the institutional system of another discipline or occupation.

Again we encounter duality. It is clear that social work has made a place for itself in the minds, if not always in the hearts, of administrators of a wide variety of agencies and institutions. Again, the social worker may encounter a complex of trust and fear. To amplify this point would be to repeat what has been said of social work's singular relationship to its community. Traditionally, social workers have been prone to respond to any demand for their services. When social work is administered by another system, it is inevitable that it must use and be used by that system. Hence, its charge is to determine whether, along with an avowed social welfare purpose, that system's policies, regulations, and provisions defeat or fulfill the aims of social work. When these belie the social welfare purpose, it should be ascertained whether the administrative staff can and will work for change in the program's ways of working, so that its use of social work can be reconciled with the profession's ethics and aims. . . .

Under the administration of another profession in collaboration with other disciplines, social work often is termed an adjunctive service. It is implicit in the very nature of its contribution, however, that it cannot be adjunctive. In a program where there are multiple services available to individuals and groups, the social worker's function is not only that of understanding need in order to meet it through its own services, but it is also that of helping people make productive use of other services, as well as sometimes that of bringing a variety of services together in an economical and appropriate procedure. For this, social work cannot be added on but instead it must serve as an integrative force while becoming an integral part of the program. In the give and take of its multidiscipline practice, it is difficult for social work not to be incorporated by that which it incorporates as it lends itself to use, aligns with the concerns and attempts to carry forward the aims of other disciplines. In association with other professions, social work does not have the problem of inbredness characteristic of the older sacrosanct professions. Instead, it has the problem of promiscuity. Insofar as identification has occurred as a defense against our lack of status, other disciplines are not well served, because in such instances social work subordinates itself, lends itself to misuse, or competes through exploiting its similarity and minimizing its individuality.

It is essential that social work not lose its identity, which implies the realization that it does not serve other disciplines through its likeness to them as much as through its difference from them. With consciousness of professional function and an unwavering identification with their profession, social workers will not invalidly take over that which another discipline does, and fail to do that which they are responsible to do. To engage flexibly and differentially in a working relationship implies the capacity to identify without loss of identity. For this, professional maturity is demanded. . . .

A third respect in which social work is singular is that its helping relationship is different in certain respects from that in other professions. Individuals by and large do not expect to educate themselves, to heal themselves, to conduct their legal affairs without counsel, or to get to heaven without benefit of clergy. The recipients of social work are expected to help themselves. While the active participation of the recipient of services increasingly is being stressed in other professions, still the need for help has full acceptance by both recipient and community. There is no attitude that one should be able to do without teacher, doctor, lawyer, or clergyman. Social work to a peculiar degree is charged and charges itself with the responsibility of helping people to help themselves. For the most part, the services for which people seek aid from social work represent a failure in their expectancy of themselves and in the community's expectation of them. Consequently, the "give" of social work is taken with more humiliation, fear of social consequences, resentment, and resistance than ordinarily occurs in other professional services, psychiatry perhaps excepted.

As a result of these feelings and attitudes on the part of the recipient and of the community, the dependency component implicit in a helping relationship often is feared and denied instead of being acknowledged and respected. The social worker, from the policy-making level of administrative practice to the direct service level of casework and group work practice, knows that adequate, responsible giving is essential for the fulfillment of social work's rehabilitation aims. While knowing this, out of response to the feelings of others he may guiltily and constrictively enact an attitude that in helping people help themselves he must help meagerly.

This complexity in the helping relationship, produced by the conflict between the social worker's knowledge and what he is pressed to feel, exerts several demands on him; notably, that he understand his own feelings and attitudes about dependency and about the particular failures in man and society which bring people into the social services; that he separate himself from the feelings of the recipient and the community in order to effect change in the attitudes of both; that he permit his psychological knowledge to guide his helping hand. This implies recognition that his initial charge in helping people is to help them feel positively about taking help. For the attainment of or for the renewal of the capacity for self-help, feelings of inadequacy must give way to a sense of adequacy, humiliation to self-respect, resentment of help to emotional acceptance of one's need for it. It is demoralizing to be the recipient in a relationship in which one feels hostile. The social worker knows through repetitive experience that the helping hand which hurts is clung to and bitten with resultant guilt and self-contempt, which foster further hostile dependency. Self-dependence emerges through the meeting of dependency in ways which nurture rather than impoverish the ego.

Throughout the life of a helping relationship, it is demanded of a social worker and his program that the recipient be afforded adequate essential services in the context of a relationship which is flexibly oriented to his changing needs, capacities, resources, motivations, and behavior responses. Experience has made indisputable the fact that the relationship afforded the client is a decisive component in his use of help. In social work, therefore, to a greater degree perhaps than in some other professions, the relationship is regarded as an integral part of the helping process. We have been peculiarly concerned with what is done to people, as we do for them. We have been peculiarly aware that the recipient's response embodies something of himself and something of the worker himself and of the agency's regulations, policies, and procedures. The conduct of the helping relationship has been a major rather than an incidental responsibility. Other professions more recently are becoming concerned with the part played by the relationship in the recipient's use of their services. Perhaps it is in social work's problematic significance to those who support it, administer it, and use it that we early identified this dynamic element. Perhaps, moreover, due to our very nature—shaped by our place in society—greater concern with the relationship as an integral part of the helping process than obtains elsewhere will continue to be one of social work's peculiarities. . . .

A social worker, if he continues to function as a social worker, performs much the same at the practice level in casework or group work from one casework agency or group work agency to another. He performs much the same as an administrator from one agency or program to another. He performs much the same as an organizer from one community to another. He performs much the same as a researcher from one project to another. . . .

As we have come to know and to accept our own nature, it becomes clear that social work "specialties"—insofar as there are any—center around processes determined by function; that is, administration, organization, research, supervision, casework, and group work. And even here there is widespread conviction and mounting evidence that the major processes in the practice of social work have much basic knowledge, understanding, and skill in common.

New Developments
in Social Casework

THIS IS A COMPANION piece to "Some Aspects of Modern Casework," different from it, however, in that it attempts to identify and appraise new trends in relation to the old. Thus it offers comparisons and perspectives, forward- and backward-looking, by a seasoned and perceptive overviewer.

Among the trends Charlotte Towle recounts are those of the rediscovery of the social in social casework, the reunion of social work with its old ally "social science" for aid in understanding the individual in his social transactions, the rediscovery of the possible objective nature of any problem brought by the client in some contrast to our former total immersion in his subjective interpretation of it, the effort to probe and detect the nature of health and problem-solving strength rather than concentrating largely upon pathology. What Charlotte Towle makes clear (even through her moments of wistful weariness that she had *always* known and *always* said what was now being hailed as newly discovered) is that the ebb and flow, flux and reflux of casework's allegiances and styles of operation result in new

Excerpted from a paper presented in the *British Journal of Psychiatric Social Work* (June, 1955), reprinted in *Some Reflections on Social Work Education* (London: Family Welfare Association, 1956).

emphases and new integrations. They go not in a grooved circle but in a spiral, upward.

H. H. P.

I am asked to discuss new developments in social casework in my country at a time when much that is old is being revived. Since an old eye is prone to retrospection, I might well mistrust my impression that the current scene could be described as one in which we are coming full circle in many aspects of our practice. Perusal of the social work literature over the past several years, however, will show many references to our near forgotten pioneers and notably to Mary E. Richmond. Relatively young social workers are among the reminiscent. Of course, American-wise, we have a slogan for it: "Let us put the social back into social work."

Inevitably the reactions to this trend vary widely. Many a weary old stager has a dim view of it. To him it is history repeating itself in futile fashion. Others are irked or even momentarily infuriated—that their discards, re-evaluated by others, are given greater place than they had the sense to give them. Perhaps feeling shortsighted they are defensive and cling to their departures from tradition. Or because these departures have met their need they feel any return to the social work fold as a frustrating regression. On the other hand, many of the profession's elders, through having integrated the past with the present, see this development as a stage of reintegration following a period of some disintegration. And this is strongly suggestive of growth towards maturity. They are heartened by the prospect that social work seems gradually to be coming of age, and characteristically is emerging more fully conscious of its function in society and with a renewed and enlarged sense of its identity as a profession among professions.

I have selected a few specific developments which seem to me to represent progression in social work's collective learning rather than a defence against it. This is not to say that the growth depicted pervades our social work thinking and practice. The new integrations which I shall depict are sporadic, but it is to be hoped that they will prove to be nuclear.

It is important first to sketch two earlier movements which have had a direct bearing on recent developments.

Social work educators and practitioners have long been aware of the common denominators which obtain in the theory and practice of social work in all its branches, and hence of the fallacy of a high degree of specialization within education for social work. Conviction about educational specialization, derived in part from medical education, has been breaking down. We are finally facing the fact that there is more difference, for example, between surgery and psychiatry than obtains either between the administration of social work services and the practice of casework, or between psychiatric social and family casework. This awareness has slowly been forced upon us by the mobility of social caseworkers in practice. Beginning in the late 1920's, the migration of psychiatric social workers from hospitals and clinics into general social casework practice and into other specialities had soon reached proportions which made necessary an attempt to define psychiatric social work and to differentiate it from psychiatrically oriented social casework. This attempt, begun in the early thirties, was published in 1940.[1] Almost concurrently hospitals and clinics, deserted by psychiatric social workers, began to employ workers trained in family casework and child welfare work, and furthermore some pre-war psychiatrists soon came to value highly this background to the extent that frequently they expressed a preference for these orientations on the grounds that the workers brought to the clinical team a social orientation rather than a "too psychiatric one."

Because psychiatric social work at first held the knowledge and skill which the whole field of social casework wanted and needed, the rapid permeation of casework prac-

---

1. Lois Meredith French. "Psychiatric Social Work" (New York City: The Commonwealth Fund, 1940). See also: Helen R. Wright. "Employment of Graduates of the School of Social Service Administration." *The Social Service Review*, vol. 21, no. 3 (September 1947).

tice with a deepened social insight can be attributed in large part to the psychological orientation contributed first by psychiatric social workers. Somewhat later this contribution was supplemented by socially oriented psychiatrists both through their service as consultants to social agencies, and as their clinical staffs served social agencies through co-operative programmes. In these early years a rudimentary integration of the psychiatric and the social occurred to which we are now returning, and it is worth noting for use again today that the psychiatric social worker then played a large part also in socializing the psychiatrist, a responsibility early shared by her colleagues in other branches of social casework.[2] Prior to the war, social caseworkers had attained considerable skill in the application of psychiatric concepts, both in rendering casework services and in direct treatment through the interview. Recognition of their skill in diagnostic and therapeutic interviewing created an extensive demand for their services as practitioners in the time-limited, relationship-limited contacts of the high-pressure programmes of the depression and war years, and also as teachers of interviewing to members of other professions. A noteworthy feature of their skill was a growing ability to focus on the client with close reference to his current problem and to engage him in problem-solving, through dealing with his conscious production in the light of considerable understanding of unconscious motivation and the deeper significance of his behaviour.[3]

During and after the war the shortage of psychiatrists led them to need to duplicate themselves several times over, and to foster a subprofessional group composed of social caseworkers, nurses, psychologists, and a few sociologists. Among these, social caseworkers, notably psychiatric social

2. A review of the literature will show that this integration obtained in early child guidance days. It was notable particularly in the team work, in which each professional function retained its identity but was affected by the other.

3. During this period there was much concern with levels of treatment in an attempt to differentiate the social caseworker's treatment role and methods from those of the psychiatrist. Among numerous articles see: "Direct Treatment in Social Casework" (Paul Sloane). Discussion by C. Towle. *American Journal of Orthopsychiatry*, vol. 7, no. 2 (April 1937); "Therapeutic Criteria in Social Agencies," (Section Meeting) *American Journal of Orthopsychiatry*, vol. 9, no. 2 (April 1939); Psychoanalytic Orientation in Family Casework," *American Journal of Orthopsychiatry*, vol. 13, no. 1 (January 1945).

workers, were selected because of their skills in psycho-therapy. Other determinants, rational and irrational, oper-ated to render these professions receptive to the role of psychotherapist. This trend fast created a situation in some communities where everyone but the psychiatrist has been doing psychotherapy, while he has been serving on the side lines, except in his private practice, as super-diagnostician, supervisor, and consultant. (And, ironically, it is the psychi-atrist, perhaps nostalgic for his traditional role, who has been most responsive to the rediscovery of the importance of the social component in psychotherapy and who has been pressing the social worker to give as of old.) Although this development has produced distortions which we are now concerned to rectify, it has had its positive aspects, a notable one being the deepening of psychological understanding to give a new dimension to the social insights essential in the helping processes of social casework. The regaining of our professional function is our current concern to the extent that it is seen as a new development in social casework.

More recently, other professions directly concerned with individual human welfare have come to see social intelli-gence as essential for professional competence and have become concerned with the social component in profes-sional education. A new awareness has emerged that re-sponsible, intelligent professional help must increasingly be oriented to the individual in the context of his social situ-ation, with added perception of what the service is doing to the person while doing something for him. There has been growing agreement that, granted differences from profes-sion to profession, determined by needs peculiar to the func-tion of each, they all want to impart some understanding of the individual in his social context; of society and of the pro-fessions' place in society. This has led the professions to the social sciences, and to the behavioural sciences. Concur-rently, and perhaps reciprocally, the social sciences have been drawn into a down-to-earth movement and are eagerly absorbed in studying the professions as a social system, and professional education as an acculturation process, as well as the effects of professional services upon the recipients of them.[4] Communicate—lay the vestments of vested interests aside—come together in the common cause of solving the problems of man in society for the survival of both—this is the current trend. Obviously this movement could not but lead social work to reappraise its heritage and to renew its identity as a contributor to the application of the social sciences in practice.

Proclaimed in large letters as new is our current emphasis on treating the individual with close reference to his external reality, his family, his culture, his community. Individual dynamics within group dynamics is the latest cry. Traditionally, social casework was primarily concerned with the impact of the environment on the individual. With relatively little knowledge of human nature, we believed nevertheless that nurture to a considerable extent fashioned man's nature, and we set about to understand the stresses which operated against him, in order to alleviate them. The family was regarded as the "unit of society," and it was our charge to safeguard family life in order that the individual might be conditioned to live a socially useful life. We soon recognized that the nature of a child's relationship with his parents formed his relationship responses elsewhere, in marriage, as a parent, to his employers and to his colleagues.

Social work among professions was the first to receive Freudian thinking and to accept it almost unquestioningly for use. It was not the further light on sex alone that attracted us to psychoanalytic psychiatry. We found the concepts compatible on other grounds, notably in that the Freudian dynamics of family life confirmed our observations and extended and deepened our insights into family life. In contrast, the sociologists' classifications of that early period were not as useful to us. In helping troubled individuals in disturbed families with the problems which bedeviled them, we had come to see that the outcome of our helping efforts did not vary as widely in relation to socio-

4. Charlotte Towle. "The Learner in Education for the Professions," (Chicago: University of Chicago Press, 1954), pp. 200–233; and E. M. Goldberg. "Some Developments in Professional Collaboration and Research in the U.S.A.," *The British Journal of Psychiatric Social Work*, no. 11 (Spring 1955), pp. 4–12.

economic levels as in relation to such factors as these: resources in relationship available to the individual, alignments between family members, responsibility roles and the dynamic interplay of the personalities involved in a problem situation.

In the twenties, when psychiatric social work and medical social work brought the social worker into touch with a wider social economic range than formerly, we found that certain patterns of family life, from the points of view of relationships, obtained from class to class, and that, for example, the delinquent child from Chicago's "gold coast" often emerged from essentially the same soil, in terms of his family relationships, as the youngster from Chicago's deteriorated west side. A review of the literature of the twenties and the thirties attests our orientation to the dynamics of family life and our concern to focus our helping efforts on the meaning of individuals to one another, with regard for the significance of a social problem to those in close relationship to the individual under care.[5]

I will not attempt to depict the factors and forces which gradually brought widespread but not total breakdown in our psychological emphasis in helping individuals. Sufficient to say that as social caseworkers became increasingly absorbed in studying and treating the individual, they withdrew more and more to the individual as an isolate in terms of their helping efforts, even though their diagnostic portrayals were rich in family dynamics. And a strange thing happened—as many social caseworkers became more and more individual-centered in their treatment efforts, as they manfully strove to assume the role of the psychiatrist, at the same time the psychiatrist himself became more socially oriented as he served as consultant and teacher in social

5. Among numerous articles, the author for convenience sake cites several of her own as typical of the times: "An Evaluation of Homes in Preparation of Child Placement," *Mental Hygiene* (July 1927); "The Social Worker"—Symposium on Treatment, *American Journal of Orthopsychiatry*, vol. 1, no. 1 (October 1930); "Marital Situations in Foster Homes," *American Journal of Orthopsychiatry*, vol. 1, no. 5 (April 1931); "The Social Worker and the Treatment of Marital Discord Problems," *The Social Service Review*, vol. 14, no. 2 (June 1940). The focus on dynamics of family life has been held to steadfastly by a good many social caseworkers, as typified in my monograph, which has been widely used in social work education and practice, "Common Human Needs," first published in 1945 by U.S. Printing Office and republished by the American Association of Social Workers, New York, 1951.

agencies and other institutions in the community. Along the way he came into contact with the social scientist, and a recent union of the two makes the social science of today more compatible and more useful to the social caseworker. And now in the '50's we have this picture in my country, illustrated by the following examples. An eminent sociologist mentions social casework as a psychoanalytically oriented helping method which is limited because it treats the individual as an isolate.[6] A long-established social agency which has played a leadership role in fostering psychiatric permeation of its casework practices now employs a social scientist to teach its volunteer staff the dynamics of family life, and to train its workers to perform social services with nice reference to the family group as a whole.[7] In an interprofessional conference on medical education in which the educators were concerned that physicians of the future should have some understanding of the individual in his social context, projects were delineated in which medical students are visiting patients' homes, nurses are visiting homes, social scientists are visiting homes, psychologists are visiting homes. The social work educators were embarrassed by the question: 'Do social workers observe clients in their homes?' Of course they do—but with sufficient infrequency to create an impression that they see the social situation only through the clients' subjective eyes rather than through objective observation; sufficiently infrequently too to create an impression that it is not the social worker who brings to the clinical team knowledge of the patient's social setting and of the social forces which play upon his personality or operate in his illness and recovery.

This distortion of social work practice has occurred to some extent in all branches of social casework. What part have psychiatric social workers had in this? Because early on they played a vital leadership role which won them very real respect in the social work world as the exponents of the

6. Talcott Parsons. "Psychoanalysis and the Social Structure." *Psychoanalytic Quarterly* vol. 19, no. 3 (July 1950).

7. Otto Pollak, *et al.* "Social Science and Psychotherapy for Children" (New York: Russell Sage Foundation, 1952).

best in social casework, their participation in this movement probably has been deeply influential. Had they not lost their social work identity in the interprofessional scene, it is conceivable that other caseworkers would not have done so to the same extent. It would be unfair to leave the impression that all social caseworkers and all groups have experienced the disorientation described. Many practitioners and educators have contended steadfastly against this tendency.[8] The generic trend in social work education represents an effort to make social work as a whole a speciality—but this is a story I will tell another day.

Happily, we have now come full circle and returned to a more comprehensive point of view in the performance of our function as social workers. This function I would define as a charge to help the individual and his family to make productive use of their environment; environment being broadly conceived. It is also our charge to help individuals, and often also those in close relationship to them, to make more productive use of themselves in solving problems occasioned by social stress and/or by personal limitations, through means which are not identical with those of the psychiatrist even though they have some elements in common. Once more to see and to serve the human being as a complete organism in his total setting poses a large task. The complexity of knowing and helping individuals in social situations in terms of total personality in the total situation, I believe, explains in part why social caseworkers got absorbed in one almost to the exclusion of the other. For mastery of learning one must partialize. For competent practice one must focus. *A new development in casework has been our attempt to find our focus. In a comprehensive approach on what does one centre?* The current trend is to focus sharply on the problem of concern to the client with an eye to its meaning for him, and with regard for those in close relationship to him who affect or are affected by the problem-solving effort and its outcome.

---

8. After the war concern to differentiate the caseworker's and the psychiatrist's treatment roles and methods was revived and gave rise to many discussions. Among others published see: "Psychotherapy and Casework," (Symposium of the Boston Psychoanalytic Society, February 1949), in *Journal of Social Casework* (June 1949).

Here we come full circle again with a great difference from the past. Social casework has always been a problem-solving process, in terms of having an orderly procedure of thinking and doing. Originally it was narrowly concerned to attack social problems. Mary E. Richmond stressed the importance of engaging the client in the helping process, but because the work was more agency-, worker-, and procedure-centred than client-centred, it fell short of its aim in that there was not nice reference to the person who had the problem. There followed, as we gained some psychological understanding, a period of emphasis on the person. The slogans then current were: "Treat people not problems"; "treat causes not symptoms." Problems in terms of their objective factual aspect became beneath our notice. The psychological reality of the client filled the horizon to the exclusion of his social actuality to such an extent that we frequently did not appraise his emotional responses correctly. Soon we were making the person the problem, when often he was a person *with* a problem to which he was responding commensurately. Intent on the total personality and bent on changing it, we often lost the problem while we worked happily on personality, without benefit either of the diagnostic import or the therapy implicit in mastering a current stress. When this occurred, both differential diagnosis and differential treatment were impeded. This happened because we did not promptly test the individual's motivation and capacity to use help through focussing on the problem of concern to him. We had not become aware of the helping process as a means to understand the individual.

Gradually we have become less diffuse in our approach, and are focussing immediately on both the meaning of the problem to him and the meaning of the helping relationship. This implies first appraising what he feels and the strength of his feeling, on the assumption that the nature and size of the affect load will throw light both on motivation and on the integrative task involved for him in solving his problems. Second, we note his ways of dealing with his feelings and the effectiveness or futility of those ways, in order to appraise his capacity, and the degree of change involved if he is to solve his problems. Finally, in the light of current social and psychological circumstances, notably his relationships, his past experiences operating in the present, and his aspirations for the future, we try gradually to understand the purposes served by his behaviour. This approach, used systematically, tends to engage the client actively and in so doing gives us more quickly a picture of how he functions, of his behaviour patterns both normal and pathological; in short of his motivation and capacity for problem-solving. Diagnostic skill in appraising capacity as well as incapacity, health as well as pathology, is highly valued today because we realise that we cannot actually motivate people to use help nor provide them with the capacity to solve their problems. We may deal with people in ways which lower or break down motivation and capacity or we may provide an opportunity which uses and strengthens them.

This focus on the individual's problems is productive today in contrast to yesterday because of what our profession has learned meanwhile. Our ability to engage the individual in attacking his problems, as well as to discern the significance of his responses throughout a helping process, is due not only to the worker's more skilled use of psychoanalytically oriented knowledge and experience, but also to his use of certain generalizations at which the profession has arrived. He can anticipate reactions because of his profession's knowledge that certain vital life experiences create common problems in relation to common human needs, age, and types of prior life experience and current circumstances. For example, he knows the common significance of asking for and taking specific kinds of help, of illness and physical and mental handicaps, of failure in school, work, marriage, of losses in relationship through death, separation; and sharing. Such experiences have constituted a repeated refrain in human maladjustment. Likewise, certain kinds of life situation have been repetitive. . . . Hence the worker's early formulation of the client's need and capacity has been shaped in large part by the significance which the client's responses have for the worker in the light of generalization. Quick and accurate diagnostic insight is thus frequently made possible. Real misunderstanding of the client as a unique person may, however, result, unless the worker continuously reaches out to know him as an individual, and progressively to check impressions against early tentative assumptions.

It is as worker and client proceed together in the solution of difficulties that early impressions are corrected and understanding deepened. It is thus that the individuality of the client will become more clear, so that it will be possible not only to differentiate his characteristic ways of responding from situational responses, but also to gauge his strengths and capacity for change. Precise understanding of the ego structure, of its adaptive mechanisms, with differentiation of strengths from precarious or flimsy defences is decisively important in some forms of help. It is around this perception that helping methods become more precisely differentiated and are used with a surer touch and a more predictable outcome. A noteworthy feature of a continuous focus on problems in relation to the person, is that it tends to help the worker to integrate social and psychological factors as he and the client proceed. This is because he is schooled to look at every problem in terms of both its objective factual aspect and its subjective aspect. This operates against a common tendency to concentrate ambivalently on one or the other aspect—the external reality or the inner psychological reality—and hence to focus help on person or situation without sufficient reference to interaction. . . .

We are becoming more differential in our helping efforts. This has come about in part through the focus described. It has also come about as we are refinding our social work identity. In this, generic education has played an identifiable part, as has the union of the social scientist and the psychoanalytic psychiatrist. Because of our insecurity as a young profession we have been prone to great dependence on teachers who speak with the authority of more secure professions. This has produced much conflict and confusion for social caseworkers. Now that their leaders in social work and elsewhere speak as one on the importance of the social component in the helping processes of the professions, social caseworkers can be themselves because they are valued as such. They could not so readily return to a social work focus, however, had not the schools of social work long been giving students a sound generic base, as well as teaching the specialities with a prominent emphasis on the generic process of social work. . . .

Some of the relatively new elements in our conduct of the relationship show that as we have been experiencing some emancipation, we have been finding our own style rather than emulating the psychoanalyst's style, even though we are still guided by psychoanalytic understanding. Hence we are making headway in attaining a more reality-oriented relationship, in the sense that it is being fashioned by our social work aims, function and capacity, as well as by the needs, motivations and capacities of the individuals whom we serve. . . . What our clients need and want in the relationship and have the capacity to use is wide. Our range is from the normal right through more abnormal individuals than the psychiatrist would select for deep uncovering insight therapy. Furthermore, the psychiatrist's patient brings his personality as the problem, whereas the social worker's client brings a problem in which his personality may or may not be extensively involved, and which he may or may not be ready to identify as a personality difficulty. A very real difference in immediate focus is that the social worker and the client get down to work on a problem, drawing in the personality implications in a partial way. The psychiatrist and his patient get down to work on the personality sometimes shelving the solution of specific problems for the time being.[9] Our growing awareness of these among other differences is now making us keenly aware that we must abandon many stereotypes, which we had annexed and used rigidly because of the insecurity implicit in trying to behave like psychiatrists when we are not psychiatrists.

9. In brief psychotherapy as practised by many psychiatrists the immediate problem approach is used in some instances. Hence there is some overlapping in social casework and psycho-therapeutic methods. The psychiatrist however tends to go further in dealing with the personality implications.

Accordingly, with an eye to understanding need and capacity, we are relinquishing rigidity in such practices as maintaining that unless a client seeks help we cannot help him; unless he will come to the office we cannot work with him. We have returned to an old practice of initiating contact with clients referred by others, and we are again visiting clients at home—all this proclaimed as new and dignified by the name of "aggressive casework." We no longer refrain from the use of authority, sometimes actually in the form of judgments as to right and wrong. To the extent that we use this authority in response to the client's need and his incapacity to appraise and regulate himself, rather than out of our own need to be authoritative, we are finding it a helpful measure. We support the client in many instances, more freely than formerly, with advice and guidance, in response to his capacity to use it, or his incapacity to function without it. . . .

Out of the emancipation process described it is to be hoped there may come new developments in interprofessional teamwork. Originally in the clinical team the functions of each profession were well defined. The problem of segmentation of the patient presented itself, but this factor and others resulted in combined effort to co-ordinate and integrate the services. Coalescence rather than integration resulted. We have had a period in which there has been too little differentiation of function as each profession has subordinated its traditional role to playing the psychiatrist's role. An effective team implies that each discipline performs a different function but that learning is interchanged, for intelligent co-ordination of the parts and for the common use of certain generic elements. It implies also that the professional person who is leader of the team must have a grasp and an acceptance both of the specific and the generic usefulness of each discipline. It is time that there should be some redefining of function, with careful delineation of our different responsibility roles and of activities which validly overlap.[10] Social caseworkers could well initiate this in

10. See Charlotte Towle, *The Learner in Education for the Professions* (Chicago: University of Chicago Press, 1954), pp. 217–23.

interprofessional programmes conducted within social agencies to serve as a pattern for use elsewhere. . . .

An important new development for social casework is the professions' growing realization that individual human welfare is the test of every programme and of every service. Thus from the standpoint of administration it is the test of social policy. To the extent that this concept is accepted, social casework is given a new relationship to administration, community organisation and research. Administration should draw on the findings of social casework in making social policy as related to agency services. Social casework has a charge to know and to make known the import of the agency's services to clients. Administration has a charge to seek counsel and to take into account the findings of casework. This implies social work research, participated in by social caseworkers. Second, the insights of social casework are beginning to be drawn into the managerial policies of administration for more effective performance by the agency as a whole. Third, where administrators have a sound grasp of social casework, as a heritage from prior education and experience, the incorporation of certain principles and working concepts implicit in social casework for imparting and sharing feeling and thinking contributes to wisdom in communication at the administration level. . . . I would also mark as new the development in social casework of its own research. . . . A noteworthy occurrence is that some caseworkers are becoming candidates for a Ph.D. degree, in order to specialize in social work research. Thus in the future we may be able to assume responsibility for our own research.

Finally, I . . . envisage that we may increasingly use our knowledge of educational method to help clients to learn to solve their problems more competently. As the insights of casework have been used adaptively by social work educators in understanding the learner, so as to afford him an educational opportunity which contributes to the development of social intelligence, these educators have deepened their understanding of the ego as it functions in the problem-solving, goal-striving situation of professional education. They have become acquainted with the normal protective function of the ego as it operates for the integration of learning, as differentiated from defences which interrupt it. In order to arrive at a sound educational methodology they have gradually learned to differentiate the student from the client, and the educational process of helping individuals to learn from the casework diagnostic treatment process. Some years ago Gordon Hamilton reminded us that casework lies midway between education and therapy. There are many instances in which clients can be helped by educational means as differentiated from therapy. The principle that a new intellectual orientation may produce a change in feeling, and thus facilitate learning and also contribute to greater competence in doing, is a familiar one to educators. Hence, well-timed interpretation, advice and guidance which produces understanding, insight and "know how" for problem-solving may ease disturbed feelings. This has a threefold result for the client; first, energy previously tied up unproductively may be released for productive purposes; second, the client may gain the intellectual wherewithal for realistic self-direction; and third, this should result in a sense of mastery of self in relation to people and circumstances. The long and short of this is that just as what we have learnt in casework has been used adaptively, so in education what we have learnt as educators may be used adaptively to a greater extent than formerly in our casework. . . . It is highly probable that many more clients than we realise could quickly use an intellectual approach as a means to problem-solving, though we fear this method because of our earlier indiscriminate use of it.

In conclusion, the new developments in casework are heartening. To many of us they signify change in a growth direction, in that casework as a basic generic process is contributing to the profession as a whole. Social caseworkers are more fully conscious of their function and of their responsibility to the profession and to other professions. Ralph W. Tyler, an eminent American educator, has said that a profession is coming of age when its principles and processes are viewed in a widening and deepening context. We are glad to see the day when this can be said of social work, and when it can be said also that social case-work has played a vital part in the development of the profession as a whole.

Reflections
on a Teacher

THE ORIGINAL OF THIS article was written as a eulogy to Dr. Marion Kenworthy, a psychiatrist, an indefatigable worker for social causes, a memorable teacher for all who experienced her, and a long-time friend of Charlotte Towle.

It is included here, because it holds interest, I believe, even for those who never knew Marion Kenworthy. That interest lies in the revelation of what one deeply influential teacher drew from one of her own deeply influential teachers, and treasured. More, it reveals the consistency over time with which Charlotte Towle understood, valued, and conveyed to all who learned from her the integration of the psychic and social, of past and present, of rigorous thinking and its practical application in the problem-solving efforts of casework, and the affirmation of the special identity of social work.

H. H. P.

I write as one who was a student upon whom Dr. Ken-worthy left a deep imprint. No student, despite lapse of time, can write with complete objectivity about an influential teacher. Much of the teacher dwells in the student and

Excerpted from "Marion Kenworthy: A Social Worker's Reflections," *Social Service Review*, vol. 30, no. 4 (December 1956). Copyright 1956 by The University of Chicago.

all the more when the teaching has been put to use. The teacher grows and changes in the life of another in terms of his usefulness. Thus one risks portraying what one has made of a teacher rather than the teacher himself. But, in the last analysis, one of the earmarks of the great teacher is that he lends himself to others for their use through teaching in ways that free the learner. He is not all things to all men, but he has had different values for different men, and his greatness lies in having fostered the individuality of the learner. In presuming to speak for Dr. Kenworthy's social work students over the sweep of almost forty years, I assume that her meaning for me was not unique: other students might specify some other values or give greater or lesser significance to the attributes which I have prized.

First, I recall that social workers—her students and her collaborators—left her tutelage proud to be social workers. To gain a feeling of adequacy in the professional scene we did not yearn to be psychiatrists. We could not comfortably slough off the responsibilities peculiar to our social work role, because the enraged shouts of this forceful teacher, when on occasion we overlooked the psychotherapeutic import of environmental factors and forces, would have rung in our ears. Students are seldom, if ever, lastingly held in check by the "don'ts" of their mentors. Instead, they are more prone to incorporate positive instruction, the "dos" rather than the "don'ts." In the last analysis, our identity as social workers was established and strengthened in part through the fact that Dr. Kenworthy herself was a social worker at heart, with a fine grasp of the individuality of social work and a concern to strengthen its identity. She was an imaginative helper, one who saw possibilities in all the everyday services and resources upon which a social worker could draw. She insistently taught nice use of social services in the light of the individual's need, capacity, and response to help. She valued social opportunity as a means of renewing and strengthening the individual's motivation and capacity for goal-striving. She valued highly an educational approach as a means to effect change in feeling, thinking, and doing. She did not leave the social worker with little other than the magic of catharsis, or lure him toward deep uncovering insight therapy as the universal means to effect behavior changes. She insisted that, whatever was done, it must be done with close reference to individual differences in motivation and capacity and to the purposes served by behavior in the current situation.

She persistently challenged easy generalizations, categorical thinking, and routinized help. I can still hear her repetitive inquiry: "What are you doing to *this* person in *this* family now in doing something for him? What is this desired change in Johnny's behavior meaning to *this* father and what reverberations is it causing in *this* family, either to create additional problems or to solve other family-relationship problems?" In short, families were individualized and a given patient was never regarded as an isolate.

The student's professional identity was strengthened through identification with a teacher who respected social work's ends and means. Dr. Kenworthy emphasized the knowledge and skill implicit in effective use of social work measures at a time when social workers were gropingly engaged in refashioning casework practices in the light of new psychological insights. . . .

We were challenged by and deeply impressed with the possibilities of psychiatrically oriented casework as differentiated from "pure psychotherapy." This new approach to casework made a demand on us and, in the light of subsequent developments, perhaps such a great one that we did not develop our own professional skills to the utmost. In the stress wrought by the complexity of our task, it became the line of least resistance to follow in the wake of the psychiatrist, emulating his role and methods. Most psychiatrists could help us, in the performance of *their* function, to use the knowledge derived from them, whereas they could not readily help us apply it in social work. Insufficient grasp of the psychotherapeutic import of social work's ways and means of helping led them either to devaluate our ways or to be oblivious to them. Out of his own absorption in becoming oriented—or perhaps at times disoriented—by the psychiatrist, the social worker sometimes failed to orient the psychiatrist to social work's role. This failure was inevitable in a period when social work was in the making as a profession and in transition in its practice.

Today, our social work self is being revived; in fact, it constitutes the "new" in social casework. . . . We have been refinding our own style in our casework focus and treatment emphasis rather than emulating the psychoanalyst's style. Although we are still guided by psychoanalytic understanding, we are challenged anew by the knowledge and skill entailed in the competent performance of our comprehensive function as social workers. There is no ego-deflating simplicity in the return of the social component into social casework practice. Many social workers and psychiatrists, prominent among them Dr. Kenworthy, rejoice that the current social work scene can be described as coming full circle in many aspects of practice. We see this development as synthesis following a period of specialization essential to extend and deepen the profession's learning. . . .

Our hope that synthesis may not be a long and uncertain process is based on the fact that some social workers continuously have kept the psychological and the social together in the practice of social casework as well as in the profession's educational process. (This they have done against odds—against the propensity of many not only to set the two apart but to create a hierarchy in which the psychological smiled down on the social.) [For these integrations] we are indebted to such psychiatric instruction as we experienced with Dr. Kenworthy and others, not only in those early years, but continuously into the present. The younger generation will again have the opportunity to integrate Dr. Kenworthy's teaching because increasingly now it will be supported in social work practice. In the light of current trends her retirement is untimely, and one looks back with regret on those in-between years when hers was to some extent one of a few voices in the wilderness crying for social work to be itself.

There were many ways in which Dr. Kenworthy promoted

the social worker's identification with his own profession and fostered his self-dependence. One of her means has been stated, namely, her own grasp of and respect for the social worker's aims and means. Because of our insecurity as a young profession, we have tended to identify as a defense, and hence we have been subject to great dependence on teachers who speak with the authority of more secure professions. Consequently, the social worker has been prone to appraise his heritage through the eyes of the psychiatrist rather more than through the eyes of his own mentors. Although social work educators, recognizing this, have persistently and systematically taught full-fledged social casework, the student's identity with social work has often been fragmented in his practice. It is very important, therefore, that social work and psychiatric educators be of one mind and heart about the social work profession in the important pattern-setting period. Dr. Kenworthy's colleagues in education can well feel indebted to her, for she gave enviable support to their teaching of social work. . . .

In 1926, I had the privilege not only of being a student in Dr. Kenworthy's classes but also of experiencing her instruction in my fieldwork placement at the Bureau of Children's Guidance, of which she was director. Later, I was a member of evening seminars, attended by agency and clinic staffs, in which we sought her help on tough cases. I have recently learned that a life-long motto of hers was drawn from Emerson's essay, "The Conduct of Life": "Our chief want in life is somebody who shall make us do what we can. This is the service of a friend."

Her assumption, right or wrong, was that social workers could think, and she befriended us in large-handed fashion by holding us strictly accountable to think. She had no fear of infantilizing us by giving us the knowledge with which to think—knowledge of common human needs, of normal behavior under stress, of psychopathology, as well as a method of case analysis for orderly thinking—but she did not think for us. This was ours to do, and how deeply we became engaged in it and what preparation this was for our subsequent practice as caseworkers and teachers! Dr. Kenworthy was a masterful teacher of case analysis and synthesis for problem-solving. She bore patiently with us through the diagnostic process, but she pressed us urgently on the "what to do." I shall always remember her "so what" attitude at a nice formulation: "Well now, what are we going to do about it?" And her angry impatience at indifference to this, at those moments when we rested on our oars, savoring our hard-won insight. No art for art's sake was permitted us. I recall also her exactitude at this stage. The doing must be oriented to the knowing and thinking. There almost invariably followed reflection upon the broad implications of a case with some formulations for use elsewhere. . . .

Her teaching lent itself to integration for use in social work practice because she focused sharply on the individual in his dynamic social situation. Not only did she teach students a method of case analysis which facilitated orderly thinking, but her respect for environment as treatment and her perception of the psychotherapeutic potentialities in the gamut of casework services grounded me in social work and committed me to use psychiatric insights in the helping processes of social work as differentiated from those of psychiatry. It followed naturally that I used them also in the teaching-helping processes of social work education. Hers was an outstanding contribution to those social workers who became the first-generation teachers of modern social casework.

We rightly attribute modern social casework to Mary E. Richmond. She gave it to us conceptually, but we could not practice it overnight, and we could not teach it. Hers was a pioneer contribution in which we were given the rudiments of much to come. She gave us the concept of systematic method and a start in its first steps—those of gathering the facts, weighing the evidence with the purpose of putting two and two together to arrive at a social diagnosis to serve as a basis for treatment. She gave us the concept that knowledge of human behavior is essential to understanding the individual, family life, and our working relationship—"the effect of mind upon mind." She gave us the concept of social work process as a democratic process if it was to fulfill its "character-building" aims ("ego-building" in subsequent parlance).

She did not have the knowledge of human behavior essential for effective use of the scientific method. Without it we could not reliably weigh evidence, and we could not put two and two together for differential social diagnosis with a view to discriminative treatment. Without knowing the meaning of the facts to the individual or the purposes served by his responses to them, not to mention the meaning of the facts and the evidence to ourselves, we could not practice client-centered casework as differentiated from worker-centered casework.[1] The decisive point is that at that stage in the development of social work we looked to the psychiatrist not only for knowledge of human behavior but also for the methodology of systematic clinical thinking. The social casework courses of the late twenties and early thirties could not give us this. How well do I remember the casework instructor's attempts to analyze the prodigious array of facts in those asset-liability columns which served as a basis for social diagnosis.

From Dr. Kenworthy, the clinical psychiatrist, we learned to deal with configurations of factors in the light of their meaning to the patient as shown in his behavior, rather than in the light of our own value judgments. Dr. Kenworthy's ego-libido case-analysis method moved our charting forward a great step when we appraised an individual's experiences and his responses in the light of their constructive or destructive import for him. . . .

The new method of analysis helped us to separate the client from ourselves, thus moving us toward the development of self-awareness. Whether we adhered to or abandoned the specific charting procedure which Dr. Kenworthy taught, the important point was that students experienced a discipline in thorough analysis and orderly thinking with focus on the client's values rather than their own. . . .

"Use what he's got as a means to remedy his deprivations, always taking the latter into account for a realistic appraisal

1. For elaboration of this see Charlotte Towle, "Social Case Work," *Social Work Year Book, 1945* (New York: Russell Sage Foundation, 1945), pp. 417–18.

of what he can do," was a repetitive refrain. "Our chief want in life is somebody who shall make us do what we can" was translated into "Help him do." . . .

Teaching the methodology of systematic thinking was one way through which Dr. Kenworthy fostered the professional self-dependence of social workers. . . .

In her early experimental work at the Vanderbilt Clinic, and later at the Bureau of Children's Guidance in New York, Dr. Kenworthy initiated the collaborative relationship of the child-guidance team and the educational methods of the child-guidance clinic as a training center. An important feature in the educational pattern was that social work was given full-fledged professional status. Social workers were trained to think, speak, and act in responsible fashion for their profession, rather than to serve as technicians subordinate to psychiatry. The training of psychiatric aides or of subpsychotherapists was not the educational objective. We are indebted to Dr. Kenworthy, therefore, for her influence on her colleagues in setting the pattern for psychiatric teaching concerned with the development of social workers, a pattern which has broken down in many situations but has been maintained in others throughout the years. . . .

Now that leaders in social work and other fields are beginning to speak as one on the importance of the social component in the helping processes of the professions, social caseworkers can be themselves because they are valued as such. It would have been more difficult for them to hold to a social work focus, however, had it not been for the teachings and response to social work of Dr. Kenworthy and her kind among psychiatrists and the fact that many schools of social work have long been giving students a sound generic base, as well as teaching the specialties with a prominent emphasis on the generic. So the time arrives when Dr. Kenworthy's contribution to social work educators gives promise of coming into full flower.

Out of her interest in social work education and her continuous connection with it as a member of the faculty of the New York School, Dr. Kenworthy early became concerned with the selection of students who could use the educational process as a means to personality change and growth essential for the demands and responsibilities of social work.[2] Over the years, she served the faculty as adviser on problematic students and as consultant on admissions. She was not satisfied with anything short of helping the faculty develop knowledge and skill for this work, despite the fact that the personality appraisals involved might have led a psychiatrist to regard this skill as his province. Instead she saw the social caseworker, versed in the case study method and oriented to the individual in social context, as peculiarly equipped not only to assume the major responsibility for selection in his own profession but to contribute his learning in this area to be adapted and used by other professions. Studying and developing selection methods was a dream which she brought to fruition through inspiring others to take action. The New York School–Columbia University Pilot Study, instituted in 1947, was made possible by a grant in commemoration of Dr. Kenworthy's twenty-five years of service. It has been directed and manned by experienced social caseworkers with Dr. Kenworthy serving as consultant and as a member of the faculty advisory committee. A sound precedent was set through this psychiatrist's wisdom in serving as consultant rather than in participating in the actual interviewing of applicants or in holding that other psychiatrists were needed for the task. . . . One sees Dr. Kenworthy befriending social work through expecting it to do what it could do.

Finally, among her contributions to the identity of social work, was Dr. Kenworthy's wartime work which led to the establishment of a military occupational specialty designation for psychiatric social work, first in the regular army and, later, in the Women's Army Corps. At the beginning of World War II there was no authority to use the specialized skill of members of our profession. . . . It was Marion Kenworthy who helped set up the first mental hygiene clinic in a basic training camp at Fort Monmouth in 1942. The success of social work in the pilot venture led to its acceptance

2. In 1929, the problem of selection of students was acknowledged and action in studying and developing selection methods was urged. See Porter R. Lee and Marion E. Kenworthy, M.D., *Mental Hygiene and Social Work* (New York: Commonwealth Fund, 1929), pp. 257–63.

as an essential service. Characteristically, Dr. Kenworthy was concerned to intrench and expand social work's gains. Accordingly, with the guidance and help of social workers themselves, as well as with the help of others, she worked for official recognition of social work. This was the first of a series of changes that made it possible for social workers to be used more fully and to be given officer status essential for leadership. . . . This is not to claim that this development was a one-man achievement. Dr. Kenworthy has never been a solitary worker. This effort, like so much of her work, bespeaks her genius for setting a movement in operation, for working with people, and for inspiring accomplishment.

On her retirement from social work education, we, her fellow educators, can well say that we have valued particularly the nature of Dr. Kenworthy's relationship to us. Her appreciation of the worth of social work and her propensity to foster its self-dependence through concern to give it place in the interprofessional scene, together with her high expectancy of it, have strengthened pride in calling for many who have studied and worked with her. For the service of this friend who has unwaveringly related to our need and want, social workers far and wide are deeply and gratefully obligated.

On the
Contemporary Scene
in Social Work

FROM THE LARGER ARTICLE that dealt with student selection, I have excerpted those sections that assess the social work scene—of ten years ago, yet not dramatically changed—into which social work students enter.

Excerpted from "Implications of Contemporary Human and Social Values for Selection of Social Work Students," *Social Service Review*, vol. 32, no. 3 (September 1959). Copyright 1959 by The University of Chicago.

"Duality marks our times," says Charlotte Towle as she assesses the good and the evil of social conditions. Duality marks her opinions and attitudes too, as it must mark those of any thinking person who sees the tensions and strains inherent in rapid change and who is knowing enough to recognize that the sweep of each social solution churns up new problems in its wake.

Past her troubled appraisal of the social scene, Charlotte Towle looks into the smaller world of social work itself and questions some trends therein. One is the apparent scramble —heightened today—to meld all social work's processes as if they were not different in some ways from one another and as if there were no special kinds of knowledge that needed identification and transmutation. Some fusions, she says, produce confusions. And coalescence, she warns, is not the same as integration. Further, she points to the ambivalences in the community that supports social work, which gives with one hand and withdraws with the other. In response, the professional self-concept of social work is in continuous shift and conflict, and there results a heavy emotional stress for the social work practitioner: in one moment he is his client's advocate, in the next his agency's defender. The recurrent theme of social work's struggle for secure identity threads through this piece. "I long to make it known," writes Charlotte Towle earnestly, "that the social worker has had, and still has, a reality problem to solve, . . . that his making known his plight may be indicative of good ego functioning," rather than some neurotic insecurity.

Finally, typically, Charlotte Towle sums up the firm advances social work has made against its many odds and asserts that "there is much to conserve and carry forward."

H. H. P.

. . . Duality marks our times, these daring but fearful times. This is not new. Throughout the ages the dual nature of man, his propensity to love and to hate, has been manifested in the affairs of the times. But today for many reasons this duality is extreme in many areas of life. Its manifestations are conspicuous. There is evidence to suggest that we have more mental health than ever before. Alongside this, we seemingly have more psychopathology than ever before. On the one hand, we are more civilized than we have ever been. This is evidenced in many ways, notably in the unprecedented extent to which we are concerned to make the benefits of civilization available to all mankind. On the other hand, we are more primitive; and what daring and fearful forms, what devilishly sophisticated forms our hostile aggression takes, individually and collectively! Swinging from hope to despair we live in a state of doubt. A sense of urgency pervades the scene, an urgency which has motivated many to deny the threat and to live euphorically, while others have been motivated to do something to avert disaster.

. . . [One] manifestation of our "survival anxiety" may be the current urgency to get together. As I reflect upon this "one world" trend, I do not see it wholly as a response to the universal concern to solve relationship problems, now that they are seen as the root of the evil. Our coming together may ease that anxiety, and may have been accelerated by that anxiety. . . . It is as if at the same point in history the professions and disciplines concerned with human and social welfare are coming of age, as evidenced in readiness to view their principles and processes in a widening and deepening context. . . . As a result, a number of unions and some fusions (to produce confusion) are occurring. Periods of synthesis are decisive in that they bring new integrations which determine future developments. They also imply considerable sloughing off of the old. What is retained is the nub of the matter, making for progress or retrogression. . . . I specify a few integrations which have had import for all concerned.

As psychoanalysis has been drawn on extensively it has undergone changes, but perhaps it has caused more change elsewhere than has occurred within itself. It has been drawn on by dynamic psychiatry, by child psychiatry, and by medicine to establish psychosomatic medicine as a major speciality. It has been applied in non-medical professions, first in social work and subsequently in education, nursing, psychology, theology, the law, and the social sciences. It has lent itself to use in other individual case-method processes and more recently in group work. All this cross-fertilization has served as an integrative force in providing a common conceptual framework which, in approximating the generic, has served as a means of communication and collaboration among disciplines formerly incompatible in their thinking on human behavior.

The social worker and the social scientist are experiencing a reunion (and it is not in Vienna, but right here). Some say it is a sort of status-striving remarriage (at least for case-workers), by reason of the fact that the psychoanalyst has, in embracing the social scientist, prompted caseworkers to do likewise. The social worker and the social scientist parted company at that point in social work's development when we perceived that to help man cope with his environment we had to understand man. The sociologist had knowledge and theories about people en masse, but he did not know them individually. He was absorbed in categorizing, whereas the social worker was bent on individualizing. Until our own experience was sufficiently intelligible to us to permit us to generalize validly, we could not relate to the social scientists' abstractions. Furthermore, we had a mission. We also were in quest of scientific method, but for the scientific missionary the social scientist had no category. Science and the sense of mission were irreconcilable. Today, it looks as if the social scientist, in studying the missionary, risks becoming one. And well he may in some measure, if he is to be an understanding and hence a useful collaborator.

Let me say parenthetically that it was the social worker, not just the caseworker, who broke with the social scientist on this and other counts. Social work has always been of one piece, both in its conviction that the test of any welfare program lay in what it did to the individual, and in its sense of having a mission. We turned to the psychiatrist who, as a member of a profession with a mission, could identify with our aims and means. As a result, the breath of human life was breathed into social work processes at a time when they were more procedure-centered than person-centered. If we are finding the social scientist compatible, I assure you it is not entirely on a status-striving basis but rather because he, perhaps through his relationship with psychiatry, has had human values breathed into his work so that he now can relate to the helping processes of a profession. We come together at a different stage of development with promise of ability to nurture one another. There is evidence that the social scientist has much to contribute to social work, in part out of our greater ability now to receive and use his contribution. There is evidence also that social work has much to contribute to his education, if we are to work together productively. New insights from the social sciences should lower that stress which has stemmed from lack of knowledge and understanding with which to be competent. . . .

In this period of coming together there is considerable exchange of methodology. Long ago Gordon Hamilton identified social casework treatment as lying midway between education and therapy. In some quarters social casework increasingly has seen itself as a re-educative process. Today many psychiatrists are characterizing some of their work in terms of an educational approach as distinguished from a therapeutic approach. So we have education as therapy and therapy as education, and education as education and therapy as therapy, and we all, social workers in casework and group work and psychotherapists from other disciplines, in the give-and-take of learning together are becoming less distinguishable in our ways of doing.

To add to the many-faceted picture the social scientist brings us the social role, a new conceptual frame of reference to serve as a diagnostic tool in our study of the individual and the group, including the family. I had always thought that in any attempt to understand an individual we appraised his behavior in the many aspects of his life—as husband, as father, as worker, as member of his community, and importantly as client or patient. Perhaps greater clarity will come to us in casework through the use of the "role" concept. Man as a complex of factors is graphic. The group as a complex of factors functioning together in ways which produce a good or a poor production is also graphic. The graphic is not necessarily simple. The real diagnostic task still is to be done—that of weighting the roles and bringing the parts together both to see the significance of the whole and to determine our focus in helping.

Group method is being widely used. The caseworker and the individual therapist in other professions with whom he is associated increasingly are seeing members of families together and holding family councils. I appreciate the efficacy of the group approach in casework when used appropriately, but in this renewal of an abandoned practice there is a demand on the caseworker to modernize his skills both in the conduct of group sessions and in diagnostically determined use of the method. We know out of past experience that there is a time for seeing family members together and a time for seeing them alone. The danger of overdedication to new method is well known.

Furthermore, in a range of settings social caseworkers are conducting groups—group therapy, group education, and perhaps group work. How much and what of group process and method is appropriately within the caseworker's function, and how much of this function can he responsibly carry? Likewise, group workers are moving into considerable use of casework method, with comparable implications and questions. Can we realistically train people for both functions within the time limits of a Master's degree program? Is there not a danger of overpushing the generic principle in order to solve staff shortages and to condense educational process? Those who contended for generic social work education did not conceive of it as a means to this end. Instead, they saw it as a means gradually to bring social work from its inchoate state into a coherent whole.

Among professions social work has had very little stability. It has been continuously in the making and remaking. It has never really had a chance to jell. Its orthodoxies have been relatively weak and its segmentation, as implied in specialization, short-lived. The tempo of its growth, always under necessitous circumstances, disposes it to ready identifications, both as a means to learning and as a defense. It is an avid consumer of nurture afforded. It is vulnerable to new integrations; herein lies its potential for growth or regression. Therefore it will take the best of us to keep our bearings in these eclectic times in which new integrations will take place. It is to be hoped that in synthesizing we will not become synthetic; that in retaining and sloughing off we will continue to build social work as an organic whole. This implies maintenance of the difference of the parts. Integration is not to be confused with coalescence. There is nothing like fusion to gum up the works. It is a time for judicious extensions and discards.

In portraying the stresses of social work numerous writers have given considerable weight to that wrought by the community's ambivalent convictions about social work. The social scientists also have identified this as a stress which explains certain attitudes and responses of social workers. I closed one such discussion, in which I had noted the freedom of the physician, the clergyman, and the teacher from this burden, with the statement:

> Perhaps it might be said that in some professions the student is under the stress of approximating the ideal which the community has of him. In social work the student must find within his profession his ideal of himself and must struggle not merely to attain it but to contend for the profession's ideals in a world which frequently contests them. He must prove not only his own worth as a professional person but his profession's worth as a profession.[1]

This dual attitude of half-hearted support of the aims and means of social work has been encountered not only in the community at large but also in the administration of the very agencies and institutions in which social workers have been employed. Often it has been encountered in collaborative work—among colleagues in other professions who have gone through the motions of working with social work but

1. *The Learner in Education for the Professions* (Chicago: University of Chicago Press, 1954), p. 16.

who could not really identify with it enough to permit it its proper place or to support its functions. Social workers have sometimes been driven to submit and to adapt to that which was expected of them or permitted them. In the inter-professional scene this has been a discernible determinant in our desertion of social work function for the functions of those who could accept us only as extensions of themselves or in some role other than full-fledged social work.

What is the situation today? It may always be that people will be ambivalent about social work because they cannot identify with the group it traditionally has served and will continue to serve. Because of the ego threat implied, they cannot envisage themselves as needing this help. The fact that there are welfare programs galore and a demand for social workers that far exceeds the supply does not mean that these attitudes are fast disappearing. In the very communities and institutions clamoring for and employing them, social workers have been put on the defensive. It is difficult to put one's cause across when on the defensive at home. We channel tension and anxiety to productive ends when we have hope and confidence. The professional "self concept" inevitably is affected by the conception others have of us. Social work's relationship with its larger community cannot possibly be better than its relationships in the agency. The real emotional stress for the social worker —a stress that affects his performance adversely—has been the dual attitude and response with which he has had to live in his daily grind. The stereotypes of the social worker which the community at large holds are forged in part by his workday associates. They will be changed by them to the extent that social workers respond positively to their changing attitudes and expectancies.

Where are we at home? There is evidence of progress within some social agencies. Increasingly the profession's human and social values are permeating the agencies' administrative process as understanding of human needs, of the dynamics of individual behavior, and of group behavior is held to be as useful to the administrator as to the social caseworker or the social group worker. It is clear that effective service can occur only as the profession's values are not violated by the agency in its policies, procedures, and regulations. Many problems due to the incompatibility of these two cultures want solution. . . .

There has been considerable comment in recent years on social work's absorption with its identity. The social worker in a variety of functional roles at various operating levels is continually focused on the relationship of man to his environment for the purpose of effecting a constructive relationship. In so doing he continuously uses other agencies and resources, and often he works from within other agencies. Continuously also other agencies and institutions turn to him. In these manifold two-way relationships, other professions commonly consider him adjunctive: he belongs to them. Frequently they would put him to any old use. He is serving other agencies and institutions and in using them he must identify with their aims and means sufficiently to understand them. It is not surprising that at times he has been more identified with than related to those with whom he works. It is inevitable that social work has had a problem in keeping its sense of direction and in defining its function in the interprofessional scene. When I read that the social worker's concern with professional identity is excessive, and note that it is interpreted as psychological insecurity due to status-striving, I long to make it known that the social worker has had, and still has, a reality problem to solve, that his anxiety is reality-based rather than phobic, that his making known his plight may be indicative of good ego functioning. Unless he identifies the problems involved and gets help in coping with them, his problems will not be solved. It may well be that our mastery of the social scientist's concept of social role can help solve our "role diffusion" problems.

In summary, a number of developments bespeak social work's potential for solving the problems implied. They may be summarized as follows:

1. Headway has been made in defining the function of social work.

2. Educational issues regarding specialized knowledge

and technical skills versus broad basic education have been resolved, to result in "generic education." As social work has been seen as more of one piece than some other professions, generic education has been regarded as an appropriate means to maintain its "wholeness." But social work has not been seen as a whole without differences in the skills of its specific functions, given knowledge, basic principles, and concepts in common.

3. The educational process has shifted from a job-focused approach to the teaching of generic concepts and principles. We have made headway in hypothesizing and applying our theoretical formulations, to serve as a basis for social work research.

4. Very recently social work research has made an impressive start and a notable feature in it is its recognition that, while social work can get much valuable help from the social sciences, it will have to be responsible for its own diagnostic and treatment typologies. The social sciences might willingly attempt to provide them, but, if they are to illuminate and hence contribute to effective helping efforts, they must evolve from within the profession.

5. Advanced education programs in a number of schools give promise of providing better qualified people than formerly for teaching, research, and administrative posts and, in time, for basic practice.

6. Social work anticipated other professions in transferring its psychological and social insights into its educational process. Its theories of personality organization have been incorporated within its general theories of learning. It has been looked to recently by other professions even though it has not solved its particularly difficult educational problems.

7. In its selection practices, social work has been in a position of leadership rather than of dependence on other disciplines and professions.

8. The weak links in social work as a profession have been twofold: first, until recently its practitioners in its basic helping operations have been disadvantaged in salary, prestige, and often in training. Consequently, the seasoned

practitioner has tended to leave practice. As the status of a profession in the last analysis rests on the performance of the rank-and-file of its practitioners, this removal from practice has been a serious defect. This problem has been recognized, and measures have been taken gradually to solve it. Second, the agency and the profession have been and in some instances still are incompatible cultures.

9. Social work has established its identity as an integrated whole in forming the National Association of Social Workers and the Council on Social Work Education. In these organizations it has potential instruments to further its development in many ways. One of these ways may be to conserve our resources through giving leadership to the appraisal of agencies and to job analyses. Social work services have been spread as thin as human need is widespread. It seems clear that we cannot function competently everywhere and that the time has come for deciding where we shall serve. This will imply making known under what conditions we can and will work; it will imply appraisal of agencies, in terms of what they can use of social work services, what education is required for limited services, and where it should be given.

We have come a long way. There is much to conserve and carry forward. There is much with which to fulfill the greater expectancy of us. There is much to give us a greater expectancy of ourselves, and much to motivate us in carrying on. . . .

Social Work:
Cause and Function

Now, IN 1961, Charlotte Towle entered the closing years of her career. Sage as she had been even in her youth, she had

Reprinted from *Social Casework*, vol. 42, no. 8 (October 1961). Copyright 1961 by The Family Service Association of America.

added to sagacity the knowledge and judgments of years of active participation in all aspects of social work. The question she asked herself as she looked back across the past and toward the future was "What needs most to be re-affirmed, reinvigorated in order to revitalize social work?" Her answer is here. It is *cause;* it is to care, to be concerned, to feel committed, to carry not simply an informed head but "an informed heart."

In this paper one sees Charlotte Towle's concern that in becoming "professionalized" social workers were beginning to value their public image and their technical skills beyond the causes for which, she staunchly believed, they must be the advocates, even the missionaries. Briefly she proffers some reasons why the sense of cause has been lost, and briefly she suggests some ways in which a cause may become reality and in which there may be union of cause and function.

Toward this end, and true to her lifelong labors and love, she presents the potential contributions that social case-workers can make to social causes and social action. Her hope asserts itself once again when she reminds herself— and us—that "the over-all cause of social work is now a world cause." It may be long in its fulfillment; it will bring new problems to be solved; but, as Charlotte Towle saw, it is probable that today more people come closer to social work's values and cause than ever before.

H. H. P.

Porter R. Lee at the annual meeting of the National Conference of Social Work in 1929, voiced prophetic concern on the eve of the great depression. As he looked to the future, he defined an outstanding problem of social work as that of "developing its service as a function of well-organized community life without sacrificing its capacity to inspire in men enthusiasm for a cause."[1] He held that social work, a move-ment largely dominated by motives, had developed into one in which motives compete with intellectual conviction. Once, charity had been the mainspring of social work. Now the driving power was a conception of social welfare. Social work had added to its character as a cause the character of a function of well-organized community life. Lee differen-tiated cause and function as follows:

... causes ... have been inspired more frequently by a desire to get rid of evils than by a desire to bring in a specific new order of things. ...

... The momentum of the cause will never carry over adequately to the subsequent task of making its fruits permanent. The slow methodical organized effort needed to make enduring the achievement of the cause calls for different motives, different skill, different machinery. ...

... A cause is usually the concern only of those individuals who accept its appeal. ... A function ... implies an organized effort incorporated into the machinery of community life in the dis-charge of which the acquiescence at least, and ultimately the support of the entire community, is assumed. ...

... Zeal is perhaps the most conspicuous trait in adherents to the cause, while intelligence is perhaps most essential in those who administer a function. The emblazoned banner and the shibboleth for the cause, the program and the manual for the function; devoted sacrifice and the flaming spirit for the cause, fidelity, standards and methods for the function; an embattled host for the cause, an efficient personnel for the function.[2]

Porter Lee drew lines sharply, as one does in order to throw issues into bold relief. If, however, it is true that progessively, since 1929, charity—in the sense of love of mankind and social justice—has given way to a conception of social welfare as the mainspring of social work, we are indeed in a plight. I have small faith in an intellectual con-cept as a driving force when it is not infused with the emo-

1. Porter R. Lee, "Social Work: Cause and Function," *Proceedings of the National Conference of Social Work (1929)* (Chicago: University of Chicago Press, 1930), p. 5; also in *Readings in Social Case Work 1920–1938*, ed. Fern Lowry (New York: Columbia University Press, 1939).
2. Porter R. Lee, *ibid.*

tionally meaningful purposes that constitute a cause. It is widely claimed that even in the domain of the exact sciences the scientist is passionate and persuasive about his discoveries.[3] In social work we know the limitations of the informed head. The union of cause and function implies an informed heart.

The informed heart, at least as implied in a rudimentary union of cause and function, was attained in the late nineteenth and the early twentieth centuries. A review of the works of Jane Addams and Mary E. Richmond, and of what has been written about them, shows that professionally they had much in common. This is not surprising, for they both embodied the spirit of the times. It was a period when the central concern of enlightened leaders in social welfare and its related fields was to develop the social dimension of the democracy that the preceding century had sought and won in politics.[4] Respect for individuality was pitted against worship of rugged individualism. Cause was now directed toward bringing about a new order of things as a means of combatting social ills and eliminating evil.

Jane Addams and Mary Richmond had an abiding faith in the principles of democracy. They were truly disturbed by the human condition, and their strong feelings motivated their strivings. This emotional intensity might well have interfered with their perception; but the records of their work indicate that, by and large, it gave depth to their perception of the meaning of stress and of the significance of forces that were breaking down man's capacity to cope with stress. Unafraid of their own feelings, they spoke for man and to the community simply, clearly, and with deep conviction. In terminology that was definitely not bloodless, they made known the values to which they adhered in their work. They had ideals, but I doubt that either of them had an image of herself or of what she ought to be in order to typify the profession.

Both of these women were devoid of professionalism.

3. For one discussion of this see Michael Polanyi, "Intellectual Passions," *Personal Knowledge* (Chicago: University of Chicago Press, 1958), pp. 132–202.
4. Donald Meiklejohn, "Jane Addams and American Democracy," *Social Service Review*, vol. 34, no. 3 (1960), pp. 253–64.

They were intent on doing what they could—or helping others to do what they could—to give the living something to live for. They gave to their colleagues and subordinates a vital sense of something to work for, not just something to do in the way of performing a task. I doubt that either of them had a fear of being more an advocate than a scholar—and no mean scholars they were! Their fearlessness in making known their feelings doubtless stemmed in part from the fact that their thinking was arrived at through the scholarly discipline of knowledge put to use and appraised in terms of what it taught. This discipline gave them faith in what they knew and freed them to speak with conviction. They were pragmatic idealists. Thus these leaders and their cohorts had, by the early twenties, laid the groundwork of philosophy, of method, and of a system of values that could serve social work in the stage of accelerated growth into which, almost concurrently, it was plunged.

This year we are commemorating the 100th anniversary of Mary Richmond's birth. Many of today's developments testify to her great foresight; many unsolved problems bring her back both to hearten and to haunt us. I therefore presume to look at some aspects of the problem of the union of cause and function from the Richmond point of view.

Brilliantly emblazoned on Mary Richmond's banner was the keynote of the times: "Respect for Individual Differences." She held that the very mark of professional service was the social worker's assumption of responsibility for its effect on the people served. . . . She held that the gift without the giver is bare; that money and services extended without the gift of understanding of individual need, want, and capacity not only pauperize the personalities served but also beget mutual mistrust. She held staunchly to the principle of the economy of adequate giving. She made known the high cost, both in human values and in money, of mistrust. In 1920 Mary Richmond deprecated the undue emphasis on the investigative process in social work which followed the publication, in 1917, of her book *Social Diagnosis*. She commented that "there is no dividing line between investigation and treatment. . . . What we need is a fusion of the two which will lead to more pene-tratingly helpful action than we are yet able to achieve. . . ."[5]

In the wide range of her activities as caseworker, administrator, teacher, scholar, social welfare and social action leader, she insistently contended for the individualization of the person, the family as a small group, and the community.[6] She steadfastly made it known that she was for "banners not blankets."[7] She was against programs and measures that blanket individuals or groups, subjecting them to routine procedures and services. In speaking of social casework in relation to social reform, she stated, "Social case work . . . specializes and differentiates . . . social reform generalizes and simplifies by discovering ways of doing the same thing for everybody."[8] In speaking on social justice, Miss Richmond held that equality before the law implied treating unequal things unequally.[9] This conviction, among others, led her to oppose giving money to clients on a public-relief basis where eligibility requirements were uniform and fixed money grants were required. In relation to the prospect of the growth of public responsibility, the assertion she had made in 1915 remained unchanged:

> Whatever else social reform eradicates, abolishes or prevents, the two great facts of human variation and of variable human response to stimuli would seem likely to remain. Whatever the legislative and governmental changes of the next fifty years, whatever the industrial changes, whatever the improvements in conditions and in folks, it will still be necessary to do different things for and with different people, if the results of our doing are to be more good than bad.[10]

Miss Richmond's reservations about the giving of public money to people in need were as follows: (1) It was incon-

5. Mary E. Richmond, "Steps in Social Treatment," in *The Long View*, ed. Joanna C. Colcord and Ruth Z. S. Mann (New York: Russell Sage Foundation, 1930), p. 491.
6. *Ibid.*, pp. 484–91.
7. Richmond, "Banners Versus Blankets," in *The Long View*, pp. 536–38. In this paper the author took issue with legislation proposed for setting aside certain regulatory measures to protect groups of women in favor of measures that would enable all women to compete more nearly equally with men in the labor market.
8. Richmond, "The Social Case Worker in a Changing World," in *The Long View*, p. 374.
9. Richmond, "Banners Versus Blankets, in *The Long View*, p. 537.
10. Richmond, "The Social Case Worker in a Changing World," p. 376.

ceivable that public agencies would pay adequate salaries and have high standards in the selection of personnel. (2) There would be no responsibility for results. Not knowing the family, individually and collectively, the worker would tend to continue to give relief without making efforts toward rehabilitation. (3) Money payments would tend to be inadequate for the same reason. Unless workers knew the families, they would not know their needs or care enough for them to fight for what they needed. (4) If mothers' pensions were granted on a basis of right, husbands would be encouraged to desert their families, and thus pensions would fail in their purpose of safeguarding family life.[11]

Thus Mary Richmond broke with many of her colleagues on the issue of movement forward toward public responsibility, and took a stand with which we are not in sympathy. She took a long view, however, in identifying problems that have defied solution—problems that must become *cause* in a near tomorrow.

It is to be regretted that many of Miss Richmond's professional descendants did not come to know her through her many papers, which show the range of her concerns and activities, and her social vision. Many have known her largely through *Social Diagnosis*, a work that gave much substance to social casework as function.[12] Like many pioneers, she thought beyond the boundaries of her time, with the result that her followers were unable to use her book with discrimination. The investigative process was overemphasized by her followers to the point where they elicited more facts than were relevant to the social problem or than could be used in diagnosis. Likewise, her concern with what is done to people in serving them was violated because the client often was subjected to an intrusive inquisition.

Making social investigation an integral part of treatment was Mary Richmond's goal, but this goal was not attained

11. Richmond, "Discussion" of paper by Frederick Almy on "Public Pensions to Widows," *Proceedings of National Conference of Charities and Correction (1912)* (Fort Wayne: Fort Wayne Printing Co., 1912), pp. 492–93.

12. Mary E. Richmond, *Social Diagnosis* (New York: Russell Sage Foundation, 1917).

until, years later, social workers gradually learned to utilize psychiatric insights. There was actual misinterpretation of her emphasis on the use of collaterals and the weighing of evidence. To many workers, this emphasis meant that the client was the least reliable informant because he was biased.

Discriminating use of Mary Richmond's methods of social investigation required the application of psychiatric insights that made the social worker aware of the importance of the client's psychological reality. Miss Richmond's recognition of this limitation is shown by her repetitive comments that social work practitioners should turn more and more to psychiatrists for help in analysis of the mental mechanisms of the individual. As a result of this limitation, the way in which Mary Richmond's work was used made social casework more worker- and agency-centered than client-centered. And so, later, one finds it being said in various ways that knowledge and understanding of human behavior derived from psychiatry breathed the breath of human life into social work's helping processes.[13]

In the initial stage of the impact of psychiatry on social casework, the psychological and social aspects of human problems were integrated for a brief period.[14] In recent years psychiatrists have again affirmed Mary Richmond's emphasis on viewing the individual within the social context. Between these two periods, however, social factors were subordinated to psychological factors to such an extent that there was a reaction against casework's absorption in the individual as an isolate. This reaction brought a reunion with the social scientist and a reunion with Mary Richmond, who had truly incorporated in her teachings much from the social sciences. These three—*generic social work, consideration of the individual in his social context, and the adequate meeting of individual and common needs*

13. One such statement was made by the author. See Charlotte Towle, *Common Human Needs* (New York: National Association of Social Workers, 1957), p. xi.

14. For a statement on this integration in the late 1920's, see Charlotte Towle, "Marion E. Kenworthy: A Social Worker's Reflections," *Social Service Review*, vol. 30, no. 4 (1956), p. 449.

through the close interrelation of social movements—were Miss Richmond's major causes.

I now move to the present, which happily gives some promise of soon becoming the past, not in the immediate solution of global problems, but in terms of attitudes toward reality. These civilized-primitive times are difficult to epitomize because of their duality. Much of the past high valuation of individuality takes the form of worship of exceptional ability for leadership. Presumably the common man may entrust himself to the superb leader and, thereby, may enjoy the "good life." This adulation coexists with a high valuation of conformity.

Faith in man, with the resultant expectation of a better day, has been shaken. The dark clouds of mistrust of man and uncertainty about tomorrow enshroud us. Conditional faith and conditional confidence mark these wishful times. We find mankind individually and collectively absorbed in projecting acceptable images. This is the age of the corporate image—the age of the adaptable conscience. Loss of hope has led to defenses against anxiety which take many forms. The relationship of cause and function in social work inevitably has been affected by this state of mind.

I shall define the term "cause" as I conceive of it today. Cause is the purpose, the reason, and the motive for providing the means by which social ills may be prevented, abolished, or remedied through social action. Not emotional need alone, but knowledge, ideals, moral values, and ethical principles prompt individuals and groups to instigate and to espouse a cause. I emphasize knowledge as the element which has shown particular growth in the present century; it could well serve as the primary impetus for championing a cause. Instead, it seems to have served as a deterrent. For example, our social work experience, enlightened by insights from psychiatry and the social sciences as well as by research, has extended, deepened, and confirmed our earlier understanding of the social import of family life. Intellectual conviction based on our increased knowledge could well support us in making greater cause than ever before of the correction of policies and practices that violate family life. Much has been written about our failure to use what we know, but I should like to indicate here some of the reasons for the fact that knowledge can act as a deterrent to rallying us in support of a cause.

1. Knowledge exerts a sobering influence; it curbs zeal. We do not instigate or espouse causes that cannot be implemented.

2. The uneven development in our knowledge has created lags. I cite Bertram Beck to the effect that if there had been a body of theory pertaining to social change equivalent to that pertaining to individual change, social change would have been incorporated into the social reform process with consequent growth of both cause and function.[15]

3. Knowledge begets a need for more knowledge. Action may be blocked by the conviction that more specific knowledge and more research will be needed before anything can be done. On this I quote Lydia Rapoport's discussion of man's pursuit of the myth of specific causation: "In social work we shall always operate with less than full and certain knowledge. This is one of our built-in professional stresses. Because of the mandate given to us by society and because of the nature of our social commitment, we cannot afford to wait."[16] When we adhere to our commitment to do whatever is humanitarian, we shall not be led far afield in solving many of the problems in social functioning—problems that are the central concern of social work.

Today we are faced with great inequalities in social work as function. Our profession, which long has labored to bridge the gap between the "haves" and the "have nots," is itself divided into these two groups. There are not only "have" and "have not" agencies but also "have" and "have not" clients. In some large agencies that serve masses of people the clients either are or feel themselves to be case numbers rather than human beings. These "have not" agen-

---

15. Bertram M. Beck, "Shaping America's Social Welfare Policy," *Issues in American Social Work*, Alfred J. Kahn, ed. (New York: Columbia University Press, 1959), p. 198.
16. Lydia Rapoport, "The Concept of Prevention in Social Work," *Social Work*, vol. 6, no. 1 (1961), p. 8.

cies, with their inadequate salaries, untrained or partially trained personnel, and their restriction on differential giving, serve mainly the "have not" clients, who suffer from great deprivation and can muster few resources to bulwark the help social work can give them. These clients vary greatly in the extent to which they are troubled; they probably vary greatly in their potential for making productive use of help. I say "probably" because, in many instances, this potential has not been tested. We do know, however, that many of these clients display great fortitude and resilience. By doing nothing for them, we highlight their potential for getting worse rather than better, since people tend to internalize the effects of prolonged social disruption.

In contrast, the medium-sized and small agencies can be characterized, in many instances, as the "have" agencies. They serve a relatively advantaged group. In some of these agencies, the number of fee-paying clients is increasing steadily. Compared with the clients of the "have not" agencies, these clients are in a favorable condition in terms of income, education, potential employability, and resources available to support social work help. They may be equally or more troubled, although sometimes they may only appear to be more troubled because the workers know them better as individuals. Their potential for using the more adequate help available varies widely.

The "have" agencies are in a better position to serve clients well because their caseloads are of a size that makes them more manageable, though not as manageable, in some instances, as would be desirable in view of the quality of work undertaken and the shortage of personnel. Many of these agencies, however, are in a position to control intake as one way of maintaining standards. These agencies often pay relatively adequate salaries. Because they have higher salaries, better staff morale, and more opportunities for staff development, and because the nature of their work and of their clientele is more congenial to workers, they can secure and retain better-trained staff members than can the "have nots." They can adhere more closely, and in some instances very closely, to the principle of adequate and differential giving in money, in services, and in helping relationships. The family can be individualized—often with the help of medical, psychiatric, and educational consultants—both as a unit and as separate family members. Because the agencies know their clients, they are in a position to make differential use of community resources; thereby, they often discover lacks in resources available to meet both common and individual needs of the family. They have the freedom to experiment with methods, with types of problems, and with whatever their work indicates would merit investigation. Some of them are in a position to secure support for research and to participate in it.

Because of these advantages and because they serve clients who arouse less prejudice than do the "have not" clients in those who support their programs, the staffs of the "have" agencies are in a better position to instigate and to implement a cause and thus to maintain the union of cause and function. Some workers assume responsibility for social work as cause both within and beyond their own programs; others do not. Many factors foster function as an end in itself to the extent that in some agencies the program fails in its purpose by not keeping faith with cause. I refer to the "retreat to the technician" at all operating levels. This has been an essential developmental stage in social work for the mastery of learning, but it has been reinforced by the trend toward using the expert to solve many problems in our mass society. The deepening of technical proficiency may, in fact, expand our vision of social reform. Now we are on the threshold of making social statesmanship a cause.[17]

Sustained compatibility between cause and function is contingent on three factors: (1) administrative leadership in tune with cause, both through comprehension of its implications and through identification with it; (2) appraisal of the continued vitality of the cause; and (3) accountability. The second factor, appraisal, implies that cause must be modified as the agency's function grows and changes

17. Alvin L. Schorr, "The Retreat to the Technician," *Social Work*, vol. 4, no. 1 (1959), pp. 29–33.

either in response to social change or through fulfillment of the original cause. Just as problems solved beget new problems, causes fulfilled beget new causes. In Porter Lee's opinion, good social work creates the necessity for more social work.[18]

In regard to the third factor, accountability, one can say that we appraise in order to learn and to hold ourselves accountable to ourselves. As we hold ourselves accountable, we may be more reliable and less defensive informants when held accountable by the community that supports our endeavors. It is as we do this that we assume our responsibility to educate the community. Whether we are pushed around or supported is contingent on our behavior in being held accountable.

Technical competence in administration is an important skill for the administrator of a local program. If he has this skill, he will adhere to the principles of the democratic process in the conduct of the agency. He will draw on the opinions of the total staff in appraising the agency and the community. Implicit in competent democratic leadership is the recognition that leadership means using authority—the authority of one's position, of one's professional commitment, and of one's special knowledge. In order to assume responsibility, the administrator must have resolved his own authority-dependency conflicts to the extent that he can accept his staff's dependency on him for leadership and, in turn, can depend on his staff for guidance that is based on their experience in serving clients and in working with the community.

Grim reality, the massive work load under which all staff members stagger in the "have not" agencies, militates against the happy outcome I have envisaged for the well-qualified administrator, trained or untrained in social work. Responsibilities that are continuously beyond the time-energy capacity of an individual or a group to discharge force a retreat into task-centered activity. A small margin is left for learning from one's practice or for contributing to others what one's practice could teach them. The vision

18. Porter R. Lee, "Social Work," p. 9.

imparted by cause is blacked out when one is entombed in function. And the professional life of the social worker—whether administrator or practitioner—becomes more a treadmill than a pilgrimage. Treadmills do not ordinarily afford a humanizing experience to those served or serving; they lead to the mechanization of both worker and client. Furthermore, they leave the staff, at all operating levels, in poor shape to hold themselves accountable to themselves or to be held accountable by the community. . . .

Unless the administrator is staunchly identified with the cause, he may respond to community misconceptions, suspicions, and prejudices by taking action that violates not only the mores of social work but the ways of democracy. I am referring here to those investigation squads which, without due process of law, have searched the homes of suspected "relief chiselers" in Gestapo fashion. Since the public assumes that the staff of an agency knows its clients, such action gives credence to the distorted image it has of public assistance clients. The attitude toward recipients of Aid to Dependent Children grants is a case in point. "The public image of the typical ADC family is erroneous. This image . . . handicaps the operation of the program, impedes public support, creates pressures upon staff and induces in the ADC mother and her children a feeling of fear, rejection, and inferiority."[19] The administrator's defensive identification with pressure groups can have an equally disabling effect.

Fortunately, such drastic action as that described above has not been widespread. However, administrators in many places have sanctioned less severe punitive action that has had some of the same effects on those served. When the administrative staff is identified with community value judgment rather than with the purpose of the program, it may employ various restrictive practices as a defense. Anxiety regarding accountability to the community has led certain administrative staffs to defend their programs rather than to confront themselves and others with the

19. *Facts, Fallacies, and Future, A Study of the Aid to Dependent Children Program of Cook County, Illinois* (New York: Greenleigh Associates, Inc., 1960), part 2, p. 5.

shortcomings. A notable example has been the way in which the process of determining eligibility has been conducted. Pervaded with the spirit of "finding people out" rather than with finding out how to help them, workers tend to find the eligible ineligible rather than the reverse. I recall Mary Richmond's opinion that there is no dividing line between social investigation and treatment, an opinion that has been validated in casework practice. Since people are prone to act as they are treated, mistrust can engender misrepresentation. When we succumb to mistrust, we violate a basic value of social work, a basic element in our cause of promoting democracy as a way of life—respect for the individual. This respect has been expressed in the best social work practice, at all operating levels, through what has been termed the therapeutic attitude essential in all working relationships—that of assuming the individual is honest, competent, and educable until he has been proved otherwise.

When we defensively shelve cause in order to maintain the stature of function we can well ask ourselves: To what extent are our fears realistic? To what extent are we assuming that the public is more uneducable or more unresponsive than it actually is? The public's questioning concern about our program may be evidence that the public has a sense of cause. The true motive behind many an accusation may be one of reform.

If the true motive is reform, we may use public criticism as a means of achieving socially constructive ends. We shall have to see our work and our values through the eyes of others, as a first step in promoting the mutual understanding inherent in effective agency-community relationships. Programs and agencies belong to the community; in the end, they must have the community's support. Laymen will make the decisions by which their programs and agencies will march forward, limp, or fall. They cannot be expected to make wise decisions without the help of those whom they have employed to administer the programs. Their misconceptions are a means of engaging them in thinking anew. In helping this process of rethinking, the social worker has a responsibility beyond that of merely providing the technician's specialized knowledge. He has a responsibility to try to effect changes in feeling and thinking about disadvantaged and troubled people. Doing this does not mean that he should manipulate people by using arguments that exploit their values—arguments that will appeal to them even though we ourselves find them unconvincing. Instead, he should affirm, supplement, or differ with the layman's thinking in the light of his own special knowledge and commitment.

Unafraid of his own feelings, the social worker will speak clearly, simply, and with true conviction. (Fear of feeling often begets obscure language and noncommittal responses that make no impact on the layman's emotion-fraught convictions.) The worker will make known the aims of a program, the values to which he must adhere, and his reasons for adhering to them, all in terms of the effects of services on people. He will be forthright in stating *what* his agency is financed and staffed to do and *what*, in the light of its limitations, it cannot do. He will freely concede, for example, that the Aid to Dependent Children program may be fostering unmarried motherhood, not by giving these women financial assistance, but by *not* giving them other services. He will use every opportunity to demonstrate both the economy and the humanity of adequate giving.

We show that we trust the layman when we treat him as an intelligent, educable, and humane individual. Whether or not he proves to have these qualities, his image of social work and the social worker will be more favorable than it will be if we convey a mistrust of him. Our mistrust is shown by talking down to him, by seeming to compromise, and by telling him only what he wants to hear. In the long run, if we behave toward people in this manner, they will feel betrayed, and in their eyes the image of the social worker will arouse contempt. More important than our image, however, is what we do to people in patronizing them. We perpetuate ignorance when we sacrifice valid arguments to our false conception of what will be appealing.

The task of interpretation and education that confronts board members, advisory committees, and social workers is a massive one. To both serve and re-educate masses of people is a formidable undertaking. Our emotional investment in our subject matter can be both an asset that motivates us and a liability that frustrates us. Our "learners" may not prove to be learners. They have the potential for being either strongly attracted to or deeply resistive to the cause of social welfare because of their strong feelings about the people social welfare programs serve and the cost of the services. The task of educating the public is particularly difficult in relation to the "have not" clientele served by the "have not" agencies, but the entire profession shares the responsibility for accomplishing it. Today the charge to educate the public is particularly difficult to achieve because segments of the population may be unreceptive as a result of emotional resistance. Society's long-standing propensity to set the poor apart has been intensified by provisos compounded of racial prejudice and moralistic judgments made in an age that has become frighteningly amoral and immoral.

The social worker is likely to encounter at least three adversaries in his attempts to explain and interpret the need for extended social welfare services:

1. The individual whose misconceptions stem primarily from misinformation and lack of knowledge. His feeling and thinking change readily in response to intelligible interpretation unless the information he receives runs counter to deep convictions and values. When he finds that the new orientation is both intellectually and emotionally compatible with his old orientation, he presents no problems in learning.

2. The individual whose convictions and values are so incompatible with those of social work that he will have to undergo a change both in feeling and in thinking. When adherence to the past is rooted in loyalties to old causes and alignment with past mentors, the nature of the individual's relationships with the persons imparting new thinking and with those engaged with him in acquiring it are important. Furthermore, the appeal to the head must also touch the heart; a new cause must replace an old one. Therefore, such

a person is responsive to the social worker who is inspired by a sense of cause and who makes known the purpose, the values, and the ethic that underlie the agency's program. The spirit of the times and the response of the individual's own group may either play into or play against the social worker's point of view.

3. The individual who is uneducable because he has deep-rooted convictions and prejudices that serve his own purposes. He is rigidly protected against change in feeling, thinking, or doing. Often he is a man of small conscience who is not motivated to function for the common good. On the social worker's horizon, the number of such persons, often vocal, may loom larger than it really is. Actually, as headway is made with the first two types of individuals and community sentiment changes, particularly at the leadership or power-group level, this person's overt resistance may be lowered.

Finally, an educational approach to which in time the third type of individual may succumb is the will of the community as expressed in law. Robert M. Hutchins cites child labor legislation, which as a cause was bitterly opposed. Today, as law, its opponents and their psychological descendants do not take issue with it. It is now part and parcel of the way of life to which they have adjusted, and perhaps, in the long run, have even adapted themselves. Hutchins comments in another context that one might well remember the educational force of law, that "the importance of law is not that it is coercive, but that it is pedagogical."[20] I should like to add that it is coercive at first, but in the long run it is pedagogical. The educational element in law is the limitation it imposes on the acting out of feelings that run counter to the common good. In conforming to law, the person is subjected to experiences that may both correct misconceptions and make new behavior satisfying. How a man acts can alter what he is—or at least can make it possible for the next generation to feel as their elders professed and acted.

20. Robert M. Hutchins, "The Nurture of Human Life," *Bulletin of the Center for the Study of Democratic Institutions, Fund for the Republic*, March 1961, p. 3.

An issue today is that of the responsibility of the casework practitioner to engage in social action in his role as
social worker apart from his role as citizen. The traditional
position on this issue, as handed down by Mary Richmond,
was that the social caseworker had a "before and after"
responsibility. Using as an illustration the caseworkers' activity in relation to the child labor law in Pennsylvania, she
showed that they had compiled and made available facts
from case records for the use of a committee formed to
draft a bill and advocate its passage. These facts proved to
be decisive. Later, when hardships caused by the law produced a clamor, "the leading family welfare agency of Philadelphia was called upon—not for facts this time, but for
plans by which, in co-operation with the local public education association, every alleged case of hardship could be
provided for while protecting at the same time all young
children from premature employment."[21] Mary Richmond
claimed that if this follow-up had not been guaranteed, the
law doubtless would have been repealed before the community could have adjusted to it. Therefore, she saw social
caseworkers as having played a vital part in this social
action through the performance of their own function. She
held that it was not within their competence or their function to assume responsibility for the conduct of all stages
of a social reform movement.

Applied to the current scene, this point of view would
require the caseworker to be responsible for initiating or
instigating social action by making known unmet needs and
social ills as revealed in his practice. He would contribute
his findings, through agency channels, to those writing social policy, conducting publicity campaigns, drafting legislation, and working with legislators and laymen in the
community.

Despite the casework findings available for their use,
those who have these more specialized functions may not
have sufficient grasp of social casework to perceive the
specific import of their policies and legislative drafts for
social work practice. I therefore hold strongly that social

21. Mary E. Richmond, "Possibilities of the Art of Helping," *The Long View*, p. 588.

casework personnel in administrative or subadministrative positions should be used as staff consultants. As consultants in the administrative line they are in a position to speak with the authority of their knowledge. The social caseworker may inherit later the individual and family problems created by social change consequent to social action. In the fulfillment of his agency's responsibility for social casework practice, he plays a part in entrenching the gains made through social action. In addition, I would expect caseworkers to participate as social workers in professional deliberations on social issues and to take a stand on social action proposed by the National Association of Social Workers.

It is said that the social caseworker has alienated himself from the broad concerns of social work and has tended to practice his technique solely for its own purposes. If this means that he is not assuming the responsibility I have delineated, I believe that his retreat may have come about through other factors than lack of concern about social conditions that support social work. The conditions described in Mary Richmond's example of the caseworker's part in child labor reform in Pennsylvania may be lacking in some agencies today. It is manifest that the staff of the social agency she described was not bogged down in function to the exclusion of cause. Because its administrator stood ready not merely to instigate action but to use the practitioners' findings in support of a social welfare measure, the casework staff had the inspiring experience of seeing their action at home travel all the way up the line to both the state and the national levels.

The work I have envisaged will make a demand on the caseworker's time, but a sustained focus on the broad social implications in specific case situations could well produce beneficial effects on casework performance. There will be a variation in the extent to which caseworkers will assume this responsibility. In those programs in which practitioners are at the bottom of the pile, in the position of "little man, what now," subject to the dictates of the administration but not valued as informants, their potential for social action will not be developed. They will not participate because (1) they will lack the opportunity; (2) when occasionally given the opportunity, they will find it difficult to give play to imprisoned ideas; and (3) in some settings, not having individualized their clients sufficiently, the caseworkers will not be reliable informants.

The problem of treating unequal things unequally has not been solved. The central principle in social work at all operating levels is that of individualizing persons, groups, and communities. Except as we follow this principle, we cannot be responsible for what we do *to* people in doing *for* them or in collaborating *with* them. Without adherence to this principle, social workers manning a program are administering a public facility but are not doing social work. The problem of getting the spirit, the mores, and the major methods of social work into public assistance practices has been a continuous concern of enlightened leaders who have pioneered in these programs.

In the very beginning of broad public assistance programs, it was recognized that agency services could be geared to common needs and that there would be certain fixed elements. Eligibility requirements and money grants would be the same for all; grants would be modified in a uniform manner in relation to exceptional need. It was hoped that people could be treated differentially as they made known their need and rights and as they used the services. The aim was to make the regime therapeutic in order to help people under stress maintain healthy ego functioning. It was hoped also that as individuals and their families became better known to the workers, a limited but sound casework service might be rendered in relation to problems other than need for financial assistance.

It probably could be said that these aims have been attained in some measure in some programs. From all accounts, they have not been fulfilled in many quarters because of adverse factors known to us all. Restrictive practices, which defeat the purpose of the programs, have flourished because of the inadequate opportunity for knowing people as well as ignorance about how to learn to know them. There is growing recognition that the time has come to define the functions of these programs realistically. Can they provide social work service? What of all that constitutes social work practice can be undertaken reliably? Making these determinations is essential in recruiting and training personnel. It is essential also in confronting ourselves and our communities with the reality that if we are to practice what we profess the means must be provided.

Hope for the future lies in the fact that self-deception has not been pervasive within the profession of social work. Over the past 25 years, professional literature has recorded our awareness of unsolved problems, our discontent, our search for solutions, and our tenacious efforts. There has been commendable persistence in protecting and defending social work's stake in these programs—commendable in that it has been motivated not by vested interest but by the conviction that human need must be met if these programs are to fulfill their potential as a force operating for the common good rather than for widespread social evil. One can take hope in much that is going on today—demonstration projects, reorganization proposals, in-service training plans and research grants made by the Social Security Administration and private foundations. Certainly our cause today could well be that of defining and implementing the function of social work in great public programs that are decisive in maintaining democracy as a way of life. Many in this generation who have pioneered, and still are pioneering, in these programs will go down in social welfare history as equal to the best of our forebears as men and women devoted to a good cause that they have been striving to implement in unreceptive times. The fruits of their labor must await a better day.

Let us now look to the future. In the midst of a scientific age, when man's wits have all but outwitted him in producing a universal death threat, a great humanitarian movement has emerged as a defense against destruction and as a means to world peace. As early as 1907, Jane Addams, in her advocacy of world peace, noted that "men of all nations are determining upon the abolition of degrading poverty, disease, and intellectual weakness. . . ." She believed that "peace would no longer be an absence of war, but the unfolding of worldwide processes making for the nurture of human life."[22] The over-all cause of social work is now a world cause. The mission of our country is envisaged as that of making the world a fit place for human beings to live in—a mission unfulfilled for many at home but one that we can hope will give impetus to social work's lifelong cause at home as well as abroad.

The spirit of our times is in tune with the humanitarian professions and, prominently, with the entire health, education, and welfare movement. Now is the time to respond to the call to greatness and to make inspiring demands on ourselves as well as on our communities. There will be weakness in our leadership at home and abroad to the extent that we are motivated by fear. Fear gives rise to precipitous, indiscriminate, and selfish giving—giving that centers on building up the self-concept of the giver. It arouses mistrust and will fall short of its opportunistic aims.

This is a time for the social work profession to have faith in its cause, to reaffirm its humanistic values, and to work positively for conditions of life that will promote man's humanity to man. In this endeavor we can be reassured by the knowledge that scientific studies are increasingly validating humanistic values. In turn, the sciences on which social work has drawn have served as a humanizing force in deepening man's understanding of man in society. The union of cause and function within social work will be a natural outgrowth of the progressive union of science and humanism. Similarly, the world cause—the nurture of human life as a means to man's survival, which today is synonymous with world peace—is contingent on leadership through which science becomes a humanizing force.

22. Jane Addams, *Newer Ideals for Peace* (New York: The Macmillan Company, 1907), p. 238.

Bibliography
of Charlotte Towle's
Publications

Books

Social Case Records from Psychiatric Clinics—with Discussion Notes. Chicago: University of Chicago Press, 1941.

Common Human Needs: An Interpretation for Staff in Public Assistance Agencies. Public Assistance Report no. 8. Washington: U.S. Government Printing Office, 1945. Reprinted by University of Chicago Press, 1947. Revised edition published by American Association of Social Workers, 1952, and by National Association of Social Workers, 1957 and 1965.

The Learner in Education for the Professions: As Seen in Education for Social Work. Chicago: University of Chicago Press, 1954.

Articles

1. "Case Work with Neuropsychiatric Patients." *Red Cross Courier*, February, 1926.

Items in the Bibliography are listed in order of publication.

2. "An Evaluation of Homes in Preparation for Child Placement." *Mental Hygiene,* vol. 11, no. 3 (July 1927).

3. "How to Know a Foster Family." *Child Welfare League of America Bulletin,* April–May 1928.

4. "Treatment of Behavior and Personality Problems in Children: The Social Worker." *American Journal of Orthopsychiatry,* vol. 1, no. 1 (October 1930).

5. "Changes in the Philosophy of Social Work." *Mental Hygiene,* vol. 14, no. 2 (April 1930).

6. "The Evaluation and Management of Marital Situations in Foster Homes." *American Journal of Orthopsychiatry,* vol. 1, no. 3 (April 1931).

7. "Psychiatric Approach in Home Finding." In *The Social Worker.* Boston: Simmons College School of Social Work, 1931.

8. "Mental Hygiene of the Social Worker." *Proceedings: Illinois State Conference of Social Welfare,* 1935.

9. "Factors in Treatment." *Proceedings: National Conference of Social Work.* Chicago: University of Chicago Press, 1936.

10. "Direct Treatment in Social Case Work." Discussion of paper by Paul Sloane, M.D. *American Journal of Orthopsychiatry,* vol. 7, no. 2 (April 1937).

11. "The Individual in Relation to Social Change." *Social Service Review,* vol. 13, no. 1 (March 1939).

12. "Changing Concepts in Visiting Teacher Work." Discussion of paper by Gladys Hall. *Visiting Teachers Bulletin,* vol. 12, no. 1 (September 1936). Reprinted in *Readings in Social Case Work,* ed. Fern Lowry. New York: Columbia University Press, 1939.

13. "Therapeutic Criteria in Social Agencies." Discussion. *American Journal of Orthopsychiatry,* vol. 9, no. 2 (April 1939).

14. "Teaching Psychiatry in Social Case Work." *Family,* vol. 20, no. 10 (February 1940).

15. "Professional Skill in Administration." *American Asso-*

ciation of Psychiatric Social Workers News Letter, May 1940.

16. "The Social Worker and the Treatment of Marital Discord Problems." *Social Service Review*, vol. 14, no. 2 (June 1940).

17. "Some Basic Principles of Social Research in Social Casework" *Social Service Review*, vol. 15, no. 1 (March 1941).

18. "Underlying Skills of Casework Today." *Proceedings: National Conference of Social Work*. New York: Columbia University Press, 1941. Also in *Social Service Review*, vol. 15, no. 3 (September 1941).

19. "Some Notes on the War and Adolescent Delinquency." *Social Service Review*, vol. 17, no. 1 (March 1943).

20. "The Effect of the War upon Children." *Social Service Review*, vol. 17, no. 2 (June 1943).

21. "Common Human Needs in Public Assistance Programs." *Social Service Review*, vol. 18, no. 4 (December 1944).

22. "Psychoanalytic Orientation in Family Casework." *American Journal of Orthopsychiatry*, vol. 13, no. 1 (January 1943).

23. "The Place of Social Casework in the Treatment of Delinquency." *Social Service Review*, vol. 19, no. 2 (June 1945).

24. "Social Casework." In *Social Work Year Book 1945*. New York: Russell Sage Foundation, 1945.

25. "Social Casework in Modern Society." *Social Service Review*, vol. 20, no. 2 (June 1946).

26. "Economic Aspects of the Reunited Family." *Social Service Review*, vol. 20, no. 3 (September 1946).

27. "Public Welfare and Democracy." *Public Welfare*, vol. 4, no. 6 (June 1946).

28. "Social Casework." In *Social Work Year Book 1947*. New York: Russell Sage Foundation, 1947.

29. "The Training of the Social Worker for Child Guidance."

In *Handbook of Child Guidance,* pt. 5, ed. Ernest Harms. New York: Child Care Publications, 1947.

30. "The Emotional Element in Learning in Professional Education for Social Work." *Professional Education.* Pamphlet. New York: American Association of Schools of Social Work, 1948.

31. "Case-Work Methods of Helping the Client to Make Maximum Use of His Capacities and Resources." *Social Service Review,* vol. 22, no. 4 (December 1948). Also titled "Helping the Client to Use his Capacities and Resources" in *Proceedings: National Conference of Social Work, 1948.* New York: Columbia University Press, 1949.

32. "The Classroom Teacher as Practitioner." *Social Work as Human Relations.* New York: Columbia University Press, 1949. Also in *Social Service Review,* vol. 22, no. 3 (September 1948).

33. "The Client's Rights and the Use of the Social Service Exchange." *Social Service Review,* vol. 23, no. 1 (March 1949).

34. "Issues and Problems in Curriculum Development." *Social Work Journal,* vol. 30, no. 2 (April 1949).

35. Discussion of "Why a Nurse Mental Health Consultant in Public Health?" by Katherine Brownell Oettinger. *Journal of Psychiatric Social Work,* vol. 19, no. 4 (Spring 1950).

36. "Looking Ahead in Orthopsychiatric Research." Symposium. *American Journal of Orthopsychiatry,* vol. 20, no. 1 (January 1950).

37. "The Contribution of Education for Social Casework to Practice." *Social Casework,* vol. 31, no. 8 (October 1950). Also in *Social Work in the Current Scene: Selected Papers, 1950.* New York: Columbia University Press, 1950. Also in *Principles and Techniques in Social Casework: Selected Articles, 1940–50,* ed. Cora Kasius. New York: Family Service Association of America, 1950.

38. "The Significance for Social Workers of the Multidiscipline Approach to Child Development." Discussion of paper by Peter B. Neubauer, M.D., and Joseph Steinert. *Social Service Review,* vol. 24, no. 4 (December 1950).
39. "Client Centered Casework." *Social Service Review,* vol. 24, no. 4 (December 1950).
40. "Reinforcing Family Security Today." *Social Casework,* vol. 32, no. 2 (February 1951).
41. "The General Objectives of Professional Education." *Social Service Review,* vol. 25, no. 4 (December 1951). Prepublication of chap. 1, *The Learner in Education for the Professions.*
42. "The Distinctive Attributes of Education for Social Work." *Social Work Journal,* vol. 33, no. 2 (April 1952).
43. "Evaluating Motives of Foster Parents." Discussion of paper by Irene Josselyn, M.D. *Child Welfare,* vol. 31, no. 2 (February 1952).
44. "The Selection and Arrangement of Case Material for Orderly Progression in Learning." *Social Service Review,* vol. 27, no. 1 (March 1953).
45. "Aims and Characteristics of Advanced Education, Differentiated from Master's Degree Education." In *Social Work Education in the Post Master's Program. No. 1, Guiding Principles.* New York: Council on Social Work Education, 1953.
46. "The Learners." Ibid.
47. "To Our Offspring in the Netherlands." Commentary on a European experiment in casework teaching by Dr. Jan de Jongh. *Social Service Review,* vol. 27, no. 2 (June 1953).
48. "The Selection of Students for Schools of Social Work." *Collected Papers from Workshop on Admissions, St. Louis, January 1953.* New York: Council on Social Work Education, 1955.
49. "The Use of the Written Autobiography in the Selection of Students." Ibid.

50. "Social Casework in the Post Master's Program." *University of Chicago, School of Social Service Administration, Newsletter,* vol. 1, no. 3 (July 1953).
51. "New Developments in Social Casework in the United States." *British Journal of Psychiatric Social Work,* vol. 3, no. 2 (1955). Also in *Some Reflections on Social Work Education.* London: Family Welfare Association, 1956. Also available from Council on Social Work Education, New York.
52. "Generic Trends in Education for Social Work." In *Some Reflections on Social Work Education.* Ibid. Also available from Council on Social Work Education, New York.
53. "Professional Education a Humanizing Process." In *Some Reflections on Social Work Education.* Ibid. Also available from Council on Social Work Education, New York.
54. "Notes on the Teaching of Psychology to Social Work Students." In *Some Reflections on Social Work Education.* Ibid. Also available from Council on Social Work Education, New York.
55. "Marion E. Kenworthy: A Social Worker's Reflections." *Social Service Review,* vol. 30, no. 4 (December 1956).
56. "American Social Worker on British Soil." *Goucher Alumnae Quarterly,* vol. 34, no. 4 (Summer 1956).
57. *Proceedings of the 1957 Institute on Teaching Psychiatric Social Work.* Pamphlet. New York: National Association of Social Workers, 1958.
58. "Implications of Contemporary Human and Social Values for Selection of Social Work Student" *Social Service Review,* vol. 33, no. 3 (September 1959).
59. Essay review of Werner Boehm, *Objectives for the Social Work Curriculum of the Future.* Vol. I of *Social Work Curriculum Study: Council on Social Work Education. Social Service Review,* vol. 33, no. 4 (December 1959).

60. "A Social Work Approach to Courses in Growth and Behavior." *Social Service Review*, vol. 34, no. 4 (December 1960).
61. "Social Work: Cause and Function." *Social Casework*, vol. 13, no. 7 (October 1961).
62. "The Role of Supervision in the Union of Cause and Function in Social Work." *Social Service Review*, vol. 36, no. 4 (December 1962).
63. Essay review of *Jessie Taft: Therapist and Social Work Educator*, ed. Virginia P. Robinson. *Child Welfare*, vol. 41, no. 10 (December 1962).
64. "The Self Expectancy of Social Work." Louisville and Western Kentucky chapter, National Association of Social Workers, and Kent School of Social Work, Louisville, 1963.
65. "The Place of Help in Supervision," *Social Service Review*, vol. 37, no. 4 (December 1963).
66. Essay review of Bertha C. Reynolds, *An Uncharted Journey. Social Casework*, vol. 45, no. 1 (January 1964).
67. Preface to *Social Casework: A Psychosocial Therapy*, by Florence Hollis. New York: Random House, 1964.
68. "Ethics and Values in Social Work." Pamphlet. Chicago: Loyola School of Social Work, 1965.
69. "Helping the Casework Practitioner Become a Classroom Teacher." *Education for Social Work Proceedings, 1959*. New York: Council on Social Work Education. Reprinted in *Source Book of Reading*. New York: Council on Social Work Education, 1965.